The Sociology of Early Childhood

The Sociology of Early Childhood brings a new perspective to the field of early childhood education, offering insights into how children's diverse backgrounds shape their life chances. This book will be invaluable for all early childhood educators and students, who want to explore the complexities of contemporary society.

The book takes us through the lives of children from birth to eight years of age, highlighting key issues for babies, for toddlers and for older children, as they grow and learn. Exploring key aspects of inequality, such as gender, social class, race, disability, Indigeneity and sexuality, the sociological insights of this book help educators navigate their role as guides, mediators and advocates for young children. Whether it is understanding children's emotions, working with families, or understanding the challenges of climate change, this book will help, with practical and relevant knowledge.

Traditional approaches to early childhood focus on individual children, often missing a critical awareness of social relationships. There has also been a narrow understanding of children's abilities at a given age or stage, which has ignored the significant impacts of power, privilege and disadvantage. Using sociological theory, the authors unpack how these big issues affect all aspects of children's lives, showing how children struggle to overcome the negative stereotypes which operate to diminish the life chances of many children. This book gives all those who care about or for young children the tools and understanding to become powerful advocates for a better childhood, and a better world.

Yarrow Andrew is a lecturer in early childhood education within the College of Education, Psychology and Social Work at Flinders University, Australia, having worked previously for fifteen years as a preschool educator.

Jennifer Fane is a lecturer in health education within the College of Education, Psychology and Social Work at Flinders University, Australia, after training and working as a primary school teacher in British Columbia, Canada.

The Sociology of Early Childhood

Young Children's Lives and Worlds

Yarrow Andrew and Jennifer Fane

LONDON AND NEW YORK

First published 2019
by Routledge
2 Park Square, Milton Park, Abingdon, Oxon OX14 4RN

and by Routledge
711 Third Avenue, New York, NY 10017

Routledge is an imprint of the Taylor & Francis Group, an informa business

© 2019 Yarrow Andrew and Jennifer Fane

The right of Yarrow Andrew and Jennifer Fane to be identified as authors of this work has been asserted by them in accordance with sections 77 and 78 of the Copyright, Designs and Patents Act 1988.

All rights reserved. No part of this book may be reprinted or reproduced or utilised in any form or by any electronic, mechanical, or other means, now known or hereafter invented, including photocopying and recording, or in any information storage or retrieval system, without permission in writing from the publishers.

Trademark notice: Product or corporate names may be trademarks or registered trademarks, and are used only for identification and explanation without intent to infringe.

British Library Cataloguing in Publication Data
A catalogue record for this book is available from the British Library

Library of Congress Cataloging in Publication Data
A catalog record for this book has been requested

ISBN: 978-1-138-08953-2 (hbk)
ISBN: 978-1-138-08957-0 (pbk)
ISBN: 978-1-315-10916-9 (ebk)

Typeset in Bembo
by Out of House Publishing

Contents

List of figures and tables   vi
Acknowledgements   ix

1 Being born   1

2 Becoming ourselves in relationships   23

3 Agency and resistance   43

4 Choice and constraint in children's health   61

5 Child wellbeing – contested views   79

6 Understanding emotions in context   98

7 Learning environments   115

8 Spirituality and young children   135

9 Guiding behaviour in an unequal world   156

10 Working with diverse families   176

11 Sustainable education for dangerous times   194

12 Changing the world   212

Glossary   230
Index   233

List of figures and tables

Figures

1.1	Source: Pixabay	1
1.2	Judy Horacek cartoon showing people's unwillingness to let go of privilege	4
1.3	Regardless of racial background or economic circumstances, all children deserve a peaceful and secure upbringing	8
2.1	Source: Jennifer Fane	23
2.2	It is never too early to introduce a child to the natural world	32
2.3	Natural phenomenon, such as a caterpillar turning into a chrysalis, can introduce children to a sense of wonder	39
3.1	Source: Elizabeth Baker	43
3.2	Basic art activities allow young children to feel some control over their environment, as they shape the materials, and explore the textures and patterns they can create	51
3.3	Natural materials of a wide variety are usually easy to source, and can enrich ordinary activities, such as using clay or dough	54
4.1	Source: Jennifer Fane	61
4.2	The structure–agency continuum	66
4.3	Engaging children in food growing helps children to understand where food comes from and to take risks in trying new fruits and vegetables	68
4.4	These preschoolers from Madagascar are taking part in International Handwashing Day, a United Nations project designed to raise awareness of accessible health strategies	74
4.5	Sociological Imagination Template	76
5.1	Source: Yarrow Andrew, with thanks to Flinders University Childcare Centre	79
5.2	Joyful group activities are always a good way to encourage physical activity in children, and these can happen indoors or outside	88
5.3	Small Worlds play helps children make sense of their social relationships, and can help build a sense of emotional wellbeing	94
6.1	Source: Pxhere	98

6.2	All children need skills at naming emotions, and we need to name positive emotions as often as more negative ones	106
6.3	Hugging a friend can be a useful strategy for children to know, when they are feeling fearful or anxious	112
7.1	Source: Alyssa Bagley	115
7.2	Building on the existing mature tree as a landscape feature, this skilfully designed rocky mound and platform can be a cave, a castle, a mountain and more besides	119
7.3	Whatever the climate in your area, you can make the outdoors accessible with the right clothing	122
8.1	Source: US Department of Agriculture	135
8.2	Many spiritual traditions have rituals connected with the seasons	147
8.3	Children can learn many good lessons through their connections with animals	149
8.4	Art can be a meditative process for young children, allowing them time and space to develop their ideas	150
9.1	Source: Pixabay	156
9.2	This educator is taking time to talk through a minor dispute between these children, ensuring their feelings are honoured, and good solutions found	168
9.3	An older OSHC child paints the face of a younger one, building trust and community	171
10.1	Source: Yarrow Andrew, with thanks to Flinders University Childcare Centre	176
10.2	There are many ways to communicate with families	184
10.3	This community garden and outdoor pizza oven has been created with the school community to support the wide involvement of families in the life of the school	189
11.1	Source: Pixabay	194
11.2	This young child is being given the opportunity to explore a local watercourse, and ponder the mysterious role of water in human life	196
11.3	This school aquaculture project raises fish and freshwater crayfish for food, with the polluted water cleaned up by filtering through an outdoor bed raising herbs for human consumption, before being recycled into the tanks	201
11.4	This childcare site is making the most of a generous yard by growing a range of fruit trees, as well as vegetables in raised beds	207
12.1	Image: Pixabay	212
12.2	These student teachers in Canada were activists of their day, carving out new roles for women in education in the 1890s	218
12.3	Demonstrations can still be an effective way of making change, and activism on behalf of children can attract wide-ranging support	226

Tables

4.1	The sociological imagination template	77
5.1	Child wellbeing and development constructions	85
5.2	Child wellbeing indicators derived from the five selected child wellbeing/development constructions	86
5.3	Child protection orientations	90

Acknowledgements

We would like to thank the people who read early chapters and provided feedback or contributed to the process other ways; Vittoria Barbara, Connie Lent, Denise Rundle, Claire Lace, Brian Newman, Hannah Chapman-Searle, Chris Jacques, Alyssa Bagley, Pamela Leach, Katherine Purnell, Andrew Plaistow, Fiona Strahan, Lara Corr, Susan Banks, Flinders University Child Care Centre and Alberton Primary School. Yarrow would especially like to thank Emily Chapman-Searle, who read the entire manuscript and made many invaluable suggestions, as well as walking alongside me on the long road to publication. I am blessed by such amazing family, friends and colleagues.

1   Being born

Figure 1.1
Source: Pixabay. Licence: Creative Commons CC0

Introduction

The Sociology of Early Childhood takes you on a journey into the lived experiences of young children from birth to the age of eight. Drawing on sociological research, which explores the social factors that influence every human life, this book will illustrate the powerful and persistent pressures which act on children, wherever in the world they are born. Differences among human beings are often refreshing or interesting, but they have been used throughout history to treat certain groups of people unfairly. We ask you to look again at these differences, as an educator, and decide for yourself what impact they have on the children you are teaching, and what you can do about this.

Each chapter will begin with questions which aim to draw you into the big issues – giving you an immediate sense of what you will be learning in that section. Next we'll give you a story – a narrative about the social world of children – to ground you in the daily work that we are discussing. Then we will dive right into what will be most useful for you to know as an educator, in dealing with the complexities of each aspect of teaching in a modern and diverse world. At the end we have questions, activities and resources to help you make connections between what you have read, and how you might use it in your educational work with children from birth to eight.

We know that as an educator you care deeply about the wellbeing of the children that you work with. As the chapters unfold, you will learn about what it means to be a baby, to grow older and to become part of educational systems and societies, from a sociological perspective. You will learn about the importance of a holistic view of health, about the significance of environments and emotions, and the ways that families, communities and local contexts all play a role in the lives of young children. Throughout all of this our aim is to help you feel confident in dealing with the complexities of young children's lives, so you can teach every child in ways that respect who they are, and help them thrive in your classroom. So let's get started …

Questions for consideration

- What sorts of ideas is sociology interested in, and why are these important for early childhood educators?
- All societies are webs of relationships among people, at a particular time and in a specific place within the natural world. How do the effects of power and privilege shape these relationships in your society right now? Which people are most marginalised in your community, and why?

Vignette from practice

Kahlil is a four-year-old child in your class, where you teach in a childcare service run by your local municipality. You have always found Kahlil to be a happy child, although fairly quiet, and are glad to have the chance to work with him again this year. During outdoor play on a mild day near the end of first term, you are sitting digging with Kahlil in the sandpit. It is near the end of the day, with the sun slanting through the trees, and many children have been picked up already, making this a peaceful moment in an otherwise busy teaching day. Perhaps triggered by a particularly vivid memory from the previous year of digging in that same space, Kahlil starts to tell you something that shocks and saddens you. Hesitantly at first, but then with increasing intensity, Kahlil tells about his experience of two older children – both boys – who he was terrified by last year. It has taken him some months into this new year, but he has realised he can start to feel safe, and that his tormentors will no longer be around to make his life miserable.

You know that sometimes children can be cruel to each other, but what bothers you most is that you did not notice any of this going on in your class last year. Your mind races; 'How did I miss this? Why didn't I protect Kahlil from this bullying?'

Giving Kahlil a hug, you tell him how sorry you are that he had to live through this, and that you did not realise what was going on and do something about it. You want to remind him to tell you when anything is bothering him, but realise this is only going to burden him further. Perhaps he did try to tell you last year, but you were too preoccupied to notice, or misunderstood his hesitant efforts. You have work to do, you can see, in how you handle conflict and meanness in your group, and to find ways to make your classroom a safer space for all children.

The sociology of early childhood

As authors, we believe that early childhood education has not paid enough attention to sociology. Sociology is the study of society, and the ways that power shapes and reshapes both large societal structures (the government, media, education) as well as individual interactions between human beings. Sociologists acknowledge that the world is not an equal place, and believe that understanding how inequality originates and is maintained is vitally important. As early childhood educators, whether new or very experienced, this sort of understanding is valuable. It will help you to see why relationships with some families may be unexpectedly difficult, or why children react so differently to the same sorts of behaviour guidance. We believe that attending to sociological aspects of our experiences provides perspectives that otherwise would go unnoticed. This book draws you into the world of early childhood practice, and gives you a sociological take on children's lives, on pedagogical practice, on relationships with others and on our curriculum choices.

The story above, about Kahlil, reveals the everyday power relationships that occur in early childhood settings. It talks about how Kahlil has felt marginalised within this learning community, and has been bullied by two other children, so that he felt silenced and terribly afraid. This is a direct manifestation of power, through violence, intimidation and threat (although power is often wielded in more subtle ways). To a sociologist, there are particular questions raised by this incident. Has this child been targeted because they are from a non-dominant ethnic background, or because they are from a Muslim family? Maybe it is because Kahlil is a quiet child, who prefers to do things like drawing, rather than join in the active and aggressive games that many boys in this group seem to prefer? Has this educator been unable to see this violence and intimidation because their privilege as a 'white' person has allowed them to be blind to possible manifestations of racism? Have ideas about children's innocence, based on myths about age and experience, also worked to make such violence unthinkable, and so invisible? Or is it simply that Kahlil has been overlooked in favour of other children who demanded more attention, who were more verbally competent or outgoing, or were more familiar culturally to the educators present?

These sorts of questions are central to the practice of sociology, because they are about recognising that some forms of inequality will have significant impacts on the life chances of particular people. In this case, Kahlil may have been unable to take advantage of a year of rich early educational experiences, because his attention and energy were absorbed by fear and working out how to feel safe. If these sorts of experiences are repeated for Kahlil throughout his educational journey (as is true for many children from marginalised backgrounds) then he will not be able to learn as effectively or become the person he might have been without these repeated negative experiences.

Inequality impacts on everybody, but it has the hardest and longest impacts on those who are most disadvantaged in our communities. We believe that as educators you care about unfairness. We want you to have the knowledge and the skills to deal with it more effectively, so that your efforts will make the world a better and safer place for all the children under your care.

Figure 1.2 Judy Horacek cartoon showing people's unwillingness to let go of privilege.
Source: © Judy Horacek 2016. First published by Fairfax Media. Used with permission

The big issues – power, privilege and marginalisation

One of the most important ideas we are talking about in this book is power, and how we can see this operating in society through the unearned privileges some groups of people have, while others do not. Why do we call them 'unearned' privileges? Most people are comfortable with privilege that can be earned, such as people being rewarded for their skills, hard work, good behaviour or special qualifications. When we talk about unearned privileges we are thinking about things like the colour of your skin, the gender you were assigned at birth, the wealth of your family or even being conventionally attractive according to the standards of the country and era you were born into.

One example of unearned privilege you may not have noticed (unless you are reading this as someone whose first language is not English) is the privilege that comes with being born into particular language communities. Across the world, some languages are used by many people because they were once the language of trade (e.g. English, Spanish, French), as a result of histories of colonisation. At the moment English is a particularly influential language because it is the dominant language in the United States, which has been the world's most politically influential and wealthy nation for much of the last century. Being able to speak English fluently and comfortably is a form of privilege, because you will find this language used by others wherever you travel on the globe, within many educational institutions and in much of the world's publishing.

We will be talking about privilege, and the power that comes with this, throughout this book, as well as the absence of privilege, which can be called marginalisation, powerlessness or disadvantage. When particular groups are marginalised, we are using a metaphor about being pushed to the edges of society, from where it can be difficult to be noticed or heard. Sometimes this is literally what happens, when refugees are forced into internment camps away from major population centres, but more often it is about lack of access to services, support or mainstream public discourse.

It is hard to talk about privilege because those who are privileged do not want to think about the unfair advantages they have received. There will be times in this book when you will be asked to notice your own privilege. You may find this uncomfortable, and in some cases it may even make you angry. This is okay! It is normal to feel defensive when you start to realise the advantages you have grown up with, without ever noticing them. This is a form of *resistance*, and is something we will talk more about when discussing the theory that underpins this book.

Dimensions of inequality

Before we do so, we need to explain about the differences that tend to become a focus for privilege and disadvantage in most countries, which we call *dimensions of inequality*. Any person from a privileged group is likely to have more; more money, more influence, more time to speak and so on. People tend to think about these dimensions of inequality simplistically as absolute differences, rather than just varying experiences of being human. We hope we can help you to see more complexity in each of these dimensions of inequality, as well as the important differences between them in the impacts they have on our societies. This complexity means that within any given category – 'women', 'able-bodied people' – there will always be considerable variation, because these dimensions of inequality intersect with each other (see breakout box).

Intersectionality

Theories of intersectionality, based on the foundational work of Kimberlé Crenshaw (1991), help us to understand that different dimensions of inequality can sometimes reinforce each other, making their effects more harmful. In other circumstances the effects of inequality may be lessened, such as when male privilege might offset some of the disadvantages of racial prejudice. Crenshaw sought to show that the impacts of gender, race and sexuality on the lives of Black women in the US cannot be understood separately, but only through observing the material impacts of these dimensions of inequality in aggregate, and their differential effects for individual women and their contexts.

While we cannot always draw attention to these intersectional effects in our examples, as an educator it will always add to your understanding of a situation to think about how a particular child or family might be impacted by multiple dimensions of inequality.

Gender – unexamined lives

Within education, one of the most important of these dimensions is gender. This is the idea that there are only two types of people in this world; women or men, girls or boys. When we are born we are usually put into one of these categories without having any say in the matter, based on a casual inspection of our external genitalia by medical staff. However human bodies are not simple, and what we tend to think of as gender is actual a complex inter-relationship between our chromosomes (containing genes), the hormones circulating in our bodies, the appearance of our bodies and our emerging identity in relation to current expectations of gendered behaviour. Increasingly we know that many people's bodies do not fit neatly into one of these two gender categories (some of these people would describe themselves as *intersex*), and there is emerging awareness that many people's identities as human beings do not fit easily into categories of female and male either. Some people will transition from their assigned gender to another one. Some will continue to experience their gender as changing (*genderfluid*), undefined, or absent entirely (*agender, neutrois*).

An increasing proportion of the population see themselves as *genderqueer*, or *non-binary*, a gender different from either female or male (see online link to these gender definitions, at the end of the chapter).

Whatever you believe about gender, we know that for most of history, and across nearly every society, men are privileged at the expense of women, earning more money, doing less domestic and emotional work, and wielding more political power. Education plays a role in this, and we will see throughout the book the ways in which education often reinforces social expectations of gender, either consciously or unconsciously, through differing expectations of behaviour, school dress codes and preferential treatment.

Social class – let's not talk about this!

Many people would like to believe that social class is not an issue in their society, and that we all live in countries where there is equal opportunity. As a result there is resistance to talking about social class, as if it is only a historical issue. Unfortunately it is a very real phenomenon, and shapes all our lives, whether we acknowledge it or not. Social class is a measure of economic privilege, of wealth and poverty, but it is not *only* that. How much wealth we have influences who we spend time with, the sorts of places we live and the sorts of things we tend to know about. These are all aspects of class privilege, or the absence of it.

When talking about class, we will tend to use language such as *working class* to describe those with least economic privilege, *ruling class* to describe those with most economic privilege and *middle class* to describe those who fall somewhere in between. There are no perfect ways to talk about social class, and many arguments about how many classes there are, or how we should identify these groups. It is worth knowing that economic privilege (having more money) will moderate the effects of other types of disadvantage, particularly within the educational system. For example, in the UK all people from an Afro-Caribbean background will experience some racism, and will be less likely to be part of the ruling class, but those who are will benefit from class privilege (e.g. elite schooling) which may offset race-based disadvantage (e.g. discrimination in job interviews). Social class also tends to shape whom people socialise with ('people like us'), as well as the expectations we have about the types of jobs we will do or neighbourhoods we might live in.

Race and cultural heritage – acknowledged, but still damaging

Many people are familiar with the idea that racism is wrong, or damaging. This is certainly true. What is less often acknowledged is that racism is a structural phenomenon, not just a form of personal animosity, and perpetuates through unacknowledged biases and covert mechanisms (Mueller, 2017). Whether a person is personally racist or not in their behaviour, they may benefit from forms of structural racism if they match privileged norms such as lighter skin colours.

8 *Being born*

Scientifically it is now well-known that 'race' is not a useful way of describing types of human beings, although it remains a common way to describe people with particular sorts of body types or skin colours (Warmington, 2009). Instead, we know that human beings are remarkably similar across the planet, with historical and ongoing intermingling of populations, in response to migration, travel and so on. While populations of people from particular parts of the world may superficially appear similar, individuals within those populations may genetically be more similar to individuals from very different-looking populations across the globe, due to the complexities of human history.

From a sociological perspective, what is important about race in today's world is that light-skinned people experience forms of privilege, not only within their own country, but also globally. This is due to the historic dominance of European powers during centuries of colonialism and empire-building. White privilege is a persistent advantage for those whose appearance matches a European norm, and often confers advantage in getting paid employment, accessing housing or other forms of social privilege.

Lastly, race is also closely connected to culture and ethnicity, because we can be said to share our race with other members of our family, even if they do not look similar to us. Race connects us to our ancestry, and the sorts of cultural practices and religious beliefs that exist within our extended family. In this way it is unlike gender, because we do not tend to share the same gender with our whole family.

Figure 1.3 Regardless of racial background or economic circumstances, all children deserve a peaceful and secure upbringing.

Source: Pixabay. Licence: Creative Commons CC0

Connection to land – indigeneity and migration

Related to the idea of race is the concept of indigeneity. To be Indigenous is about connection to a particular place, or country, and is about being part of the first known human population to have inhabited that area. Such connections to country may be as long as 60 000 years for Australian Indigenous people, 12 000 years for First Nations people in the US, or 800 years for Māori people in Aotearoa. Indigenous groups have often been marginalised or dispossessed as a result of (European) colonisation. However their claims to the first and longest relationship with a place have increasingly been acknowledged and recognised through treaty processes or international mechanisms, such as the United Nations Declaration on the Rights of Indigenous Peoples (2008). Indigeneity is also significantly connected to ideas of sustainability, as Indigenous groups carry significant knowledge about how to live on and with the natural environment in sustainable ways. Recognition of the particular relationships of some people to certain places helps us all to notice the emotional and spiritual significance of landscapes and histories, ideas we will pick up in chapters 8 and 11. These aspects of human difference are becoming increasingly prominent as Indigenous nations across the globe struggle for recognition and for rights to their traditional lands. This recognition is complicated by the increasingly large movements of people across the globe, in response to the changing climate. Such migration is introducing new social stresses on the societies which are absorbing the most migrants, with locals often fearful about what impact these newcomers might have.

Ability and disability – mental and physical

Human beings slip easily into judgements, and one of the most basic judgements is 'Are you *normal*, or not?' In this book, we will not be using the language of 'normality' uncritically, because it has become associated with ideas of 'rightness', acceptability and so on. There is a great deal of variety among human beings, in the range of mental and physical abilities or challenges, and therefore no way to say what is 'normal'. Ideas of what is 'normal' also shift over time, and these shifts are always of interest to sociologists. Twenty years ago, someone talking to themselves on the street would have been considered scary and perhaps mentally unwell. In the era of the smartphone and other devices, talking (apparently) to yourself has become a common feature of everyday lives.

We do not know the futures of the children that we work with. They may appear to be developing in ways that could be considered typical, until the intervention of an illness or injury changes their experience of life. Other children will come to us with known and identified mental, physical or emotional needs that we must learn about, to educate them more effectively. Usually this involves building a solid relationship with that child, because they will know best what they want to learn or explore.

An important idea in this book is that 'disability' has a core social element. We experience the world through others' reactions to us, and through how easy or difficult it is to function smoothly in the world with the bodies, minds and assistive technologies that we may need as human beings. As educators we can use our role to reduce the social stigmas and functional difficulties associated with many impairments or other disabling conditions, so that the children we work with are more free to learn, to connect with others and to explore what their lives may become.

Sexual expression and identity – with children?

Many educators prefer not to think about sexuality, because society has traditionally constructed children as 'innocent' and free of sexual desire or practices (Robinson, 2013). This common attitude is unhelpful to young children. In this book we see young children coming into a world where sexuality and sexual identities are really significant for the adults around them. As a result, they pay attention to these issues, and quickly learn that adults do not like to talk about this subject, and often look very uncomfortable when sexuality is mentioned.

We believe that as educators we have a responsibility to provide children with the information they need, when they need it. When young children are exploring their bodies, and experiencing the sorts of feelings associated with masturbation, we can help them learn that this is something done in private, thus helping them learn the social rules of their society. When young children are experiencing strong connections with others – an early type of love – we can help them to channel these energies respectfully towards the object of their affection.

Most importantly, we need to talk about sexual expression because children are sometimes forced to participate in a range of sexualised activities by older children and adults. When we are silent about sexuality as educators we are not able to provide children with the skills they need to identify sexual involvement that does not feel good, and that may be damaging to their sense of identity. These protective behaviours can be as simple as letting children know that they are in control of who touches them, and how this happens. When anyone is trying to take away their control, then we can tell them it is okay to tell a trusted adult about this.

Finally, we know that many sex and gender-diverse children have been made to feel 'abnormal' or wrong, because their experience of the world is different from those around them. Not all of these children will grow up to identity as same-sex attracted people or as transgender, but they all need to know that their feelings are not wrong. This belief, that only cisgender, heterosexually identified people are 'normal', is called *heteronormativity* and is perpetuated unthinkingly by many people and institutions. All children, whatever their identities, need the same guidance about how to relate to others lovingly and respectfully, and to experience environments where they, and their families, are safe, and valued.

Age – who is in, and who is out?

Our last area of difference is an important one in early childhood, because it relates to age, and the ways people are judged unfairly around this. Both the very young and the very old are not believed to be capable by most adults, and often are treated poorly because of this assumption. Throughout this book, we want you to be aware that this discrimination is called 'ageism', and represents a devaluing of some groups of people unnecessarily and automatically, regardless of their abilities.

The children we work with are young (some are infants), with less physical strength or coordination, and less accumulated experience and knowledge. Nonetheless, they are learning, and learning faster than at any other time in their lives. As educators, we want you to consider treating all children as capable – from the outset – and only offering support or guidance when this is needed or wanted. When we treat others as incapable, whether old or young, they feel dismissed, trivialised and less-than-human. Many children have learnt to accept this as normal because it is the only thing they have known. As educators, you have a powerful message to offer children in your classrooms: *you know a lot, and we can help you learn more.*

Theoretical foundations of this book

We want this book to be a practical and useful resource for those starting their journey as early childhood educators as well as those who are currently working with young children. We do not want to focus so much on sociological and political theories that our main message is lost. However we know that some will want to know what theoretical perspectives are valuable to us as authors, and how we will use them to help you think about the sociological ideas in this book.

In doing so we will be talking about formal theories – which often seem quite distant from daily life – and the scholars whose ideas have shaped them. These are different from the sorts of 'folk theories' that circulate in early childhood education, such as the idea that girls and boys are 'naturally' different, or the idea that children are innocent. These folk theories have some truth to them, which is why they circulate so widely. In this book we will try and show how these everyday assumptions can be challenged or thought about differently.

Poststructuralism

One of the important theoretical frames of this book is *poststructuralism* (see breakout box). Poststructuralist ideas draw on the work of a number of scholars, but the most well-known is Michel Foucault, a philosopher and social critic writing in the second half of the twentieth century. His important insight was that power is not something you can hold onto, but something that flows through and across society, being constantly negotiated and contested (Foucault,

1977). When you ask a child in your classroom to pack up their work, and they refuse, you are experiencing the realities of poststructuralist ideas of power, and the concept of *resistance*. You may think you have 'power', as an educator, but children can and do resist that power, refusing to do what you ask or doing it in ways you did not anticipate.

Poststructuralism

We are using the word poststructuralism in this book, to capture a widespread movement of researchers, thinkers and educators, influenced by some ideas that became prominent in the last part of the twentieth century. This is sometimes called *postmodernism*, or *post-foundationalism*, and sometimes people just call this set of ideas the *'post- theories'*! In the nineteenth century (and for much of the first part of the twentieth century) there was a widespread belief – *structuralism* – that everything in the world (plants, animals, societies, languages) would soon be understood through one overarching structure. People hoped to find universal laws which explained each of these phenomena completely.

*Post*structuralist theories, on the other hand, assume that the world will be complex, and that there are multiple ways of knowing and understanding any given phenomenon. Poststructuralists assume that all theories are contested by those who have access to power and knowledge, and that some ideas come to be considered as 'the truth' because these ideas represent discourses which have become widespread, and are supported by powerful interests. Poststructuralists still believe some ideas and theories are 'true', but they recognise that because others may disagree with them, then it is more honest to call these *truth-claims*. This is a reminder that truths are not universal, but specific to particular communities and ways of knowing.

Foucault argued that power circulates through *discourse*, which represents the collective words, beliefs and actions of a particular group of people in a specific time and place. We are born into a set of discourses – a particular discursive environment – which set limits on what can be talked about, believed or done in that place. Some discourses become dominant (i.e. most people believe in them), and so play a big part in shaping our choices about what we do and say each day. Think about what you chose to wear today, or how you tend to behave. Is this random? Your choices are constrained by the discourses available to you, with dominant discourses having the biggest impact on your 'choices', and other discourses offering possible options, but ones that are less likely to be chosen. For this reason, Foucault argued that knowledge cannot be separated from power, because the more we know, the more we are able to influence or access different discourses. Following Foucault, we will sometimes use these words together, as power/knowledge, to reflect this close connection (Foucault, 1980).

Within poststructuralism, human beings still have *agency* – the ability to act and make choices. However our choices are not infinite, and are seriously constrained by the discourses that are available to us. If we are assigned to the female gender at birth, then the sorts of possibilities that are available to us in most places will be different from those children who are assigned male. Girls will be talked to more about their feelings, be dressed in less practical and more colourful clothing, and their hair will usually be allowed to grow longer, to help others identify them as female, and treat them differently as a result. Discourses do not control us absolutely, and we can and do resist their messages, but they strongly shape the likelihood of us behaving or thinking in particular ways.

One of the first people to use poststructuralist ideas in early childhood was Bronwyn Davies (1989), who used these ideas in research with preschool children around gender, and gendered power dynamics. As a feminist, she was interested in how children learn to become adults who are entrenched in gender norms and roles, and what the social mechanisms are in childhood that make this happen. By using poststructuralist ideas she showed very clearly that children are not just passive victims of 'socialisation' (see chapter 2), but actively contest the ideas of gender, and the possibilities that exist within these for some children and not others. More recently, Prasanna Srinivasan and Merlyne Cruz (2015) draw upon poststructuralist theories to look at the discursive practices of race relations in Australian schools, and the practices, such as 'othering' or 'silencing', which keep racial inequalities intact.

Critical pedagogy

Closely connected with poststructuralist ideas, particularly in the field of education, is the set of theoretical ideas known as critical pedagogy. These began with the work of Brazilian educator Paulo Freire, in the 1960s, as he worked alongside peasants and uneducated workers, teaching them literacy skills (Freire, 2014 [1968]). However he was also starting to understand what learning meant to those he was teaching, and thinking about the possibilities that become available within education for those that have traditionally been excluded from it. The central idea in critical pedagogy is that education is not neutral, and that the ways education is constructed often functions to perpetuate the ideas of the wealthy elites, and to alienate those from more humble backgrounds. Freire realised that the traditional model of education assumes that learners know nothing, which he called 'the banking model' (see breakout box). Instead he found that his students – adults from poor backgrounds – were not empty vessels, but full of ideas about how the world worked, or should work, and with desires for knowledge not traditionally found in schools. His new approach to education he called 'conscientização' (critical consciousness), and this described the shared process by which teachers worked alongside their students, helping work out what they wanted to learn, and finding ways to make that learning happen which made sense to those learners.

> ## The banking model
>
> One of Freire's most influential ideas has been his critique of traditional education, which he saw as working under the 'banking model'. Freire argued that most teachers assumed that their students were like empty bank accounts, into which they, as the teacher, had to deposit knowledge. Freire saw this as a very flawed model of education because it assumes so much power on the part of the educator. How do they know what knowledge students need? It also encourages students to be passive, as their only role is to receive the knowledge, file it away and be able to retrieve it. There is no attempt to explore deeper understanding, including why this knowledge may be valuable, and in what circumstances.
>
> Instead, Freire argued for co-intentional education, where students and educators both guided the learning, articulating their versions of reality, and coming to a shared sense of the possible problems, as well as any solutions. This model began with adults, but can be used when working with children by engaging them in conversation about what they want to be learning, and problem-solving together about ways to explore those curriculum areas. Inquiry-based learning fits in well with this model, because it does not assume that a particular body of knowledge must be absorbed, but begins from the questions children may have about the world. This is similar to the idea of 'co-constructing knowledge' within sociocultural theory, but with an awareness that sharing knowledge is explicitly about sharing power, and may meet with resistance from more privileged groups who benefit from existing systems of education.

Within mainstream sociology, there has been significant attention paid to education, because compulsory schooling plays a key role in shaping societal discourses around economic inequalities. French sociologist Pierre Bourdieu has written extensively about how educational systems work to perpetuate existing systems of inequality, through disguised mechanisms which make this seem natural, or inevitable. It is this normalising effect of education – which he argues persuades children to see themselves as 'smart' or as 'stupid' based on their origins – that functions to perpetuate existing structures of class and privilege. He uses the concept of *symbolic violence* to discuss the ways that dominant cultures in a particular society impose their own understandings of the world on all of society through education, and so delegitimise other perspectives

(Bourdieu & Passeron, 1990). He names this as an invisible form of violence against whole groups of people, including less privileged classes, because of the damage it does to their sense of themselves as legitimate or valued.

Many other educators have taken up the work of critical pedagogy, and used it to make education meaningful to all sorts of people traditionally excluded from education. For example, feminist educator and academic bell hooks (1994) is an African-American woman who uses critical pedagogy to challenge the ways that the US excludes women and non-white people from education. This happens either explicitly, in the historical exclusion of any except white men from most schools and universities, or implicitly since then, in having curriculum and reading lists dominated by the ideas of privileged men, most of whom are white.

You can see these sociological phenomena at work even in this book, because many of the theoretical ideas discussed originated with privileged European men, such as Foucault or Bourdieu. Their ideas have become well known as a result of a whole sequence of events, all shaped by power and privilege. As males they were allowed to study, and given support to do so, which is still denied to many young girls in this world. Secondly, their race and class privilege gave them access to mentors and funding bodies to help them develop their ideas and promulgate those ideas more widely. Lastly, their ideas were taken more seriously because they were male, but also because of their employment by leading universities in wealthy countries.

Theoretical perspectives are useful, but it is good to remember that ideas do not grow in a vacuum. All learning is dominated by the voices of the most privileged, usually those who are white, male, able-bodied and wealthy. As a result, although we will be using theoretical ideas that draw on the work of male scholars, such as Foucault, Freire or Bourdieu, we may explain their ideas through the writing of others, such as Davies or hooks, whose feminist and critical perspectives on the world allow them to take up these ideas and breathe life into them, perhaps seeing aspects of them that more privileged scholars may have been blind to.

Critical pedagogical researchers have developed many useful ideas that we will draw on throughout the book. When talking about curriculum – the content that we teach and how we teach it – it is worth remembering that this content, like the theories we draw on, is not neutral or universal. The *formal curriculum* within our education system will have been created by people with more access to power/knowledge, and will tend to reflect the values of the ruling classes, such as the dominance of what is called 'neoliberalism' in today's world. Critical pedagogues realise that to understand how curriculum works in school, we need to analyse the different ways it is put into practice. This has led to concepts like the *hidden curriculum* – knowledge that is transmitted accidentally within education through unconscious attitudes or unexpected occurrences – or the *null curriculum* – which represents those ideas considered taboo or dangerous, and which are actively avoided (Blaise & Nuttall, 2011).

Social and critical psychology

This book is framed around sociological perspectives, and so addresses the processes within each society that shape children's lives. Nonetheless, the history of early childhood education has been significantly shaped by its alignment with psychological approaches to human life, which focus primarily on individuals, separate from their social contexts. We will therefore be drawing also on the work of those who have developed social and critical approaches to psychological knowledge that engage in dialogue with ideas from sociology.

The most significant of these is Erica Burman (1994), who wrote an influential book critiquing the limited, culturally biased approach of child development theories (see chapter 2). She argued strongly against biologically based theories of childhood, showing that human attributes like gender – assumed to be innate – were actually socially constructed phenomena being misinterpreted by psychological researchers. Burman pointed towards more useful ways to examine human life, and how human growth continues to be embedded within wider social processes and communities. Her work examines the cultural assumptions that are embedded within many psychological theories, and how these work to marginalise and stigmatise the experiences of many human beings from different cultural backgrounds, in regard to issues such as 'maternal responsiveness', or universalist constructions of developmental stages. She criticised the narrow psychological focus on the mother–child relationship, which perpetuates a cultural assumption that women are exclusively responsible for the rearing of children.

One of the consequences of this assumption is that early childhood is one of the most gendered fields of work and research, with very few male-identified people working with children directly, or as teacher-educators. Another consequence is that women are made to feel uniquely responsible for – and often highly guilty about – the children they have jointly conceived with (mostly male) partners. The media often blame women for any perceived problems with children, whether this is fair or not.

Within education, theoretical work by Valerie Walkerdine (1990; 1989), another leading critical psychologist, has focused particularly on the experiences of girls and working-class children within the school system. She shows how schools perpetuate inequality, marginalising girls from less economically privileged backgrounds, and making it harder for them to succeed. If they do not succeed, they are taught to see this as a personal failing, rather than the result of an unfair system. In her writing around social class, her work complements and extends the work of Bourdieu, who writes about the negative effects of education on many groups of children.

The varied lives of young children – being born

Throughout the chapters of this book, we will take you through the various experiences of young children as they progress through the early childhood years, experiencing forms of childcare, schooling, family life and community involvement. Their experiences will affect their life chances, and the skills and knowledge they acquire. In doing so we show how our location within systems of inequality such as class, race or gender makes some outcomes for children more or less likely (Van Ausdale & Feagin, 2001). In doing so, we will also be suggesting the ways you can intervene as educators, interrupting some of these unequal effects and making life fairer for all children.

Pre-birth

While we might want to think that all children start life with equal chances, in reality there are many factors before birth that can have a significant impact. We now know that the age of both mothers *and* fathers can have an impact on whether, for example, a child is born with Down syndrome, a non-fatal genetic condition that can impact children's intellectual abilities. At an everyday level, many factors of family diet and lifestyle can impact on a child's later health and wellbeing. Providing good access to health services and education about healthy lifestyles are a societal responsibility, but often parents are judged as individuals for personal choices often mediated by social class and racial inequalities. Those parents experiencing the most severe economic hardship may not have access to enough food or secure housing, and this can lead to babies being born early and underweight, in ways that can impact on their health long-term. We will pick up on these ideas in chapter 4.

Wanted, or not?

One of the facts about children we do not often consider as educators is whether a child is even wanted or not within their family. This is an aspect of occupational blindness, perhaps, in that we want to believe that every child has been born into a loving and supportive family. In fact many children are born by accident, and may be coming into a relationship characterised by conflict, mental illness or other negative circumstances. In some cases, gender has an impact, as girl babies are less valued worldwide and are aborted at higher rates, or given less care, attention and education once they are born.

Who is my family?

One of the most significant factors impacting on children's life chances is the family they are born into. First, if someone is born into a family living in one of the wealthier nations (the *Minority World*), with a functioning political system and effective health services, then they will have a longer life expectancy and more access to social and economic status. Within an individual country, it will matter whether your family represents the dominant grouping, which may be defined by a particular race, ethnicity or a particular religion. Patterns of institutional prejudice in most cultures mean that parents from the dominant group are more likely to be employed, in more secure and well-paid employment, and more able to provide a good life for their children. Children born into heterosexual couple relationships will experience more social privilege than children born to single-parent families or families whose parents are in same-sex or polyamorous relationships, who may experience shame or discrimination because of their family situation.

What you will find in this book

Before we explain to you the structure of the book and what you will find, we want to let you know about the *glossary*, at the back of the book. This is a useful list of the words we use that may be unfamiliar. It is also the place where we explain some of the early childhood language we employ, because we may be employing language that is not used in your context. For example, words like 'preschool' will be used to describe multiple years of early education prior to formal schooling, in the way it is used in Sweden, rather than one year of this early education, as is the case in other places.

In **chapter 2** we will look in more detail at the lives of babies, and their rapid enculturation into the everyday cultures and norms of the place they are born. In doing so, we will encourage you to feel confident in the wide variety of excellent ways that babies are raised in different cultures, as well as their robust abilities to survive many different living situations.

Within **chapter 3**, we look more closely at the lives of toddlers, as they begin to feel a sense of their own ideas and desires, separate from those of their caregivers. We look at the idea of agency, and why we should not be apprehensive about young children's attempts to make choices about their own existence. We also look at the social structures that may limit these possible choices, through the discourses that circulate about what people of a given gender, race, class or disability should be doing.

In **chapter 4**, the idea of children's health takes centre-stage, as we investigate what young children need to flourish, in terms of their physical needs. This is impacted significantly by the dimensions of inequality we looked at earlier in the chapter, and will help you realise how closely woven these ideas are with the possibility and potential of human lives.

Chapter 5 extends this idea of health to look at how this is shaped socially, through the idea of wellbeing. We ask whether adults' ideas of children's wellbeing always match up with children's own desires for their lives, or their perceptions of what makes life worth living.

Taking up **chapter 6**, we dig deeper into children's emotional lives, exploring how these can be useful indicators of children's emerging understanding, as well as a good tool for helping preschool children learn skills like self-regulation.

Within **chapter 7**, we find ourselves in the classroom, whatever this might look like in your own early childhood context. Whether outdoors, purpose-built or a family home, these environments help shape the possibilities for our educational work with children.

Chapter 8 examines the often ignored area of spirituality, which can be expressed in many different ways in children's lives and communities. For Indigenous communities spirituality may be the foundation of their culture and wellbeing. For those who grow up within a particular religion, the rituals and practices of this religion will have an impact on their upbringing and daily experiences, and the skills that they acquire.

Throughout **chapter 9**, we take up the practical but creative task of guiding children's behaviour. Looking through a sociological lens will impact on our decisions about what boundaries we set, and how firm these are, and will keep us mindful of children's agency and diversity.

In **chapter 10**, we acknowledge the significant role that children's families of origin play in their lives, and the many different configurations of family that can nurture and raise children. In doing so, we will help you to think about the skills you need to engage with families who may be different from you, and to find points of meaningful connection from which to work together.

Chapter 11 sees us take on the key challenge of the twenty-first century, which will be how humanity learns to live sustainably and equitably within the limits of the only habitable planet we know. We explore what may be necessary for us to know as educators, and some of the positive ways we can respond to this challenge.

Lastly, in **chapter 12**, we examine what it means to think about our educational work as a form of activism, becoming advocates for the vital work that we do in our field. We look at how we might use our skills as educators to engage children, families, colleagues and the wider community in the search for better education, and a better society.

Concluding remarks

As you journey through this book, we hope you will be encouraged, through the questions at the beginning and end of each chapter, to think about who you are as an educator, and the unique combination of skills, abilities and life experiences you may bring to this role. Some chapters will make a lot of sense to you, reflecting what you know of children, the work that you do or the world that you inhabit. Other chapters may present ideas that are unfamiliar, or present them in ways that are puzzling or confronting. For example, the idea of white privilege (see online resources) is often one that educators of European heritage have not had to think about, but which will be very familiar to those readers who have grown up with brown skin, or with non-European cultural backgrounds.

Our aim, with this book, is to help you become culturally competent as an educator, in the broadest sense. This is learning that you will continue to do throughout your life, but we aim in these chapters to give you a solid grounding in the sociological issues that most impact on our shared work in early childhood. To be culturally competent is not to know everything, and certainly not to be an expert in the lives of others. Instead it is about having an open attitude, knowing enough about what you don't know to ask the right questions, of children, of family members and of colleagues, so that you can work with them effectively. We firmly believe that culturally competent and respectful educators are the key to an effective, meaningful and vibrant early childhood sector, and one which has the wellbeing of all children at its heart.

Questions for reflection

- How does theory help educators in early childhood to make sense of their work? What sorts of theories are important to you? What 'folk theories' exist around you? How can these big ideas help us to reimagine what we do, and how we go about it?
- Our lives are shaped by an 'accident' of birth, being born into a particular gender, a particular family and culture, with a particular skin colour or with differing abilities from others? What privileges or challenges have you grown up with? How do they continue to shape who you are now?
- What social changes have you noticed in your lifetime? Some of these changes may have impacted on your life, either positively or negatively, changing your everyday behaviours. What areas of social relationships have changed most rapidly, and which seem stuck in a rut?
- What sociological issues do you find most challenging to deal with, as an early childhood educator? These are usually the ones you avoid thinking too much about, or acting upon, because you feel you 'don't know enough', or 'don't want to offend'. How can you work to improve your skills of 'cultural competence', so that you can work better with children in these sorts of situations?

Activities for educators

- Make time to talk to someone who is very different from you, in terms of their experience of gender, ability, cultural background or whatever. This can be a friend or an acquaintance, and you need to be clear that you would like to ask them, respectfully, about their experience of the world. Use this time to listen carefully to what they have experienced, and how particular systems of privilege may have impacted hard on them, or not.
- In your work with children, think about the issues you do not want to discuss in the classroom – the *null curriculum*. Talk with your colleagues about difficult subjects you might need to address with the children, and how you can do so in ways that reflect best the values of your community and site. At some sites you may decide to discuss this with the parents and families

who use your service. However, remember that as an educator you are best placed to consider the general needs of all children, rather than families who are often only focused on their own child.

Key readings

Bourdieu, P., & Passeron, J-C. (1990). *Reproduction in Education, Society and Culture* (R. Nice, Trans. 2nd ed.). London: Sage.
Freire, P. (2014 [1968]). *Pedagogy of the Oppressed* [*Pedagogia do Oprimido*] (M. Ramos, Trans.). New York: Bloomsbury.
Foucault, M. (1977). *Discipline and Punish: The Birth of the Prison* [*Surveiller et punir: Naissance de la prison*] (A. Sheridan, Trans. English ed.). London: Penguin.
hooks, b. (1994). *Teaching to Transgress: Education as the Practice of freedom*. New York: Routledge.
Van Ausdale, D., & Feagin, J. (2001). *The First R: How Children Learn Race and Racism*. Maryland: Rowman & Littlefield.

Online resources

TED talk by Kimberlé Crenshaw on intersectionality and its importance. www.ted.com/talks/kimberle_crenshaw_the_urgency_of_intersectionality?referrer=playlist-talks_to_help_you_understand_s
'It's pronounced metrosexual' – useful educational site, including a list of current definitions of words connected to gender and/or sexuality. http://itspronouncedmetrosexual.com/2013/01/a-comprehensive-list-of-lgbtq-term-definitions/ – sthash.JeciXYj7.0CglXN1S.dpbs
Read about the effects of white privilege on the website for the US-based SEED project (Seeking Educational Equity and Diversity). https://nationalseedproject.org/white-privilege-unpacking-the-invisible-knapsack

Further reading

Blaise, M., & Nuttall, J. (2011). *Learning to Teach in the Early Years Classroom*. South Melbourne: Oxford University Press.
Burman, E. (1994). *Deconstructing Developmental Psychology*. London: Routledge.
Crenshaw, K. (1991). Mapping the margins: Intersectionality, identity politics, and violence against women of color. *Stanford Law Review*, 43(6), 1241–1300.
Davies, B. (1989). *Frogs and Snails and Feminist Tales: Preschool Children and Gender*. Sydney: Allen & Unwin.
Foucault, M. (1980). Truth and power. In C. Gordon (Ed.), *Power/Knowledge: Selected Interviews and Other Writings* (pp. 109–133). New York: Pantheon Books.
Mueller, J. (2017). Producing colorblindness: Everyday mechanisms of White ignorance. *Social Problems*, 64(2), 219–238.
Robinson, K. (2013). *Innocence, Knowledge and the Construction of Children: The Contradictory Nature of Sexuality and Censorship in Children's Contemporary Lives*. Abingdon: Routledge.
Srinivasan, P., & Cruz, M. (2015). Children colouring: speaking 'colour difference' with Diversity dolls. *Pedagogy, Culture and Society*, 23(1), 21–43.

United Nations (2008). *United Nations Declaration on the Right of Indigenous People*. Retrieved from www.un.org/esa/socdev/unpfii/documents/DRIPS_en.pdf

Walkerdine, V. (1990). *Schoolgirl Fictions*. London: Verso.

Walkerdine, V., & Lucey, H. (1989). *Democracy in the Kitchen: Regulating Mothers and Socialising Daughters*. London: Virago Press.

Warmington, P. (2009). Taking race out of scare quotes: Race-conscious social analysis in an ostensibly post-racial world. *Race Ethnicity and Education, 12*(3), 281–296.

2 Becoming ourselves in relationships

Figure 2.1
Source: Jennifer Fane

Questions for consideration
- How do we become social beings?
- Is the socialisation process consistent across cultures?
- In what ways do family structures, cultural practices, economic circumstances, differing abilities and trauma shape children's emerging capabilities to form successful relationships?

Vignette from practice

Rosaria and her daughter Maricella attend an infant-toddler programme that meets high quality professional standards according to quality criteria in her country. The programme adheres to suggested educator/child ratios, the environment is clean and well organised for optimal safety, with indoor and outdoor play areas and nutritious meals. The educators have university degrees in early childhood education with specialisations in infant-toddler care and education. Each day Rosaria carries her 18-month-old daughter Maricella into the infant room and sits with her on the rocker. She hugs her and holds her for several minutes while rocking, telling her how much she loves her.

Even though Maricella is able to walk and has learned to pull her sweater over her head and place it in her basket, Rosaria carefully takes the sweater off, carries Maricella with her and places the sweater in the basket. Maricella has attended this programme for six months and her mother knows that Maricella's educator, Catherine, prefers that she place Maricella on the floor, tell her goodbye and then walk out the door. Nonetheless, each day Rosaria walks over to Catherine, still holding Maricella, and reaches over to pass Maricella to Catherine. Maricella clings to Rosaria then bursts into tears as Catherine gently pulls her from her mother's arms. When Rosaria has left, Catherine comforts her and soon Maricella runs off to play. As Maricella runs off to play, Catherine comments to her co-worker, 'Do you notice how she stops fussing as soon as Rosaria leaves? We should make a time to talk about this with Rosaria, and understand what it feels like from her perspective.'

Introduction

As early childhood educators, we have a profound impact through the relationships we create with children and families. Early childhood education programmes are driven by a variety of theoretical frameworks, each situated in a socio-political and cultural context. These frameworks will impact upon how you form relationships with children and their families, through the expectations they embody about your pedagogical relationships. Relationships are critical to the quality of children's experiences in early childhood settings, and we hope this chapter will help you think more deeply about the skills you will need in this work.

At times, the ways that educators make connections with babies and their families may not be compatible with the personal and cultural practices of these families. The work of caregiving looks and feels different in group settings beyond the family context. As such, unique relational practices emerge within early education programmes, as a result of our specific knowledge-base and practice as educators. In this chapter we aim to extend your knowledge-base beyond the dominant discourses of child development, and look at alternative ways of engaging in care of infants and toddlers.

Many early childhood educators express that their passion for working with children is what draws them to this work. At times, you may find it intimidating to realise that a key part of your role involves working with adult family members, in supporting children. All children are first and foremost situated in the rhythms of their family life. This is vital learning, and we will think more deeply about this area of practice in chapter 10.

Coming into the world

From the moment of birth, infants begin to negotiate the intricacies of relationships within the context of their social setting. One infant may suckle contentedly at the breast while another is rushed to intensive care, to address the complications of drug addiction passed from mother to child. Some will have bodily or metabolic impairments requiring surgical intervention, and have to fight for their lives as their family waits in shock and disbelief. These very different beginnings will have consequences for each child's relationships, because of the reactions of those around them. A parent who sees their baby as fragile due to early health complications is likely to be more anxious than the parent of a robustly healthy child, because of their vastly different experiences of the first weeks of life.

As babies grow, they may be parented by one, two or multiple parents, of various genders, by grandparents or other relatives, by adoptive parents, or by caregivers in a foster home. These different experiences of being parented can all be successful or stressful, joyful or tragic. The emotional climates and daily rituals of these particular lives will begin to shape the habitual responses of these very young children, and some will end up approaching the world fearfully, and others confidently. Traditionally this process has been called 'socialisation', and has been a useful concept in flagging that human beings *become* who they are, rather than being born a particular way. We exist as many potential possibilities, and this potential becomes actualised in response to the families and cultures we grow up in, and the particular choices we ourselves make in our earliest days.

We hope that you will approach the concept of 'socialisation' with caution, as it is frequently misunderstood by parents and educators (Grbich, 1990). Many adults assume that they are in complete control of the process, and that if they work hard enough at socialising a child in a particular way, then that child will become the person we want them to be. Those of us who have spent more time with young children know that this is far from the truth! Children shape themselves, in response to the many messages they get from the world around (not just families, but the media, their peers and extended family), as well as their own bodily needs and processes. The result is always unique and surprising – and outside the control of those raising the child. The emerging field of epigenetics is interesting, because it confirms this 'loose framework' of development from a biomedical perspective. Our genetic heritage, it turns out, is not a blueprint, but a spectrum of possibilities, which are then actualised by particular experiences in the world. Interestingly, researchers are realising that experiences in the world can write themselves onto a person's body, causing physical changes which can then be inherited by that person's children or grandchildren (e.g. Bygren *et al.*, 2014). Our understandings of human development are opening up, revealing it as a complex process, and one which can be a two-way street. Our environments and upbringing can affect our genetic legacies, and our biology appears to offer multiple possibilities, only some of which will be manifested.

As human animals we are born into the world vulnerable and in need of nurturing, founded upon secure relationships. We have brains and bodies eager to learn, and are capable of absorbing information and connecting concepts at an astonishing rate. The physical environments we are in will shape what we learn, as we will see in chapter 7, and the social experiences we have will either support or undermine our wellbeing. This chapter explores children's earliest relationships and our roles as educators in supporting their engagement in early childhood settings. We examine this challenging transition for babies, as they negotiate personal relationships within new and unfamiliar settings.

Do babies need theory? Social structures and human relationships

Even though babies do not have any understanding of 'theory' (whatever this concept is called in their home language!), they are nonetheless forming their own theories about how the world works. As early childhood researcher Helen Hedges (2014) explains, 'working theories' are where the child draws on their creativity and current experience to understand the world around them, and help guide their future decisions. As human beings we use these working theories as part of our ongoing inquiry into the way the world works. So a baby's first theory might be, 'If I cry, someone comes and holds me, and I feel better'. For some, their experience of crying is that someone yells at them or hits them, and so their working theory becomes, 'If I am quiet, nothing bad will happen'. In the vignette at the beginning of the chapter, Maricella may have believed that if she acts more like a baby, then her mother will do everything for her. The more evidence that she gets that her theory is correct, the less effort she will make, knowing that others will do things on her behalf. This dynamic might shift when she begins the infant-toddler programme, or it may mean that she develops different patterns of behaviour from those at home, depending on the reactions of the adults around her.

We believe theory is valuable for you, as an early childhood educator, because you will get new perspectives on the sorts of situations you will encounter in your work. In this section we will look at theory from sociology around social structures, and about emotions and everyday life. We will also ask you to rethink the most common theories in our field, those of developmental psychology, and the role they continue to play in how adults relate to babies and toddlers.

Social structures and traditional sociology

When social scientists first began to study society, they focused on the most obvious institutions of power, such as governments, religious organisations, big business, education and the media. These societal structures are all sites of power/

knowledge (see chapter 1), because of their ability to wield influence over large communities, and project particular ideas about the world. Sociological research continues to explore how these social structures impact on individuals, and the sort of agency that each person can access to negotiate their influence.

Education

As early childhood educators, we are already part of one of these structures of power, the education system. We will be adding our voices to the dominant discourses which circulate within educational settings. This is not something to be apologetic about, nor do we want you to pretend that you have no power. Whatever our position in society, we all contribute to or undermine the dominant discourses in society, through our words and actions. As educators, we will be working with a particular group of children, and the close relationships we form with them and their families will give us a great deal of influence over their thoughts and feelings. Pretending this is not the case is dangerous, because we will not be taking our responsibilities seriously.

Government

We cannot help being impacted personally, and in our working lives, by other structures in society, and understanding these will help us do our work in education more thoughtfully. The traditions of critical pedagogy assist in this, by unpacking the impacts of these structures, and showing how they tend to reproduce rather than challenge existing inequalities (hooks, 2010). Governments, of course, have a direct influence in education at all levels from early childhood to tertiary, creating policy, enforcing regulations, running schools and preschools, and often creating national curriculum documents. These national curriculum documents vary in the extent to which they attempt to control the work of educators. Some are broad-based, documenting values rather than practices, such as the Swedish curriculum (Vallberg Roth, 2006). Others are much more detailed, restricting the autonomy and agency of educators by controlling the knowledge they can draw on (Cannella, 2000).

Religion

Religious organisations can wield considerable power in many countries, despite the rise of secular society and non-sectarian governments. In Ireland, for example, the Catholic church still runs the majority of schools, giving it considerable influence over the lives of educators, children and the community (Smith, 2001). Religious organisations may have a direct stake in systems of government, as in Iran, where since 1979 Shi'i Islam has been the official religion, and the constitution requires governments to take religious law into account in their decision-making, including decisions about education (Tamadonfar, 2001). The dimension of inequality most impacted by religion is sexuality and gender expression, as most religions tend to police this area of human life most strongly, enforcing discourses of heteronormativity (see chapter 1).

The corporate world

Big business increasingly wields influence in the preschool sector, through buying or building early childhood services, and running these as profit-making enterprises. These businesses have the strongest hold in countries which have been dominated by neoliberal discourses, such as the US, Australia and the UK. One of the concerns about the rising dominance of this private model of childcare provision is its impact on quality. This is less true for individual for-profit services, which may in some cases provide excellent education at a reasonable price. More often, however, the demand to create value for shareholders by large corporations means that budgets are squeezed, employing less-qualified staff and with fewer resources, impacting on the structural quality of those services (Cleveland *et al.*, 2007).

Media

Lastly, the media often play a significant role in magnifying the voices of the more privileged sectors of society, due to the editorial influence wielded by the very wealthy owners of these businesses. This may lead to more favourable views of private education over public education, or result in poorly informed criticism of well-grounded educational interventions. Where countries have introduced ways of testing and ranking educational performance, the media often magnify the impact of these, by publishing lists of the 'best' and 'worst' schools and early childhood services. Quality improvement regimes, however optimistically they are introduced, end up distorting early childhood systems (e.g. Goffin & Barnett, 2015), and usually exacerbate inequality, as informed middle-class parents come to dominate the most highly rated sites, a phenomenon called 'opportunity hoarding' (Sayer, 2011).

The sociology of intimate life

More recently, sociologists have begun to explore the impact of emotions and other human interactions. They are looking at these not as an internal and individualised phenomenon, but as clues to the norms of behaviour in our cultures, and the expectations created for different groups through the discourses circulating in society (see chapter 6). For example, most cultures share a belief that females and males are intrinsically different sorts of beings, rather than variable members of one human species. We are raising and educating babies in these environments, and they soon begin making their own working theories about gender. We know that babies start to connect related concepts and experiences from the first months of life, and they are beginning to form fuzzy impressions that the world around them might be divided into two different groups of people. As they get older, they start to associate particular types of objects and behaviours with these different groups, as well as to realise that they themselves are presumed to be in one of these two categories, as either female or male.

This is not a simple process, as human societies are complex and changeable. This is why children tend to internalise these categories (such as gender or race) slowly and imperfectly, up to about the age of eight. You will frequently hear older children's working theories around gender being expressed – 'only girls have long hair', 'only boys play football' – but we know that these theories are being formulated from babyhood onwards. As we suggested in the section on socialisation earlier in the chapter, this is a multi-faceted process, and there are many societal processes which contribute to reinforcing heteronormative behaviours (Fine, 2010). Even when adults consciously do try to de-gender their child-rearing, young children take their cues from all the cultural knowledge to which they have access. For example, many feminist-inclined parents have despaired when their daughters gravitate towards the colour pink, because this preference is pushed so strongly through mass media and the sorts of toys that are marketed to children.

Judith Butler (1990) is one of the world's leading experts on gender, and is credited with showing that gender is not something we *are*, but something we *do*, through our everyday actions and choices. She called this idea 'performativity' (see breakout box). This idea has been very useful in understanding how stereotypes persist and are replicated not just in gender, but also within racial and class communities. This idea of performativity helps us understand the choices young children are starting to make around their behaviour. As babies learn that they are a 'girl' or a 'boy' (because adults around them keep telling them this), and if they accept that this is true (transgender children may resist this notion), they then choose to act in accordance with what they believe is the right way of being a girl or a boy.

Performativity

Butler argues that phenomenon like gender take their force from their repeated inscription in everyday acts and behaviour. She suggests it is not that we are compelled to act biologically in particular ways, but that we engage in such behaviours through choosing to fit in with the norms for the gender we were assigned at birth. To say we *perform* gender is a useful way to think about this, as long as we remember that these are not performances we can easily step away from. The habitual and lifelong nature of gender behaviours makes them hard to shift, so we fall into gendered habits even when trying not to. *Performativity* attempts to capture this idea that discourses of gender are perpetuated coercively through our collection behaviour in human communities, even if the specific norms of gender differ across culture and places.

Trauma

We believe these sorts of gendered constraints on children's behaviour are unhelpful, and limit children's possibilities for flourishing as human beings. This experience of gender, however, is not usually a traumatic experience, except for children whose identity differs from the gender they were assigned at birth. Many babies grow up in traumatic situations, which can shape their lives irrevocably. Depression following the birth of a baby is common among mothers, as well as being experienced by some fathers. When this depression is persistent or severe, it is likely to impact on the quality of caregiving that baby experiences, with long-term consequences for that child's experiences of intimate relationships. Similarly, many infants grow up in situations where there is domestic violence, and sometimes this violence has resulted from that child's birth, because of a father's unjustified anger about losing his female partner's care and attention. These infants' sense of 'normal' may be of frequent loud and distressing noises or even pain, if a parent takes out their abusive or depressed feelings on that child. It is distressing to hear about the painful lives of some babies, but we want you to know it is likely you will educate many children from traumatic situations such as this, and will need to respond thoughtfully to their particular needs.

Child development and 'universal' theorising about children

Most early childhood practice around the world for the past hundred years has been guided by child development theories, based within the discipline of developmental psychology. This phenomenon has been strongest in the US, where the National Association for the Education of Young Children (NAEYC) has long advocated for 'developmentally-appropriate practice' (DAP). This has been the dominant discourse in early childhood education historically, creating the impression not just that child development is *one* source of knowledge about children, but that it is the *only* source of knowledge you will need to be a good educator.

Erica Burman (1994), whose work we noted in chapter 1, has been critical of developmental psychology, because of its narrow and simplistic approach to human existence. These theories often propose 'grand' theories about children, which link particular ages of children with particular stages of development, or ways of thinking and acting. These include Jean Piaget's (1969) theory of cognitive development, Mildred Parten's (1933) staged theories about play, and Erik Erikson's (1950) theories about 'psychosocial' life stages, from birth through to the end of life. There are two main problems with these and similar theories. First, they have a narrow evidence base, usually from research on specific Minority World populations, such as white wealthy people in the USA. Secondly, they are totalising, assuming that what is apparently true for people in one place will be applicable right across the world. When child developmental theories are taught to early childhood educators they are framed as universal truths, readily applicable to all children in any context. However, as recent work by the Open Science Collaboration (2015) project suggests, only 36 per cent of psychological studies can be successfully replicated, and even many of these results are weaker than first thought. As poststructuralists and sociologists we are not surprised by this. Any research with human populations will be highly depend on context, and subject to changing human norms and expectations, including sociological research. As educators we encourage you to be skeptical of any knowledge presented to you as fundamental truth (including the knowledge in this book), and to reflect on whether its insights match up with your own experiences of teaching children and the educational values that matter most in your context.

Some alternate models – challenging ageism

We believe that child developmental theories are often ageist, because they carry an implicit assumption that we begin life as deficient, and get better, wiser, and more capable as we get older. Such theories reassure adults that they are capable, but are often very damaging to young children, who are left feeling incapable, and so encourage passivity and helplessness. Many of these developmental theories have led to a deficit approach to education, in which educators spend most of them time focusing on what young children cannot do (by using developmental checklists) rather than what they enjoy or do well. A less ageist perspective suggests babies enter the world capable of absorbing knowledge and drawing conclusions at a rapid pace. As we age, we acquire more knowledge and experience, but we also slow in the rate we can learn, and become more limited in our creativity and curiosity.

Strengths-based education

One of the strongest challenges to a deficit approach to children's learning has been the move towards 'strengths-based' education under Aotearoa/New Zealand's 'Te Whāriki' curriculum framework. Within this framework, outcomes for children are seen as combinations of skills, attitude and knowledge, identified in two broad categories, *dispositions* and *working theories* (discussed above). Dispositions (think of *mindsets* or *competencies*) are orientations to learning, such as persistence, curiosity or learning from failure (Claxton & Carr, 2004). When we work on identifying children's orientation to learning, we understand not what they know right now, which will change, but how well-prepared they are for future learning.

Strengths-based educators document learning with a variety of tools, including videos, critical conversations, narrative documentation and reflective observations, and focus on what children do well, and what they enjoy. These strengths (in engagement and mastery) can then be used to encourage the child to extend their skills into new areas, or investigate favourite activities more deeply. It can be used successfully with babies for whom such skills

Figure 2.2 It is never too early to introduce a child to the natural world. Here a child explores a vegetable garden, touching and smelling freely.
Source: Hannah Chapman-Searle. Used with permission

are becoming apparent. When we see an infant posting a block through the same slot repeatedly, building their hand–eye coordination, then we see them demonstrating persistence and can find similar activities which they may find rewarding. One of the biggest educational problems we have is how we fail those children who are least orientated to school – often (but not always) children from more marginalised backgrounds. By building on children's strengths, we help all children develop confidence in their abilities, and a willingness to trust in the process of education, even when it seems mystifying or frustrating.

Respecting babies

Emmi Pikler was a Hungarian doctor and paediatrician who founded the Lóczy Institute in 1946, to work with children orphaned after the war. This institute still operates but now works with children that need fostering or other forms of permanent care. Pikler was aware of the potentially detrimental effects of institutionalisation, particularly on infants, and so developed a range of methods to care for them effectively (Gonzalez-Mena, 2004). These methods resonate well with the strengths-based approach above, seeing babies and toddlers as capable, and also as people whose needs should be respected. Pikler believed that babies should be allowed the ability to learn independently, and encouraged her staff not to put babies in positions they could not achieve themselves. For example, she would not put a baby in a sitting position until they had developed the ability to do so themselves. This supports babies in developing their own techniques for moving around, building their persistence and problem-solving dispositions. Most importantly, Pikler took seriously babies' emotional needs, and expected staff to be fully focused on infants within the limited one-on-one times they had with them in an orphanage setting. The aim was to make those times rewarding times, full of rich conversation, and to help that child to feel that they were loved and valued individually. In other interactions, staff made sure they asked babies for permission before picking them up, waiting for a positive response, or reassured them verbally about things that were going on (such as someone walking past them). These all help to build a sense of trust and security. Pikler herself advocated for each baby to have a key caregiver assigned to them, and many early childhood services around the world have picked up on this, particularly in work with infants. While we see the value in this, we caution that research has shown that such key caregiver programmes can be problematic when a baby's caregiver is sick or absent, because their needs often get overlooked at those times.

The infant as citizen

A final vision of children's lives we'd like you to consider is that children can be seen as citizens, rather than incapable human beings or the tender objects of care, as Gunilla Dahlberg and her colleagues (2007) have argued. They suggest that as critical educators we need to move away from the idea that children are *future* citizens, and remember they are citizens right now! Children are affected by decisions made by our governments, because these decisions impact on education systems, family poverty, gender equity or even the regulation of corporations (such as advertising junk food to children). Children are not just affected by these when they reach voting age, but are affected now. One response is to teach children to become critical thinkers, carefully evaluating the information they receive. As we will see in chapter 12. we might also support them in learning the skills of being an activist, so they can have a political voice, even if they cannot vote. What would taking babies' citizenship seriously mean for us? We think that Emmi Pikler's techniques are a good start, because they demonstrate respect for babies in a wide variety of ways, honouring their emerging capabilities. We also wonder if we can support babies as citizens by providing a social and economic safety net to support families with infants effectively, as well as resourcing well-qualified alternate caregivers for any babies whose families might be failing in their care.

Privilege and children's care needs

It might be hard to think of infants as being privileged, but this idea is familiar from sayings such as 'being born with a silver spoon in your mouth'. Babies do not choose this privilege, and do not take it for granted as adults sometimes do. Nonetheless, our children are still being brought up with widely different experiences of wealth, and in response to various markers of cultural privilege. A child born with light-coloured skin in this world is likely (but not guaranteed) to receive more favourable treatment than a sibling with darker skin colour, because of structural racism (see chapter 3). As critical educators we cannot make these differences disappear, but we can put effort into understanding these systemic inequalities, and work to minimise them in our classrooms. This section will explain why some infants and toddlers might have specific care needs, based on their lack of privilege, the societal messages they are receiving within that culture or the trauma they have experienced.

Dis/ability

New ideas about the understanding of disability, from researchers who have experience of disability themselves, demonstrate how narrowly most of us conceive of what is 'normal' for babies. This has dramatic consequences for any babies born visibly different, because of the ways that adults around them, both family and strangers, may react to them. While most parents become passionate advocates for their disabled children, the continued dominance of biomedical models of disability means that they must continue to struggle against the negative messages implicit in the standard model of child development. A child with muscular dystrophy, for example, will have a different trajectory around physical development than most of their peers, because of the impact this condition has on muscle development and control. Drawing on a social model of disability reframes this apparent problem, and reminds us that it is universalising expectations around development which are creating this situation, rather than the child with this condition. The child with muscular dystrophy still has a life, and will experience joys and sorrows like any other child.

Similarly, children who have experienced early trauma may be left with difficulties in social adjustment which make some aspects of human life more challenging for them. Labelling a child 'difficult' or 'slow to warm up' works from an individualistic framework that locates the problem in the child. Instead we can focus on our adult understandings of differing social needs, and develop our ability to cater for a wider variety of emotional experiences and behaviours. As an educator you have the challenging task of treating all children equally, despite powerful discourses around 'normality' which encourage preferential treatment of more typical children, while often having low expectations of children with disabilities. We see this even in inclusive early education settings, where the qualified educator's role is seen as working with the majority of children, while a child with a disability is often in the care of a person with few formal qualifications, and little understanding of the particular needs of that child. Instead of using the educator's skills to benefit the child most likely to experience disadvantage, their attention is given most to the children who need it least.

Remember that some impairments, such as being born without hearing (or 'Deaf', as the sign-language community might write it), may set children apart a little, but may also make them feel special and valued within their own community. It is important for Deaf babies to be raised immersed in sign language if this is to be their home language, and this will need careful collaboration with parents to ensure their child has the support they need in this critical period. While this may be overwhelming as an educator, specific children's needs offer opportunities for all members of the classroom community to learn different skills and ways of relating.

Social class

In thinking about constructions of normality, we know that most educational settings privilege behaviours which are typical of middle-class homes, and so are judgemental of children whose home lives may be very different. With older children, this means that qualities such as being able to sit still for long periods, or being confident enough to ask questions of unfamiliar adults, are seen as the defining qualities of successful learners. With babies, where there are fewer expectations on the child, this attention is focused on the child's family. Educators can fall into the trap of being judgemental about the actions of the child's primary caregiver, without taking the time to understand that family's situation, or build a better relationship with the family.

> ## Forms of capital
>
> One helpful way in which to understand family disadvantage is through Bourdieu's (1986) concept of capitals. In order to understand the complexities of social class, he built on the idea of economic capital (wealth, money), extending this metaphor to other resources, such as cultural capital (knowledge, expertise, education) and social capital (connections, networks). This theoretical framework helps understand why, for example, a ruling-class person might lose all their wealth, through a bad investment, but would still have classed advantages because they are unlikely to have lost their extensive stocks of cultural and social capital, and can still utilise them to their advantage.

Social class matters immensely, as bell hooks's (2000) work explains, with lack of economic privilege often intersecting with other inequalities. For example, a baby whose parents may be struggling with mental illness will likely have less access to professional or social support, if from a disadvantaged class background. From an educator's perspective, disadvantaged children may suffer from more frequent illnesses, due to the various social determinants of health which may be affecting their families (see chapter 4). This can impact on their behaviour, and they may cry more frequently and be harder to comfort or distract. This can cause educators to give them *less* attention, in response to the added stresses within a formal care setting. Thus lack of economic capital within families can lead to educational disadvantage, and flow on to a lack of cultural capital, or increased social isolation and less social capital (see breakout box).

Race and Indigeneity

Lastly, we hope you will always be conscious of the impacts of structural racism on the experiences of culturally and linguistically diverse babies within settings which cater primarily for children from the dominant culture. Babies will be sheltered from the direct impacts of racism by their families, but parents and caregivers will still be impacted by racism, with possible impacts on mental wellbeing or economic circumstances. Even if their families are flourishing, and are well-supported within their local communities, these parents will still be vigilant about racism, and this may make it harder for them to trust you as an educator if you are from the dominant cultural background. This will be especially true for families with Indigenous heritage, who will not only experience 'ordinary' racist effects, but also experience the effects of toxic colonial histories, and the damaging impacts of negative stereotypes, or intergenerational trauma. Educators who care about social justice will be conscious of the possible impacts of structural racism on families and be willing to hear parent concerns about these issues when they are raised, without trying to dismiss or minimise them.

'Being with' babies

We have seen some of the many ways in which babies may experience inequality, from the very start of their lives. However we know that quality early childhood settings are usually a positive intervention in the lives of all children, through our work in supporting parents and extended families, and through the respectful and warm relationships we (ideally) build with children. In this section we want to talk about positive ways that you can work with babies and toddlers, helping build competent and resilient children. We know that many of these skills and practices will already be part of your repertoire, and that this section will act as a reminder about effective ways of supporting the children you will be working with.

When working with babies we advocate keeping the focus on relationships, because it is so easy for routines (feeding, sleeping, toileting) to become dominant. While routines are important, we often forget that their main purpose is the child's wellbeing. Routines help children to feel competent by allowing them to anticipate upcoming events, and to feel capable in familiar tasks. However it is often educators themselves who are the most invested in these routines, and we want you to notice when you are sticking to routines at the expense of more important relational issues. There will always be some children, particularly those on the autism spectrum, who have a greater need for routine. You may be able to help these children by ensuring that 'handover' times in the morning are kept consistent and reassuring, to help ease them in their daily transitions.

It is easy for institutionalised forms of caregiving to become so weighed down by routines that there seems little room for joy and spontaneity. One way of avoiding this is to remember to celebrate! There are many things to celebrate when working with babies, who are learning an incredible range of skills, physical, intellectual and emotional, over the first year or two of life. Perhaps a child has managed to roll over from their back to their front, or has managed to get a spoonful of food in their mouth without too much mess! These are moments worth celebrating with that child or as a whole group, if you know this will not make that child too self-conscious. Celebrating might mean singing a joyful song, having a dance together or simply slowing down to notice and appreciate the moment. As educators you might also want to have your own quiet celebrations, on those times when everyone is sleeping peacefully or quietly engaged – these can be precious moments when working with groups of infants.

We believe that singing communicates strongly to all the children in your vicinity that the world is a safe place, and that this is a time for celebration. People rarely sing when they are scared or stressed! There are songs for every occasion (even reminders about classroom rules), and taking time to find a variety of songs from different cultures, and for different circumstances, will help you enjoy this more. Asking family members to teach you their favourite songs is a good way to build connections, increases your repertoire, while also helping their child feel safer in your care. If the song is in an unfamiliar language, take the time to write it down, both how to sing the words, as well as their meanings. We know that families will appreciate the effort.

Challenges and fears

We want you to be able to enjoy your work with babies, at least most of the time (there will always be *some* days where nothing seems to go right). If you are not enjoying your work, then this may mean you need to change your everyday practices, to make them more rewarding; for you, the children and your colleagues (see also chapter 12). It may mean you need to think seriously about finding another form of work, because babies will pick up on your unhappiness, and be less settled as a result, making your job even more difficult. Early childhood education is not for everyone, and the working conditions in the field are often less good than they should be. Our children need educators who are committed to the work, and have the desire to create engaging learning environments.

Another challenge often experienced by educators is coming to terms with the diversity of expectations and practices in how families care for their children, particularly in multicultural settings. It can be threatening for educators when their own conventional wisdoms about how to look after babies are challenged by other staff, by the different pedagogical practices in a new workplace, or by family members themselves. It is important to remember that no one culture has a monopoly on 'good practice'. Indeed, different children will respond in an incredible range of ways to the same actions, no matter how carefully thought out they are. For example, Anglo-American culture emphasises 'independence' in children, but this can also lead to less desirable qualities like selfishness or competitiveness, which can be damaging within a learning community. We want you to enjoy this wealth of human knowledge, and see it as a great resource for you, offering you always new perspectives and new practices to add to your repertoire. As Tara Yosso (2005) explains, all families come to your setting with particular forms of community cultural wealth, and learning about their experiences and beliefs will provide you with insight into other ways of embodying humanity.

Children themselves also experience many challenges, not least attuning themselves to a scary new environment, as they will be doing when starting their preschool experience. As educators we must take this fear seriously, and support children patiently, even if it takes many months for them to feel truly at home in your setting. Remember that this is not a deficit in the child, but may be a clue to how happy they are at home, or how much they feel comforted by routine.

Curiosity and wonder

As we draw this chapter to a close, we want to remind you of the joy and privilege you will have working with babies. Unlike most jobs, working with babies is an adventure, because babies are learning new things with every passing week. It is very hard to be bored when keeping up with an ever-changing, fast-growing group of infants, and your days will tend to feel like they go past speedily (except, perhaps, for those moments when an over-tired baby just will NOT go to sleep).

Babies are experiencing many things in the world for the first time ever, and as adults we need to pay close attention to what children are noticing, to remind us of what most interests them. One of the authors remembers working with babies during a long period of drought, and realising, when rain finally did come, that for some of these children they had never experienced this ordinary planetary event, despite their many months of life. In that moment, all of the group who were awake had gravitated to the window to watch this strange phenomenon! Of course they were curious when they had never experienced anything like this before. We opened the door to be able to smell the rain-wet

Figure 2.3 Natural phenomenon, such as a caterpillar turning into a chrysalis, can introduce children to a sense of wonder. Even educators will usually learn something new, as they extend on children's curiosity.

Source: Yarrow Andrew

ground, and some of the more adventurous ones ventured out to feel it on their skin – a small price to pay for new knowledge.

Research with educators shows that the greatest satisfaction comes in seeing children make leaps in their learning. Working with the youngest children, you will be reminded of the many wonders in the everyday world: a rainbow arching across the sky, an unfamiliar beetle making steady progress along a branch, a tower of blocks falling down in a noisy clatter, or a spiderweb glistening with raindrop jewels! Babies are attentive to all of these things, and show their joy without reservation. We hope you will be reminded each day of the marvels that the world has to offer – how many other jobs will offer you that?

Concluding remarks

In this chapter, we have looked at some of the social structures that impact on our educational work, and the influences that can affect our lives and the lives of children very deeply. Decisions of governments can be liberating, or catastrophic, in the workplace, in family life and in our education settings. Many decisions, whether made by businesses, governments or bureaucrats, can have unintended consequences, because human life is complex and outcomes are almost impossible to predict with any certainty.

We have asked you to think about the limits of developmental theories about children, and the ways they can restrict our vision, and constrain our imaginations. We have offered some alternate ways of working with babies which underline respect for every child, a recognition of their emerging strengths and differences, and what these can offer within a group setting. As we will continue to do throughout the book, we have reminded you of how privilege and disadvantage are at work, even in the lives of babies, with some receiving a flying start, and others being damaged by early trauma. We hope you have been given a sense of hopefulness about what you may bring to the lives of the youngest children, and the gifts of wonder and curiosity they will offer you in their turn.

Questions for reflection

- Think back to the vignette at the start of the chapter. What might be behind Maricella's mother being so protective of her? What might this handover process feel like from Maricella's own perspective? How might the educator have opened a conversation with that parent to create a handover routine that worked for the service, for her and for the child?
- What strengths did you have as a child? How well do you feel these were nurtured?
- Which social structures do you feel have the most impact on your life at the moment? How do they impact you? Would they impact in the same way if you were poorer, a different gender or elderly?

Activities for educators

- In the week ahead, try and look around yourself with the eyes of a young child. What things in your environment might be fantastical or amazing, to someone with no experience of the world. Does a vacuum cleaner sound like a scary monster? Does the sunset flood the world with an unfamiliar light? Learning to notice and feel wonder at the ordinary things of life is a good way to empathise with and be sensitive to the needs of the youngest children. Notice when you do not know something, and choose to follow your curiosity and find out more.
- In a familiar or safe environment, lie on the ground and imagine you do not have good control over your limbs, as is true for infant children. Are there others in the room around you? Can you see them without moving? Are you worried they might trip over you? What other things might infants be experiencing. Thinking about Pikler's principles in working with infants, spend a few moments imagining how you would like caregivers to be

acting in your space, if you were a baby. What would you want to tell them? Ask your friends to try this experiment, and tell you their ideas. We all have valuable experiences of the world, and our imaginations can close the gap sometimes, when communication is not easy.

Key readings

Burman, E. (1994). *Deconstructing Developmental Psychology*. London: Routledge.
Gonzalez-Mena, J. (2004). What can an orphanage teach us? Lessons from Budapest. *Beyond the Journal: Young Children on the Web*, Sept., 1–6.
Hedges, H. (2014). Young children's 'working theories': Building and connecting understandings. *Journal of Early Childhood Research*, 12(1), 35–49.
hooks, b. (2010). *Teaching Critical Thinking: Practical Wisdom*. New York: Routledge.
Yosso, T. (2005). Whose culture has capital? A critical race theory discussion of community cultural wealth. *Race Ethnicity and Education*, 8(1), 69–91.

Online resources

RIE – Resources for Infant Educarers. This not-for-profit is dedicated to spreading the ideas of Emmi Pikler about how to work with babies and toddlers. www.rie.org/
This is a useful guide for educators about how to work with traumatised children. http://education.qld.gov.au/schools/healthy/pdfs/calmer-classrooms-guide.pdf
Cultural background – This article from the *Encyclopedia on Early Childhood Development* challenges the universalising tendencies of child development knowledge. www.child-encyclopedia.com/culture/according-experts/culture-and-early-childhood-education

Further reading

Bourdieu, P. (1986). The forms of capital. In J. Richardson (Ed.), *Handbook of Theory and Research in the Sociology of Education* (pp. 241–258). New York: Greenwood Press.
Butler, J. (1990). *Gender Trouble: Feminism and the Subversion of Identity*. Abingdon: Routledge.
Bygren, L. O., Tinghög, P., Carstensen, J., Edvinsson, S., Kaati, G., Pembrey, M. E., & Sjöström, M. (2014). Change in paternal grandmothers´ early food supply influenced cardiovascular mortality of the female grandchildren. *BMC Genetics*, 15, 12–12.
Cannella, G. (2000). The scientific discourse of education: Predetermining the lives of others – Foucault, education, and children. *Contemporary Issues in Early Childhood*, 1(1), 36–44.
Claxton, G., & Carr, M. (2004). A framework for teaching learning: The dynamics of disposition. *Early Years*, 24(1), 87–97.
Cleveland, G., Forer, B., Hyatt, D., Japel, C., & Krashinsky, M. (2007). *An Economic Perspective on the Current and Future Role of Nonprofit Provision of Early Learning and Child Care Services in Canada*. Retrieved from www.childcarepolicy.net/wp-content/uploads/2013/04/final-report.pdf
Dahlberg, G., Moss, P., & Pence, A. (2007). *Beyond Quality in Early Childhood Education and Care: Languages of Evaluation* (e-library 2007 ed.). London: Routledge.
Erikson, E. (1950). *Childhood and Society*. New York: W. W. Norton & Co.

Fine, C. (2010). *Delusions of Gender: How our Minds, Society, and Neurosexism Create Difference.* New York: Norton.

Goffin, S., & Barnett, S. (2015). Assessing QRIS as a change agent. *Early Childhood Research Quarterly,* 30(B), 179–182.

Grbich, C. (1990). Socialisation and social change: A critique of three positions. *British Journal of Sociology,* 41(4), 517–530.

hooks, b. (2000). *Where we Stand: Class Matters.* New York: Routledge.

Open Science Collaboration. (2015). Estimating the reproducibility of psychological science. *Science,* 349(6251), 943–951.

Parten, M. (1933). Social play among preschool children. *Journal of Abnormal and Social Psychology,* 28(2), 136–147.

Piaget, J., & Inhelder, B. (1969). *The Psychology of the Child.* New York: Basic Books.

Sayer, A. (2011). Habitus, work and contributive justice. *Sociology,* 45(1), 7–21.

Smith, A. (2001). Religious segregation and the emergence of Integrated Schools in Northern Ireland. *Oxford Review of Education,* 27(4), 559–575.

Tamadonfar, M. (2001). Islam, law, and political control in contemporary Iran. *Journal for the Scientific Study of Religion,* 40(2), 205–220.

Vallberg Roth, A.-C. (2006). Early childhood curricula in Sweden. *International Journal of Early Childhood,* 38(1), 77.

3 Agency and resistance

Figure 3.1
Source: Elizabeth Baker (Public domain)

Questions for consideration

- How much control do you think parents and caregivers should have over children's lives?
- What choices should children be allowed to make, and at what age should we start to give them these choices?
- When children resist or defy adult direction, do you think they are being 'naughty'? Do more privileged children get given more leeway than other children in these circumstances?

44 *Agency and resistance*

- How do you think resistance manifests in young children of different ages?

Vignette from practice

This is a typical day in the babies room at Mary Davies Early Learning Centre. In this room there are eight children, ranging in ages from about three months up to eighteen months, with two educators, Anh and Jessica.

Yaminah is eight months old, and the educators, in consultation with her parents, have noticed her interest in self-feeding, and want to give her more opportunities to engage actively in the meal process. Yaminah seems excited to be sitting up at the low table where lunch is served, and to be eating with some of her classmates – the older children that she watches with interest during other parts of the day. She appears particularly interested in Chloe, a fourteen-month old, who is confidently spooning macaroni into her mouth. Jessica is offering her some mashed pumpkin on a spoon, but Yaminah seems more interested in watching Chloe.

'Why not give her a spoon of her own?' suggests Anh.

'Good idea', says Jessica, and hands Yaminah one of the rounded metal baby spoons from the wicker basket at the table.

Yaminah smiles broadly when given the spoon, and clasps it about halfway down with only a little difficulty. She immediately proceeds to bang it noisily on the table, laughing at the sound it makes on the wooden surface. After experimenting with various sorts of banging, as Jessica persists with trying to get pumpkin into her mouth, Yaminah stretches the hand with the spoon towards the bowl.

'Would you like to try feeding yourself?' asks Jessica. At this question Yaminah starts jiggling her legs excitedly.

'This is going to get messy' says Anh, smiling fondly. Yaminah tries various strategies with the spoon, but the position of her hand means the bowl of the spoon is often pointed downwards, and the pumpkin slides off. This is a fun game, lifting it high and watching it splat messily back into the bowl and surrounding table. Anh bends down and carefully moves the spoon, so that the bowl is pointing upwards, showing Yaminah how the shape makes it look different on one side and another, and how one side holds food better than the other. It isn't too long before she dumps the spoon over the side of the chair! Jessica wonders whether this was deliberate ...

'Would you like another spoon?' she says, handing a clean one from the basket to Yaminah, who grabs it, and then drops it where the first one went. 'I understand,' says Jessica, 'you have worked pretty hard on that today!'

As she is saying this Yaminah reaches into the bowl and grabs a handful of pumpkin, and brings it up to her mouth with a pleased look on her face. 'A much better solution', she seems to be saying ...

Introduction: The beginnings of agency

As we saw in the previous chapter, we do not experience a lot of control over our early lives. From our earliest days, when we need a lot of care and attention, adults tend to do things for us, around us, and to us, without asking our permission. As we get beyond infancy, and that initial period of helplessness, we start to make choices about what we do, how we spend our time, and even who we might become. In this chapter, we will be looking at some of the sociological understandings of this desire for agency, and how the possibilities for agency relate to the larger structures of our societies and cultures.

Are the 'terrible twos' really so terrible?

Within English-language contexts there is often joking about the 'terrible twos', which suggest that young children of this age are difficult to manage. Child development knowledge suggests that children of this age are going through a period of rapid change, in physical growth, in acquisition of language, in emotional expressiveness, and awareness of adult expectations (e.g. Grolnick, Bridges, & Connell, 1996). To a sociologist, the behaviour seen in children at this age is very understandable, because it represents the desire of children to start taking charge of their own lives. This is something we expect children to do eventually, but it requires the adults who are caring for them to start allowing children to have some meaningful agency in their daily lives.

Around age two is often when adults notice this active desire in children for control over their circumstances, and when adults become aware of their need to manage children differently. As babies, adults tend to do things for children without seeking their permission. The youngest babies lack the language or the physical control to resist what is being done, and can respond mostly by expressing emotion, such as by smiling or crying. As children become more physically mobile and verbally competent, their range of options for expressing agreement or disagreement becomes much larger, and this is often what adults begin to notice. Infants begin with non-verbal refusals, such as turning their head to one side to avoid food, but at some point, a child will learn the concept of 'no', however that is expressed in their first language. This is a powerful concept, allowing them directly and unequivocally to oppose the wishes or actions of their caregiver.

As adults, whether parents or educators, we are often not ready for this moment (the child is more than ready). When a child first says 'no' to us, or refuses in a very definite way to do something we want them to, we may feel affronted, in part because of the care and effort we are continuing to put in to care for this small person. We may also feel our opinion is more valuable or we have an agenda we are not telling the child (such as an awareness of time constraints). We suggest that this feeling of being affronted is not a good guide to how we should respond. This should not be about a struggle for control. As the adult, it is now part of your job to work out, and to imagine, what choices in life this child might reasonably be able to take, and which ones you still feel should be made by those around them. This will look different in different families, in different early education settings and in different cultures. What matters is that the adults understand that their role is not to suppress the child's desire for control, but to channel it in helpful directions, so that they learn the practice of making choices, and experiencing the ongoing consequences of their choices in ways that promote useful learning.

Theories around choice and constraint

In this section, we are going to look at some of the theory around agency – the choices that may be available to us – and how much control we might have over the choices we make, or not. One of the key voices in poststructuralist theory is Foucault, and there have been many educational researchers who have drawn on this theoretical work to help them understand working with young children. We will also explore Bourdieu's ideas of *habitus*, which help us understand the ways we are constrained by our upbringing in different ways. We want to feel we are in control of our lives, but it is helpful to think critically about this, and be aware of what factors in our lives may be impacting on us.

Subjectification and life as an educator

Early childhood educators are subject to a variety of influences within their working lives. These begin in our own education, as we prepare to become early childhood educators. Our sense of who we should be and how we should behave is shaped for us by the people who are teaching us, and the materials they provide within this. Our identities as educators, and the commitment and dedication we are encouraged to show, are part of our subjectification. We also experience this subjectification when our workplaces are shaped by the sorts of quality accreditation process which exist in many national contexts. These attempt to limit the possibilities for early education in particular ways, and the result is that we become subject to the disciplinary power of these systems (Foucault would probably call these *regimes of truth*). Our agency within these processes comes when we choose to shape our own identities in ways that are not expected (perhaps we will limit our dedication, and not work beyond our paid hours, for example) or if we push back against the proscriptions of accreditation systems either covertly, or openly. That early childhood education is mostly a field in which women choose to work is an example of subjectification – anyone may choose to study and work in this field (they have agency!) but in practice the highly gendered discourses of society mean that it is almost exclusively those who identify as female who choose to do so.

Foucault and the power of discourse

One of Michel Foucault's (1982) big ideas was that in the modern era our societies have moved from external repressive discipline – such as existed in the era of absolute monarchy – to an internalised self-discipline, in which most people need little obvious control, even with the comparative freedom in most contemporary societies. This sort of disciplinary process, which is called *subjectification*, involves people becoming subject to various norms and controls, which are communicated through discourse (see breakout box). There are many discourses circulating in society, but only some become dominant, while others have much less influence. All discourses are sets of ideas about how to behave, what to think and what is possible, and dominant discourses will reflect the interests of those with most power in a given society. One way of thinking about your work as an early childhood educator is that you are making particular discourses available to the children in your care. It is therefore important to be aware of what discourses you are making available and how these reflect the priorities of the dominant culture in ways that may be damaging to those who are not privileged in this way.

In most countries these discourses will involve privileging the ideas of a particular racial or religious group, as well as containing ideas about male superiority over women, the advantages of being wealthy, able-bodied or beautiful, and so on. Dominant discourses, according to Foucault are not 'true' (men are not actually better than women, for example), but act to normalise particular attitudes, and privilege particular types of people. Foucault calls these 'truth claims' to distinguish them from universalising claims about truth or 'reality'. A truth claim works to make certain outcomes more likely in society, particularly if most people end up sharing these beliefs. So, for example, in a world where men have historically been privileged, the dominant discourse makes truth claims about men being 'smarter', 'stronger' or 'better leaders'. These are not claims that are tested, but are assumed to be true by most people, and function as self-fulfilling prophecies, because beliefs are so effective in shaping our behaviour and making positive outcomes more likely (Fine, 2010). Similarly, in a world where most countries have experienced some period of colonisation by white (European) populations, dominant discourses often make truth claims about white people being more attractive, or perhaps more 'civilised'. These are not objectively true, but function to disempower those who cannot claim the privilege of whiteness, perpetuating the damage done by colonialism even in a postcolonial era. Young children encounter dominant discourses, and the truth claims that circulate within them, through their families, through the media, through religion and increasingly, through the early childhood services they attend. So a child who is not white might go from their family (where they feel normal, beautiful and secure) to a childcare setting where most of the other children do not look like them, and who might make them feel wrong, or 'ugly', due to how they look, or because of other ways they differ from the cultural norms in that setting. As educators we are often complicit in reinforcing particular cultural norms in ways that marginalise some children. In this case, where the focus is on skin colour, or attributes associated with particular human populations, this is called structural racism (see breakout box).

> ### Structural racism
>
> Vaught and Castagno explain that 'racism is a pervasive, systemic condition, not merely an individual pathology. Racism is a vast system that structures our institutions and our relationships… [R]acism adapts to socio-cultural changes by altering its expression, but it never diminishes or disappears' (2008, 99). They argue that any educator who wants to challenge inequality must be aware of the systemic nature of racist discourses, and be able to talk back to the idea that there is any sort of 'neutral' or 'colour-blind' form of knowledge. Knowledge is located within the discursive power structures of society, and so will always reflect the aims and beliefs of the dominant culture. For example, in Canada Indigenous people experience much higher rates of imprisonment, often for minor offences such as swearing or unpaid fines, because of racist discourses which impact on the individual decisions made by police and the judicial system (even when not *intending* to be racist), which accumulate to have structural impacts for Indigenous people and communities.

Bourdieu, and the constraining effects of our upbringing

Foucault's work is useful in understanding how particular sorts of attitudes, including ones that most people would claim not to support, such as racism or sexism, can be perpetuated unconsciously, through repeating the truth claims of the dominant discourse. A different way to look at this problem draws on the ideas of Pierre Bourdieu. This involves looking at the inequalities in society not from the top down, which is Foucault's approach, but from the bottom up, about how we learn to become human within particular environments.

Bourdieu (1984) was mostly concerned about social class, and the ways economic inequality continues to be perpetuated through subtle human mechanisms, including the sorts of things we claim to enjoy, or the ways we behave with others. Bourdieu says that we all grow up in a particular environment, with particular norms and expectations (calling these different sorts of environments, *fields*). Each field of human activity, whether this is a local community, a professional group, or a learning community, will have particular norms and expectations for the people within it, which Bourdieu called *habitus*, and these are sometimes explicit but often remain unspoken. When a group of people internalise these expectations within a particular environment they can be said to share a particular habitus, which means they will all tend to act and react in similar ways. We usually do not notice our habitus, because the norms of our community are so familiar to us. Bourdieu explained that we often know whether a given situation is a product of the same classed environments that shaped our own habitus, because we will feel like a 'fish out of water' if it does not, a feeling familiar to many working-class students at universities (Bourdieu & Passeron, 1979).

To have a particular habitus, as a result of a particular upbringing, is neither good nor bad, but merely a reflection of human difference. It becomes difficult when we move into new environments and must notice that our usual actions and reactions no longer fit. This is particularly noticeable in school settings. Most schools reflect the dominant culture of a society – usually the norms and expectations of middle- or ruling-class cultures. For individuals from those privileged backgrounds, school will seem like a normal and understandable environment. They will be more likely to succeed simply out of familiarity. For those from less privileged backgrounds, such as poor or working-class students, the expectations of school may seem bewildering, frustrating or incomprehensible. These students may end up feeling (or being made to feel) stupid or badly behaved through unfamiliarity with the norms of that educational environment.

Turning theory into practice

How can educators learn from these theoretical perspectives on structure and agency? One key idea from Foucault is that all of us will have grown up within a particular *discursive regime*. A discursive regime describes how in any given time and place certain discourses – ideas about human behaviour – are believed to be true or right. Our school or early childhood setting will reflect this discursive regime and operate in a particular way. We hope you will remember that this way of operating is not the only, the best or the most logical way for education to function. There are as many different ideas about education as there are human societies, and all forms of education are capable of transmitting valuable cultural knowledge from generation to generation. Knowing who you are, as an educator, and the values that were around you when you grew up, will help you get some perspective on the ways that you tend to behave within your classroom setting.

From Bourdieu, and the idea of habitus, we know that we will have a set of behaviours that feel most comfortable and familiar to us, and these usually reflect the sorts of practices that are typical within the family and community we grew up in. At any given moment we will have a variety of choices about how to act, based on what we know about the context we are working in, and the amount of education or life experience we have. But we will still tend to gravitate towards what 'feels right', and this often reflects the habitus we learned growing up. This means we will often take for granted particular ways of acting, for ourselves or for young children. We need to be wary of the pedagogical judgements that we may make when children do not act in the ways that we expect. It is always useful to ask, 'what must be true for this child, for their behaviour to make sense?'

A number of researchers within the sociology of education have taken up these ideas, and examined what they mean for the early childhood workforce. We know that the vast majority of people working in early childhood identify as female, and most do not come from very privileged backgrounds. Most educators will have been at least partly impacted by the institutional sexism, racism and class discrimination that is common in school settings, as Beverley Skeggs (1997) has explored in her work. To counteract these negative messages most women working in early childhood invest in themselves as caring and responsible people, and spend a lot of energy looking after those around them. The educator's role is to care for children, but we also expend effort looking after members of the child's family, as well as our colleagues. The profile of people working in early childhood is changing slowly, with more male-identified and qualified educators entering the field, but even today early childhood education continues to be shaped by its perception as low-value work.

Focusing on care for others may be good for the field, but it often means that educators do not pay enough attention to their own needs, and this may make them more likely to work long hours beyond what they are paid, or spend many hours worrying about children and their families outside work hours. We can think of these as 'choices' but this ignores the ways such behaviour is constrained by being raised as female or from a less-privileged background. These experiences shape us, leading us to feel less good about ourselves, more willing to doubt our own abilities and so more likely to accept working conditions that are not fair, or that do not support us to do a good job. As Rachel Langford (2010) explains, often 'child-centred' practice ends up silencing or denying the needs of the female educators working in our field, and this will not help us in creating better, more democratic educational environments.

Children and their 'choices' in educational settings

What does all this mean for children? How do we build on this understanding of theory and of our own human limits as educators to do a better job for all children? From their earliest moments, babies have some control over their actions, even if this is as simple as deciding to stop crying once they are picked up. Looking back to the vignette at the start of this chapter, we can see Yaminah making a number of active choices: expressing interest in the older children's self-feeding, eagerly reaching for the spoon, later on letting it drop and lastly her creative solution of using her hands to feed herself instead. The educators working with her made efforts to tune into what Yaminah wanted, while at the same time thinking about the consequences of allowing her more agency.

As educators, we often act as gatekeepers in children's learning, allowing some inquiries to flourish, while limiting other possibilities. There are times when what children want to do may be impractical (flying to the moon), genuinely risky (not wearing their seatbelt on the school-bus) or simply poor timing (wanting to start a painting project at the end of a preschool day). The point always is to know *why* we are allowing some choices and not others, and making sure this is not just because we do not want to make the effort, or because we see the idea as foolish. If we are to take children's learning seriously we need to be willing to support their curiosity and exploration, even when we might find this challenging. Sometimes the most exciting curriculum investigations in

Agency and resistance 51

Figure 3.2 Basic art activities allow young children to feel some control over their environment, as they shape the materials, and explore the textures and patterns they can create.
Source: Chris Jacques. Used with permission

early childhood come from children's ideas that were initially considered 'too hard' by the educators they were working with. For example, a group of Grade One students thought that their much-loved school chickens needed a birthday cake. Their educators were ready to dismiss this idea, but instead asked them to draw and label their ideas. The educators realised this was a great opportunity to extend their healthy eating unit, by supporting the children to develop an inquiry about what healthy eating means for chickens. After some weeks the children proudly made a decorative and healthy cake, which was proudly served to the chickens as part of a 'birthday party' to which families were invited. The chickens loved it, and the educators learnt that even apparently 'random' ideas can spark a useful learning journey.

The other side to remember, about children's agency, is their ability to say 'no'. Think back to earlier in the chapter, and the idea of the 'terrible twos'. Adults might think it is terrible that children want to resist the decisions they are making about that child's day. However, as we know from Foucault's theory of power, there will always be resistance to power, and we should not be surprised by this. Most children have nearly all decisions made for them throughout their day – where they spend it, what they eat and even what they wear. Is it any surprise that they want to say 'no' to some of this? At any time when children are resisting what we are asking of them – whether a baby or an eight year old – we have an opportunity to explore what they might be finding hard about it. Is it possible they feel rushed, and with a bit more time they may be willing to do what we have asked? Perhaps there is some aspect of the situation that the child knows that we do not (that the sweater we are trying to get them to wear is really scratchy and unpleasant, for example).

One of the vital skills for educators at any level is that of perspective-taking. With any activity we create for (or with) children, it is helpful to think through what it will be like from their perspective. Do they have the necessary skills to be able to succeed, even minimally, at this activity? What might they not understand, or need to know, before attempting this activity? What various ways can we explain this to cater for different learners, who notice different things about their world? Once we start to think like this, then children's resistance is often easier to understand, and sometimes seems wiser than adult perceptions of the situation. We can get children to help us solve the problems or issues that are causing their resistance, as we shall show in chapter 9, allowing them an opportunity to be creative. They will also learn more from this activity through finding ways to make it more accessible to everyone.

The limits of agency within the constraints of classroom environments

We think of play-based learning as offering abundant agency to children but 'free play' is never really free (Grieshaber & McArdle, 2010). There are always constraints – of time, of money, of practicality. There are also the sorts of constraints that come from the different ways that groups of people in our society are treated, and the different discourses available depending on a person's gender, skin colour, economic circumstances or bodily abilities. As educators our challenge is to learn to see all the different ways that children's lives are shaped by the expectations others have of them. This takes a lifetime of experience, and the few examples we give you here will hopefully shed light on the complexities of each child's situation.

The disturbing aspect of most discrimination in education – those pedagogical choices we make which advantage some and disadvantage others – is that it is unintentional. Few of us set out to damage others' life chances in an active way. Instead we have developed a particular habitus that shapes our choices moment by moment, in ways that often reflect the inequalities of the discursive regimes we have grown up in.

Gender

In terms of gender we know from classic feminist research (Spender, 1982) that in mixed gender classrooms across all educational settings educators spend more time listening to boys, and ask for their opinions more, while interrupting them less. This is one of the many ways that gender is learnt through education, with boys learning to feel privileged and as if their views are worth listening to, while girls learn to silence themselves and to feel doubt about the value of what they have to say. It is likely that you, as an educator, will still be perpetuating these sorts of patterns unconsciously, because you have grown up within a dominant discourse that privileges male speakers. If you are curious, you might want to audio-record a few of your group sessions, and note down how much of the speaking time is taken up by dialogue with boys or with girls. You may be surprised by the gap between what you remembered, and what actually occurred. As educators we have to acknowledge that this bias probably exists in our own classroom spaces, and so work harder to value the contributions and ideas of girls, particularly those girls from less privileged backgrounds. This will also require you as an educator to shut down boys who are talking, from time to time, if they are taking more than their fair share of the conversation time. This may feel very uncomfortable to you, but is an important way you can use your power as an educator in the service of an equal classroom. Of course there are many other ways that gender will impact on your educational setting, such as boys being likely to dominate outdoor spaces with particular sorts of play, or boys being assumed to be better at maths or technically minded activities, and these situations will need you to be attentive to the likely gender dynamics at play, and to work actively to disrupt them (Davies, 1989).

Disability

Over time you will work with many different children, some of whom will have a disability of some sort. As we know from disability activists (Price, 2011; Shakespeare, 2006), many disabled children will not get an equal educational experience in the classroom, because our societies do not often support full access for anyone other than able-bodied and able-minded people. There are many ways, again unconsciously, that educators discriminate against children with disabilities in their classrooms. One of the ways this happens is through what Alison Kafer (2013) describes as 'children's imagined futures'. In this pervasive discourse perpetuated by able-bodied society about people with disabilities, the future of anyone with a disability is seen as fraught with pain, hopelessness and limitations. Such a belief makes able-bodied people likely to treat that person as less than a full human being, and invites feelings of pity or sadness for the person with a disability.

This belief is far more disabling than the disability itself, Kafer argues, because it encourages all sorts of discrimination, including the sorts of overhelping that many people with disabilities experience from others. In reality, all of us, whether supposedly able-bodied, or with particular disabilities, experience a variety of challenges throughout our lives, and some of these are related to our physical and mental abilities, while others are unrelated. We all have a life, which

54 *Agency and resistance*

we experience as joyful, interesting, exciting or whatever, depending on the day, and our life circumstances. We all want to feel valued, have friends who care about us, to learn new skills and so on.

Your job, as an educator, is to learn to see all children you work with as capable, including all of those children who have a disability label. Each of those children will want you to get to know them specifically (including their strengths, and the things they find challenging) and to feel supported in learning new things throughout their time in your classroom. For play to be free for these children, you may need to work a bit harder to imagine how your environment could be altered to make their full inclusion possible. These children will want to be given opportunities to connect with their peers and make friends. They will want to take risks, and make mistakes, without the over-protectiveness or worry that so often impacts on the lives of those with an impairment. Chapter 7 will help you structure your classroom to accommodate a range of abilities, as well as find the sorts of support for children that they need to flourish in your setting. Working closely with families will be particularly useful when it comes to supporting a child with a disability (see chapter 10), because families are often their best advocate and most aware of their child's specific experience of disablement, as well as their personality and interests.

Figure 3.3 Natural materials of a wide variety are usually easy to source, and can enrich ordinary activities, such as using clay or dough.
Source: Yarrow Andrew, with thanks to Flinders University Childcare Centre

Social class

It is often hard for us to think of social class as a barrier to children's educational participation, in part because many of us have been encouraged to think of class as something that happened historically, but does not have an impact now. In fact, class may well have some of the most significant impacts on children's lives in education, but these impacts are often not talked about and so cannot be challenged, as Annette Lareau's (2003) research explains. It is worth thinking about your own upbringing, and the sorts of messages you received as a child about education and about money.

Children from more privileged backgrounds are encouraged to believe that they can be anything they would like, and often this becomes the reality, because familial wealth and social connections make a variety of life choices more possible. Children whose families struggled may feel continually anxious about money because they have watched this be an issue growing up. These sorts of worries make take a lot of their attention away from being engaged in the classroom.

Even if money is not so critical, many working-class families place strong expectations on their children to 'be good' and 'listen to the teacher'. Children who have been given these messages may spend their energy trying to understand the unfamiliar rules of the classroom rather than learning what is on offer. For those whose home lives are organised similarly to their school or childcare setting, education is easier because they understand the unspoken rules and know how to work these to their advantage. Such children are happy to ask questions, will always assume that the activities that are available are meant for them, and will often get noticed more by educators and given more challenges.

As educators, it is worth taking time to give adequate explanations about all aspects of life in our classrooms, including those things we take most for granted. It is only by giving children access to everything they need to know that we can create a more level playing field, enabling every child to participate equally. If someone has grown up being encouraged to ask questions, this may seem the most normal thing in the world. Others may need lots of support to articulate the things they want to know, or support to share the things they may already understand that others do not. Look around your group of children, and think about those children who do not seem to be as involved in your classroom, or who are flying under your radar. Nancy Fraser (2005) has argued that to create a more equal society, we should be focusing on supporting all people to participate equally, which means paying attention to anything that may be hampering full participation, such as lack of knowledge, or lack of resources, and we will look at this more in chapter 9.

It is important to remember, of course, that social class inequalities often intersect with structural racism, as will be true for many refugees, recent migrants and some Indigenous groups. For these children, their parents may experience discrimination in employment, reinforcing any economic inequalities. They may also be experiencing forms of racism or exclusion by other children, which will also take up their time and energy, making it harder for them to put effort into their learning.

Bringing it all together

Making mistakes

It is vital to remember that you will make many mistakes in your journey as an educator, especially when trying to create an environment of equality and justice in a world that is far from fair. As the examples above show, we are shaped by dominant discourses which construct inequality as natural and normal, and it takes considerable effort for us to unlearn the sorts of sexist, racist, able-ist and class-ist thought patterns we have learnt in our lifetimes. Children too will make mistakes, and it is worth remembering that when children are articulating prejudiced ideas, they are usually doing so because this is what they have learned in their own families and communities. Habitus shapes our behaviours, but we can and learn new possibilities about how to behave. You can help children to see why these beliefs are hurtful through talking about the unfairness, and which of their peers may be affected. Doing this without becoming judgmental towards them, or their family environment, is an important way to build a more respectful learning community. It will also give you practice at articulating your beliefs as an educator about what a better world might look like.

Fortunately, children are much more forgiving than adults and also quicker at unlearning negative messages, and you can help them harness their emerging sense of agency to build empathy with others. One useful strategy as an educator is to encourage children to be on the lookout for things they notice that are unfair not just to themselves but to others. You can assist them by talking openly and clearly about the things you notice that are unfair, even when this may mean admitting you have been wrong. Kai Rands (2009) talks about this idea in regard to pedagogical practices around gender, when she talks about having a 'gender-complex' approach to education. Gender-complex education draws attention to the dominant discourses around gender, helping children to question these and consider alternatives, offering resistance to this pattern of power relations. This idea can be applied more widely, and involves moving beyond just being aware of the issues and beyond admitting that they have real consequences, to taking action with the children themselves. You can help them understand the impact of these power relations in their daily lives, and help them begin to challenge moments of unfairness as well as working to repair damaging things they may have done. This is real agency, and a more profound sort of choice than is usually offered to children.

Learning to laugh

These are hard issues to deal with, and we are never going to be able to solve all the long-standing or newly emerging problems in our society within our early childhood classrooms. These are well-entrenched dominant discourses, collectively enacted right across society, and critical pedagogy is not yet the norm in our classrooms. Even if you are trying to make a learning community that is fair for everybody you will experience resistance, because those who are most advantaged by the existing system may sense the loss of some of their privilege. As we will see in chapter 6, we need to become skilled in helping children deal with their emotions, including their sense of sadness or loss when being asked to share classroom resources or educator time more fairly with other children.

Hopefully there will be times when you can see the funny side of what often seems like an impossible task. It is not always easy to see the humour in prejudice or unfairness, and we have to be careful not to be insensitive about this. Sometimes it can be simple enough to exaggerate the scale of the problem, to show the absurdity of it. When a child is struggling to share, you might say; 'What would it be like if you had ALL the Lego in the world, a whole mountain of it? Could you even play with it all? What would everyone else do? Isn't it more fun when other people can play too?' You might even want to pretend that you, the adult, don't want to share any of the resources in the classroom, because they are ALL YOURS! Seeing adults behaving in unexpected ways can often make children giggle, helping a stressful situation de-escalate and moving the conversation in useful directions.

Similarly, in working with infants, there may be times when all of them start crying, and you feel like you will never be able to calm them down or work out what is bothering them. At times like this you may need to stop, gather all the crying children in one spot, and let them know that despite the noise and the tears, you are still here and still care about them. Learning to laugh at the absurdity of a whole group of crying babies may be just the sort of unfamiliar thing to catch their attention, and distract them from what is bothering them, which is often other children's distress. It will certainly help you and the other adults around you, especially if you can make it clear that you are not laughing at the crying children, but at the craziness of the situation. Sometimes a baby may have been crying because you were too frantically busy to give them even a little attention, so doing this may actually solve much of the problem directly, including your own frazzled nerves.

Concluding remarks

There is no such thing as a perfect educator, or a perfectly patient one, despite what you may imagine. Becoming able to recognise a 'good-enough' solution to a problem, or to see any solution as a learning process (and an investigation as to whether it actually improves the problem), will help you recognise your ongoing learning as an educator in this area. Children need to develop the ability to make choices, and be guided to make better ones, and along the way they will make many choices that will frustrate or inconvenience you. At times you will be the one resisting the children's own 'good-enough' solutions to the problem, because you are stuck on what you believe to be the only right answer in this situation. At its most fundamental, education is about learning to be human, and that is no easy task. As an educator, your job is not to have all the answers, but to travel alongside children as you discover new and better answers together.

Questions for reflection

- How important is it for you, in your everyday life, to feel in control? Do you bring that into your pedagogical work, as an educator? How might this impact on the children you work with? How does it affect your relationships with colleagues?
- In which areas of your own life have you experienced marginalisation, such as being female, dark-skinned, or same-sex attracted? Can you identify any elements of the discourses which reinforced that marginalisation? You may be able to identify them through their negative impact on your life (e.g. the expectation on girls to try and be pretty, in a way that boys are not expected to) or through the prejudices that circulate about particular groups (e.g. the idea that the poor must be 'lazy').
- Think of a choice you have made recently, such as about what movie you might go and see, or what item of clothing you might buy? Now notice how your 'choices' were constrained, such as your gendered expectations about what you would enjoy watching, or others' judgements about what a person like you should be wearing? Do you feel you always choose freely in your life? What might it be like to be completely free, of others' expectations, or of economic limits?
- Which choices made by children do you find particularly challenging? What can these tell you about your own habitus, or the discourses that were dominant in your upbringing?

Activities for educators

- Start a list about things in life you have taken for granted, perhaps starting with things you may have learnt so far in this book. Make this list down the left-hand side of the page, and add to it, as you start to notice other things you may have assumed were true for everybody, but aren't. On the right-hand side of the page, next to each item, list a couple of actions you will commit to that could help you unlearn what you had been taking for granted. For example, if what you take for granted is that you will always be able to afford enough food, or particular sorts of foods, your list might include: 'Notice how expensive some grocery items I buy are, and choose a cheaper alternative'; 'Say no to eating out for a month'; 'Set a budget of …, and try to live off this for a week, without cheating'.
- Think about your social class positioning, and the places you feel most comfortable. What do you like about those places? How do you get to

act in those locations, and what feels most suitable to be wearing in those places? Now think about where you have felt most uncomfortable? Can you identify why? What 'rules of the game' in those places do you not understand? Do you know anyone who you could ask who might know? Actively learning about the lives and experiences of others is a valuable habit as a teacher, helping you relate better to all sorts of children and families. Practice being out of your comfort zone, and being respectful of others in those spaces.

Key readings

Davies, B. (2003). *Frogs and Snails and Feminist Tales: Preschool Children and Gender*. New York: Hampton Press.

Grieshaber, S., & McArdle, F. (2010). *The Trouble with Play*. Maidenhead: Open University Press.

Langford, R. (2010). Critiquing child-centred pedagogy to bring children and early childhood educators into the centre of a democratic pedagogy. Contemporary *Issues in Early Childhood*, 11(1), 113.

Lareau, A. (2003). *Unequal Childhoods: Class, Race and Family Life*. Berkeley, CA: UC Press.

Shakespeare, T. (2006). *Disability Rights and Wrongs Revisited*. London: Routledge.

Online material

Article exploring the value of mistakes in education, including how it may build the disposition of persistence. https://greatergood.berkeley.edu/article/item/why_we_should_embrace_mistakes_in_school

Online resource, with useful definitions of words like agency from a sociological perspective. www.thoughtco.com/agency-definition-3026036

TED talk by Memory Banda, a young female activist from Malawi, showing how powerful agency can be for those disadvantaged within their societies. www.ted.com/talks/memory_banda_a_warrior_s_cry_against_child_marriage?referrer=playlist-the_power_of_the_individual_vo

Further reading

Bourdieu, P. (1984). *Distinction: A Social Critique of the Judgement of Taste* (R. Nice, Trans.). London: Routledge.

Bourdieu, P., & Passeron, J.-C. (1979). *The Inheritors: French Students and their Relationship to Culture*. Chicago, IL: University of Chicago Press.

Fine, C. (2010). *Delusions of Gender: How our Minds, Society, and Neurosexism Create Difference*. New York: Norton.

Foucault, M. (1982). The subject and power. *Critical Inquiry*, 8(4), 777–795.

Fraser, N. (2005). *Reframing Justice: The Spinoza Lectures*. Amsterdam: Van Gorcum.

Grolnick, W. S., Bridges, L. J., & Connell, J. P. (1996). Emotion Regulation in Two-Year-Olds: Strategies and Emotional Expression in Four Contexts. *Child Development*, 67(3), 928–941.

Kafer, A. (2013). *Feminist Queer Crip*. Bloomington, IN: Indiana University Press.

Price, M. (2011). *Mad at School: Rhetorics of Mental Disability and Academic Life.* Ann Arbor, MI: University of Michigan Press.

Rands, K. (2009). Considering trangender people in education: A gender-complex approach. *Journal of Teacher Education, 60*(4), 419–431.

Skeggs, B. (1997). *Formations of Class and Gender.* London: Sage.

Spender, D. (1982). *Invisible Women: The Schooling Scandal.* London: Writers and Readers Publishing Co-operative.

Vaught, S. E., & Castagno, A. E. (2008). 'I don't think I'm a racist': Critical race theory, teacher attitudes, and structural racism. *Race Ethnicity and Education, 11*(2), 95–113.

4 Choice and constraint in children's health

Figure 4.1
Source: Jennifer Fane

Questions for consideration

- When it comes to the health of individuals, communities and societies, what plays a bigger part – the choices and practices of individuals (such as whether to smoke, exercise, eat well) or factors largely outside the control of individuals (economic status, race, gender)? Is it a case of one or the other, or an interplay of the two?
- What role might an early childhood educator play in supporting children's health and wellbeing? How might early childhood education and care environments impact and influence young children's health?

Vignette from practice

It's snack time on a Wednesday morning in a Year 1 class at a school in a largely disadvantaged area. The classroom teacher feels strongly about the importance of good nutrition and has explicitly asked parents to send only healthy snacks for their child and provided a list of ideal foods and food suggestions to parents at the beginning of the school year. As the children were bringing their snacks to their tables, the teacher noticed that Darren, a Year 1 student in the class, had brought a muffin from a prominent fast food chain for his snack. Speaking quietly to Darren as to not embarrass him in front of the other children, the teacher reminds Darren to ask his parents to help him choose a healthy snack next time, referencing the pictures of healthy snacks posted on the wall of the classroom.

Darren looks squarely at the teacher and matter-of-factly recounts that his parents had told him that morning that there was no money for groceries until Friday and that's all there was for his snack today. Stunned by how having little food in the house was seemingly so normalised to Darren, the educator quickly told Darren that his snack was fine, and moved on to helping another child open a yoghurt container.

Introduction: On health and being healthy

We all know that being healthy is important, but what exactly does it mean to be healthy? If you're having trouble thinking of an answer to that question, don't worry, you're not alone. While there are several widely accepted definitions of the term health, what being healthy looks like or feels like (and how to achieve this state) is a highly contested concept. The challenge in defining and understanding what it means to be healthy is that the concept of good health, or being healthy, is socially constructed, meaning this varies greatly between communities, societies and countries. Most of us would likely agree on some basic principles outlined in Article 24 of the United Nations Convention on the Rights of the Child (see also chapter 9), such as nutritious food, clean water, being active, and access to health care and childhood immunisations. However, when we consider health and being healthy from a sociological standpoint it becomes quite clear that these concepts are viewed, understood and practised very differently across different social and cultural contexts. As educators, supporting children's health and wellbeing is an essential part of our work. However, as per the above vignette, this is not always easy work. When thinking about, planning for and supporting children's health inside and outside the classroom we need to be very aware of the constraints we will face. We also need to know that there are many problematic representations and understandings of health in our society that are themselves a barrier to health.

Defining health

The World Health Organisation (WHO) defined the concept of health as 'a state of complete physical, mental, and social well-being and not merely the absence of disease or infirmity' (World Health Organisation, 1948). While this definition is still used today, it has been criticised due to its ambiguity over how this state might be reached or supported. While there are many different models and conceptualisations of health, they can be characterised under two broad headings; biomedical models and social models (see breakout box). The biomedical model is most often the foundation on which most health professions and health services are based, and these services focus on diagnosis, explanation and treatment of illness in individuals. While the diagnosis and treatment of ill individuals is of utmost importance in any health care system, a significant limitation to this approach is that it does not take into account the social and societal factors that impact on individual's health.

Biomedical versus social model of health

Biomedical model of health	*Social model of health*
The biomedical model is concerned with physical and biological factors of diseases excluding psychological, environmental, and social influences	The social model attempts to address broader influences on health (social, cultural, environmental and economic factors) rather than disease and injury
Focus is on the diagnosis, treatment and cure of disease within the medical system	Focus is on prevention through the use of health promotion, education and policy to improve health outcomes

For example, we know that smoking can cause a range of major health concerns that can lead to very ill health and premature death. We can treat individuals suffering from smoking-related illness, but using a biomedical model the course of action is to wait until someone is experiencing ill health before intervening. However, if we take a look at the demographics of smokers we can see that certain groups of people are much more likely to smoke than others. This means that to stop a health-damaging behaviour before people are ill enough to interact with the health care system, we need to take into account the social factors that impact on individual health choices and health outcomes. To do this, we can use the social health model to uncover why some people smoke even while knowing the health risks and use prevention strategies (as outlined in the breakout box) to prevent individuals from starting to smoke and to support those who do in quitting this damaging behaviour before they are ill.

The social health model (or thinking about health from a sociological standpoint) is an umbrella term referring to different approaches to thinking about health that engage with the social factors that influence an individual's health. These factors are called the social determinants of health. These are the economic, social and cultural factors that impact and influence the health of individuals and population groups, such as gender, race or social class (in chapter 1 you will remember we called these 'dimensions of inequality'). John Germov, author of *Second Opinion: An Introduction to Health Sociology*, suggests that the social health model assumes that health is a social, rather than individual responsibility. It is important to understand that using the social health model does not deny the biological or psychological aspects of disease or the need for medical assessment and treatment. Instead it focuses on the need to 'locate people in social contexts, conceptualises the physical environment as socially organised, and understands ill health as a process of interaction between people and their environments (Broom, 1991, 52). In the next section we will explore the biomedical and social health model divide further, and focus on understanding the complexities of addressing health from a sociological approach.

A social view of health

In this section we look more closely about how these different views of health impact on our work with children. In doing so we want you to think critically about the assumptions you may be making about health, as we saw in the vignette above. The social view of health takes a critical approach to health, by analysing what may or may not be possible for someone, depending on their social background or history.

A sociological understanding of child development

One of the key differences between the biomedical and social models of health is where the focus of ill health rests, at the individual level or the societal level. In early childhood services we are not usually seen as part of the health care system. Despite this the biomedical model has exerted considerable influence over theory and practice in our field as well. Developmental approaches to early childhood (as discussed in chapter 2) are pervasive in early learning and for many educators their understanding of young children's development is highly influenced by the biomedical model. A developmental approach focuses on the individual child and how the child meets (or does not meet) a number of set milestones at a certain age. This approach assumes that all children will develop along the same trajectory at similar times and anything outside this is abnormal and problematic. If we consider the interventions that are most commonly used in this approach (such as medical interventions, behaviour management, parental education) we can see that these also fall under the biomedical model. However, these interventions often do not recognise the social determinants of health that impact upon children and families. Once these factors are taken into account and understood, our potential intervention as educators or other professionals may look very different. By concerning ourselves with larger scale social and structural changes, as well as specific health needs, we are seeking to ameliorate the child's situation more broadly, thus improving the support and resources available to the family and child, as well as improving the community and environments in which the child lives.

The individual versus the social

Exploring these two models of health is important for understanding the complexity of issues and perspectives which impact on people's health and everyday lives. However, it is important to understand that neither model is 'right' or 'wrong'. In actuality, both models are needed to understand the complexities of health, as people are simultaneously individuals with specific bodies and health care needs, as well as members of social, cultural and structural groups whose choices, resources and abilities are constrained or enabled when it comes to their health.

Healthism

Healthism is a way of understanding health problems and poor health. It draws on the biomedical view of health, situating the problem of health and disease at the level of the individual. For example, if someone is in poor health, healthism is the assumption that the fault must be theirs, and that this must be due to what would be classified as 'poor lifestyle choices', such as smoking, drinking, being overweight or not exercising. As the solutions to health problems are also highly individualised, discourses of healthism essentially blame the person experiencing poor health and expect them to make better choices to rectify the problem (this is a form of *victim blaming*). While individuals do generally have some level of agency and autonomy in making health-related decisions, healthism does not take into account the social determinants of health that impact and act as barriers to individual's health.

In chapters 2 and 3 we saw how children's lives are shaped both by social structures, but also their ability to exercise agency over their lives. This parallels the differences between the social model of health, which looks at structural factors, and an individualistic approach which focuses primarily on individual's agency. There is a complex interplay between individual and social responsibility for health and health behaviours. The structure-agency continuum (see Figure 4.2) is a conceptual tool that can be used to identify factors and understand the complex interplay between individual choice (agency) and recurrent patterned historical, cultural, political, economic and social forces which limit or influence the choices available (structure) in relation to health. For example, obesity is currently a public health focus in most Minority World countries. Typically a biomedical approach is used to understand health issues in these countries, and so the obese individual and their behaviour is general identified as the source of the problem. This stance, where it is largely the individual's responsibility for avoiding ill health, is known as *healthism* (see break out box). While an individual does certainly have some choice in regards to their health and health behaviour, using the structure and agency continuum we can see that the factors at play are far more nuanced and complex. We will see that when obesity is considered in terms of individual agency as well as structuring forces, the idea that individuals are solely responsible for their health is challenged. Figure 4.2 gives some examples of how obesity may be considered from both viewpoints.

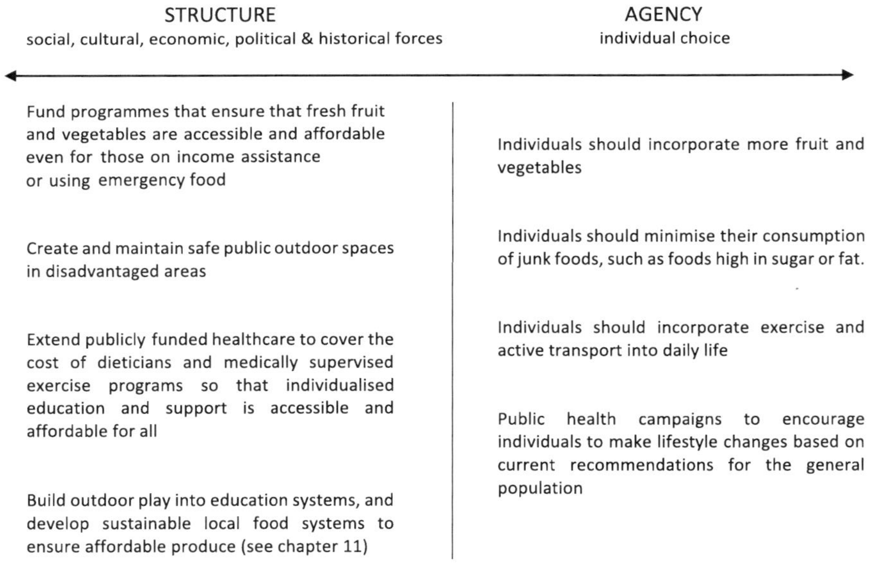

STRUCTURE social, cultural, economic, political & historical forces	AGENCY individual choice
Fund programmes that ensure that fresh fruit and vegetables are accessible and affordable even for those on income assistance or using emergency food	Individuals should incorporate more fruit and vegetables
Create and maintain safe public outdoor spaces in disadvantaged areas	Individuals should minimise their consumption of junk foods, such as foods high in sugar or fat.
Extend publicly funded healthcare to cover the cost of dieticians and medically supervised exercise programs so that individualised education and support is accessible and affordable for all	Individuals should incorporate exercise and active transport into daily life
Build outdoor play into education systems, and develop sustainable local food systems to ensure affordable produce (see chapter 11)	Public health campaigns to encourage individuals to make lifestyle changes based on current recommendations for the general population

Figure 4.2 The structure-agency continuum

Constructions of health in a health-obsessed world

Consider these two approaches to how obesity prevention and management might be constructed within society. Take a moment to reflect on the types of health messages you have come across or any health education you have received. Have these been more concerned with individuals making 'good choices' (agency) or the way in which society may create barriers to health for certain individuals (structure)? Minority World countries, particularly Anglophone-majority nations such as Australia, the UK, Canada and the US, have seen a societal shift from the idea that the government should provide strong social supports to citizens (well-funded and resourced public health system, social security and so on) to the idea that citizens should be responsible for their own health and be good citizens by staying 'healthy' (private health cover, avoiding risk factors, following health guidelines). This shift is known as *responsibilisation* (holding individuals responsible for their own health) and can clearly be seen when we look back to the assumptions behind the biomedical model. Responsibilisation is a key element in the discourse of healthism, suggesting that individuals are ultimately responsible for their own health regardless of the services or supports available to them. In this discourse the notion of a good citizen is inextricably linked with being 'healthy' and leading a 'healthy lifestyle'. This allows governments to lessen their responsibility to ensure systems and resources are in place to protect and support the health of all citizens.

Thinking back to the messages and education you have received about obesity, it is almost certain that the messages you have come across would pertain to individuals taking responsibility for their own health. We can see this in the format of television shows like *The Biggest Loser*, in the promotion of fad diets and supplements, and in the numbers of people who optimistically take out gym memberships. Inevitably, messages like this about taking responsibility for your own health become not only about avoiding disease or being proactive about your health, but also about looking a certain way, such as being fit, lean and strong. Have you ever felt guilty about eating a certain food or not exercising enough? Have you ever felt bad about yourself because even when doing all the right things you still don't end up looking like what 'health' is supposed to look like? Then you have been the recipient of internalised healthism. Unfortunately, these are the experiences of most people in societies where being healthy and 'looking healthy' are seen as synonymous with being a good citizen.

This idea that being healthy is ultimately the responsibility of the individual is a troubling message which impacts on everybody's health. We hope the children we work with are shielded from these discourses, but this is not always the case. Consider the types of health messages you may have come across in an early childhood setting while considering the following vignette.

Figure 4.3 Engaging children in food growing helps children to understand where food comes from and to take risks in trying new fruits and vegetables.
Source: Jennifer Fane

Vignette from practice

It is term 2 in a Year 1 class of 22 children who seem to be getting along well, and with the teacher's support building a strong classroom community. Dylan, one of the children in the class, has a very close friend whom his nanny organises weekly playdates with while his parents work professional jobs. Dylan has little trouble in making friends or working with other children in the class. Dylan is generally a confident child and enjoys school. The teacher was surprised one morning to find a lengthy email from Dylan's mother which explained that Dylan came home from school the day before very upset because some of the children in the class had called him fat. In her email, not only did Dylan's mother want the teacher to know what was happening in the class, she also emailed at length about Dylan and his weight. Over four long paragraphs she explained to the teacher that they focused on healthy eating in their house, and that Dylan played soccer twice a week as well as swimming lessons. She mentioned that Dylan (who was a middle child) had the same diet as her other two children but was larger than the other two. She also mentioned that she had sought a referral to a dietician and a paediatrician to further investigate Dylan's weight even though Dylan was an active child who ate a very typical diet. Not only was the teacher concerned to hear that there was bullying happening in the classroom that she had not seen or heard, but she was also saddened that Dylan's mother seemed to perceive the issue as her fault, or that there was a problem with Dylan that should be fixed. Upon reading this email, the teacher realised that not only was there work to do in addressing the bullying issue happening within the classroom, but also in thinking through how to ensure that Dylan and his family felt supported, listened too and cared for in regard to their concern about his weight.

In this story we can see how the troubling messages about health that permeate society (such as 'being healthy means looking a certain way', or that 'looking healthy is synonymous with being a good citizen') also impact on young children and their families in negative ways. If we consider both vignettes in this chapter (Darren and Dylan) we can see that there are many factors at work, both at the individual and social level, that impact on the health of the children and families we work with. As educators who build meaningful relationships with the children and families we work with, we often are aware of specific needs and details in relation to the health of each child in our care. However what are often obscured when we think about children's health from a developmental or biomedical perspective are the many structural factors that shape children and their family's health. These are the social determinants of health, which we look at more closely in the next section.

The social determinants of health

The social determinants of health are the economic, social and cultural factors that influence individual and population health both overtly and covertly. While it is often easy to pinpoint health disparities between countries, such as between Minority and Majority World nations, often the unfair and avoidable differences in health status of people from the same community, region or country go unnoticed and unchallenged. Due to individualised and responsibilised understandings of health in wealthier countries, people experiencing poor health are often viewed as responsible for their own poor health through 'lack of effort' or 'poor choices'. While individuals do have some agency in relation to their health (as per the structure and agency continuum) they are highly constrained by the *social determinants of health*. Reducing health issues to this individual level is a form of victim blaming and does not acknowledge or address the root causes of health inequalities.

The unfair, avoidable and often unseen impacts on health

In this section we will investigate various social determinants of health. Under each heading, a number of questions will be asked to help you in thinking through how these determinants impact on the lives of individuals, families and specific population groups in your own community. It is important to keep in mind that this is not an exhaustive list, nor have all points been extensively unpacked. While you read through, try and think of issues you may have encountered which are not covered.

Poverty

- Can this person and their family afford safe and appropriate housing? Is social housing available and suitable?
- Can this person afford fresh and healthy food? Are they dependent on emergency or charity-supplied food? Is this food nutritious and culturally appropriate?
- Can the person afford to see a doctor or other health care professional? Is this cost covered by the government, by social insurance or a person's own income? Can they afford to travel to receive medical care if needed? Can they take time off work to receive medical treatment without sacrificing vital income?
- Are there employment opportunities for individuals within their community?
- Are wage minimums set at a level that would allow an individual or family to live above the poverty line?
- Is social assistance available to those in need to ensure individuals and families have basic needs met?

Social class

- What health behaviours are normalised within a particular social class (smoking rates, teen pregnancies, drug and alcohol use)?
- What is the average education level of a particular social group (high school, vocational education, undergraduate, postgraduate)?
- Are all social classes equally represented in government and decision making?
- Are public services such as schools and hospitals equally funded and supported regardless of local income levels?

Age

- Are individuals unduly excluded from having some control over their own health and health decisions due to their age (under 18 years of age or elderly)?
- Are individuals spoken for by others (their families, doctors, teachers etc.) due to their age?
- Are age restrictions on health-related behaviours (age of consent, age to drink alcohol, age to make health decisions) reasonable, research-based and in the interest of the health of the individual?

Gender, sex and sexuality

- Do men and women have the same rights? How about those who identify outside the gender binary, such as agendered, or genderqueer people? Do transgender people have these rights as well?
- Do all individuals have the same rights regardless of their gender or sexual orientation (right to marry, right to conceive, raise or adopt children)?
- Do certain groups of people experience higher levels of abuse and sexual assault than others?
- Are irreversible health and body decisions made for infants without medical need (circumcision, gender reassignment for intersex babies)?
- Are health and medical services informed, inclusive and supportive of all individuals and their health needs regardless of sex, sexuality or gender?

Culture, race or religion

- Do some people experience social exclusion, prejudice, discrimination or violence due to their religious or cultural beliefs and practices or because of their skin colour?
- Is health information made available in multiple languages? Are there interpreters available if needed?
- Do health care providers and systems provide culturally appropriate care which takes into account and respects the needs and wishes of that person?
- Do all members of the society have access to health care (remote Indigenous populations, refugees incarcerated offshore)? For further exploration of these questions see *online resources* on Indigenous health.

Built and natural environments

- Are communities safe (well lit, effective police presence, traffic controlled)?
- Is social housing kept to a safe standard? Is there adequate social housing and emergency accommodation?
- Are there regulatory bodies that ensure worksites are safe and protect those who are injured at work?
- Are emergency provisions in place in the event of a natural disaster (food, water, home rebuilding)?
- Are there parks and green spaces available for use? Are they maintained, welcoming and safe?

Early childhood provision

- Is high-quality early education made affordable and accessible through public funding?
- Are early childhood spaces welcoming and inclusive of all families?
- Are early childhood educators valued and fairly compensated to support continuity for children and families?

Health education and health-promoting environments

Hopefully by this point in the chapter it has become clear to you that health is a complex and contested construct. Considered from a sociological standpoint we believe these alternative perspectives challenge the current representations and understandings of health we see and hear in the media, in health promotion campaigns, within the medical system and in education settings. In educational settings, health education and promotion is seen as essential work to be carried out by educators, preschools and schools, much of which is highly focused on the individual. As authors, we believe this is largely attributed to schools mirroring societal values as well as health education and health promotion being developed as an intervention in the biomedical model which is focused on the individual, rather than the social. There have, however, been efforts to expand the scope of health education and health promotion in educational settings.

Lawrence St Leger (2000; 2009), a leading researcher and academic in the area of school health, has played a major role in working with the WHO to create a *Health Promoting School* model for educational sites, to promote and support health more effectively in educational settings. Schools (and we would add other early education settings as well) are identified as ideal sites for health promotion and propagating health knowledge, and as such, educational sites are encouraged to support good health, not just teach about it. The idea behind this approach is that while education and health knowledge are important (curriculum), the school culture (ethos) and community support and participation are integral if the goal is to support and improve the health outcomes for all children. Further information on this model and resources can be found via a link in the online resource section.

Another way that health inequalities have been addressed in early education is in the curriculum content, such as in countries such as New Zealand (Te Whāriki), Canada (Provincial Early Learning Frameworks), Scotland (Early Years Framework) and Australia's Early Years Learning framework (EYLF). The EYLF makes use of a social view of health through acknowledging many social determinants of health, and the role an educator can play in navigating this complex terrain when supporting young children and their learning. The value of a social model of health in the EYLF is clear through the focus on children's environments and their emotional, social, linguistic and creative lives. However, despite the explicit statement that the EYLF endorses active and informed citizenship, all the examples of how an educator can promote health outcomes are individual in focus. They do not engage with community participation or advocacy, even though these are outlined as key interventions for ill health in the social health model. This individualised focus even within a framework that attempts to recognise a social view of health is, we believe, the consequence of the dominance of child development discourses in early childhood (see chapter 2). The tension here between biomedical and social understandings of human life continues to play out in all areas of early childhood, such as the continuing belief that many aspects of boys' behaviour are biological rather than social in origin.

Many curriculum documents in recent years have made attempts to include a social view of health through engaging with socially critical perspectives, as seen in the EYLF. This trend towards critical perspectives in health education is evidenced in curricula internationally such as the National Cyprus Curriculum and the British Columbian Provincial Curriculum in Canada. However it should be noted that there is substantial critique among socially critical health educators of the extent to which social perspectives have been prioritised and valued in these new iterations of health curricula.

The mixed messages about health education in many curricula mean that educators are not given clear direction about engaging young children in learning about health inequality or becoming active and engaged citizens (see chapter 12). We understand that many educators still see health only as an individual issue, and would prefer not to think about these larger inequities. However when considering health from a sociological perspective and recognising the impact health inequality can have on children's lives, we would suggest this is essential work for all educators.

Health for all: Navigating power and privilege

Our work as educators is complex terrain. This chapter opened with a vignette about Darren, a young child whose family is facing food insecurity. It showed how an apparently simple request (healthy food only at snack time), made by educators in classrooms across the globe, was alienating and unsupportive to a child who has no control over the food situation in his home. This vignette showed that even the most well-meaning health initiative (fruit time) or well-meaning curriculum (learning about healthy eating) can reinforce and entrench health inequalities in education settings. In the second vignette with Dylan, we saw the way in which our society values 'looking healthy' over reducing health inequalities. This family had significant economic and social privilege and access to many resources, such as medical specialists not covered by standard government medical provision. Despite this they felt marginalised and judged in relation to Dylan's health, through the weight stigma he was experiencing. While both vignettes speak to very different examples of how current constructions of health impact the children and families we work with, both demonstrate the power we have as educators to either reproduce these health inequalities within our classrooms, or to challenge individualised and responsibilised health messages and understandings.

It is important to cover the more individualised aspects of the health curriculum, because areas such as safety, personal hygiene, nutrition and sexual health education are all essential knowledge for young people, and we must begin to talk about these things from their earliest years. Nonetheless, we want you to know that the way we talk about bodies, the way we construct health and being

Figure 4.4 These preschoolers from Madagascar are taking part in International Handwashing Day, a United Nations project designed to raise awareness of accessible health strategies. USAID.
Source: https://globalhandwashing.org/global-handwashing-day/
Licence: Public domain

healthy, and the ways in which we engage in community service and social action all impact on children's understanding and experiences of health, and subsequently their learning and relationships in the classroom.

Engaging young children in health advocacy

Examine the way your classroom and setting engages in charity and altruism. Well-intentioned charitable acts such as food drives can often contribute to the acceptance of the idea that it is okay that some 'have' and some 'have not', and the related idea that those who 'have not' should rely on the charity of individuals rather than universal social services. Charitable drives also can serve to ostracise children within the classrooms whose families face food insecurity. Using a social health response to food insecurity with young children promotes the idea that everyone deserves access to nutritious food and that this is a social responsibility. Examples could include becoming involved in a local community garden where excess produce supplies local need, or implementing a breakfast programme that all are welcome to. Such programmes can often be made possible by pairing with a local grocery store or food supplier who can give excess food that would be wasted to the programme.

Making physical activity part of everyday learning

Many families are criticised for children not getting enough physical activity throughout the day, because fewer children walk to their school or preschools now than in previous decades. The rise in out of school hours care programmes to accommodate the long hours of working parents, and the pressure parents often feel to enrol their children in more distant but better performing schools has meant that fewer children are able to walk to school. As educators who recognise the increased pressure on parental time, we can do a lot to support young children in achieving their daily physical activity needs through their day. Make physical activity breaks a routine part of every day and throughout the day. This can be as simple as singing an action song during transition times, making a circuit or obstacle course using playground equipment, or picking a daily exercise (such as a star jump, spin or lunge) and completing a certain number on the hour every hour or whenever a bell rings.

Just because children have access to outdoor time does not mean they are being physically active. Children need opportunities to engage in moderate to vigorous physical activity every day. Some children may do this on their own through playing an organised game, but many children do not engage in this level of activity without support and planning. In preschool environments this means that there should be planning for physical activity during outdoor time that builds on children's interests and abilities. In school settings this might mean ensuring there is equipment available for children to use during recess, with games and activities taught to children that they can then play independently.

Concluding remarks

As educators, it is essential that we recognise that health disparities are unfair and often unavoidable. Without this knowledge and understanding we are likely to continue to reproduce these inequalities within our classrooms. This means that as educators, our planning, teaching and assessment of children's learning, abilities and attitudes in relation to health curriculum and behaviours need to take into account the social determinants of health. We must recognise that not all children and families have the same resources, skills, and beliefs about health and being healthy. We will continued to explore and question current understandings of health and wellbeing in the next chapter, including asking questions about whose voices are being heard in defining these terms. Challenging the individualised and responsibilised understandings of health that our societies continue to promote is the first step in ensuring that we understand the complexities and contested nature of current constructions of health. Ideally, when we engage the children and families we work with in health education, there is a focus not only on individual action, but also socially just responses to health inequalities.

Questions for reflection

- In reference to the proliferation of individualism and responsibilisation in current contructions of what is means to be healthy, in many ways society teaches us to judge. Reflecting on this idea, identify a time where you may have judged an individual or family for making a 'poor health choice'. What structural factors (such as the social determinants of health) do you think may have influenced their choice?
- What role do early childhood educators have in embodying health and fitness in the classroom? What are some key considerations for avoiding reinforcing a narrow definition of health that may impact negatively on children's perceptions of their bodies and 'healthy behaviours'?
- How might your new understanding of social determinants of health impact on how you communicate with the families of children you will be working with in the future? What are some strategies that would address some of the social determinants of health explored in this chapter?

Activities for educators

Mills (1959) created a template titled the 'Sociological Imagination Template' which can be used to deconstruct a concept or practice from a sociological viewpoint. This template can be very useful in thinking more deeply about a health issue and how it is socially constructed. In this template there are four factors, *historical, cultural, structural* and *critical,* which can be used to interrogate deeply why something is the way it is and how it has become this way.

To complete this activity, choose a health issue, such as smoking, food choices, cancer, depression, exercise and so on. Copy the template onto a piece of paper (see Figure 4.5), and fill in information/ideas/questions in each section. You

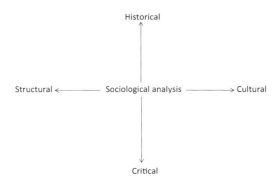

Figure 4.5 Sociological Imagination Template.
Source: Mills (1959)

Table 4.1 The sociological imagination template

Historical factors	1. When was this identified as a health issue and how was it viewed/practised/understood before? 2. Where did this issue or practice originate from? Has it or the way it is viewed/practised/understood changed? If so, how?
Cultural factors	1. Is this issue specific to a particular culture or cultural group? Are there similar isues or practices in other cultures? Are there important differences, experiences or understandings of the issue cross-culturally? 2. Is this health issue experienced differently by people of the dominant culture rather than those of a minority culture? Are there different experiences of this issue dependent on one's gender, ethnicity, age, ability, income level, etc.? 3. Are there cultural practices that either support or discourage thinking, behaviour or knowledge in relation to the health issue? 4. How do media (traditional or social) position or portray the issue?
Structural factors	1. Where do people learn about or experience this issue (schools, hospitals, families, social groups, communities)? 2. What structures such as laws, curriculum, systems (health care, schools, etc.) influence people's thinking/understanding/experiences of the issue? 3. What structures enable or constrain people's choices, access or support for this issue?
Critical factors	1. Has anything being trialled or done differently to improve people's health outcomes in relation to the issue? 2. What are some things that could be tried/made different that would make a difference in people's lives in relation to the issue? 3. Are the practices/programmes/funding in place to support people experiencing this issue well designed or implemented? Could the issue be viewed differently and different strategies employed?

might notice that some of the factors overlap slightly, or you may be unsure of where some information might go. This is because many sociological issues are interconnected, and dominant discourses work by continued reinforcement across multiple aspects of life. Don't worry too much about where something should go, instead focus on generating as many ideas or questions as possible about your chosen health issue.

Table 4.1 includes some guiding questions relating to each factor. Not all questions may be relevant to every topic, however they may offer you a starting point to help you in your investigation.

- Think back to an example of a health promotion initative you have been involved with in an early education setting as a beginning educator, or someone undertaking paid work in the sector (examples of common health promotion initatives are physical activity initiatives, healthy eating campaigns, etc.). Drawing on your own experience and engaging with the social determinants of health, list the 'pros' and 'cons' of this initative for all those involved (children, teachers, schools, families). Looking at the 'cons' you've listed, what could be changed to address these issues and make the health promotion initiative more purposeful, appropriate and effective for its target audience?

Key readings

Ayo, N. (2012). Understanding health promotion in a neoliberal climate and the making of health conscious citizens. *Critical Public Health, 22*(1), 99–105.

Broom, D. H. (1991). *Damned if we do: Contradictions in women's health care.* North Sydney, NSW, Australia: Allen & Unwin.

Germov, J. (2013). *Second Opinion: An Introduction to Health Sociology.* Oxford: Oxford University Press.

Hymel, S., LeMare, L., & McKee, W. (2011). The Early Development Instrument: An examination of convergent and discriminant validity. *Social Indicators Research, 103,* 267–282.

Leahy, D., Burrows, L., McCuaig, L., Wright, J., & Penney, D. (2016). *School Health Education in Changing Times: Curriculum, Pedagogies and Partnership.* Abingdon: Routledge.

St Leger, L. (2000). Reducing the barriers to the expansion of health-promoting schools by focusing on teachers. *Health Education, 100*(2), 81–87.

Mills, C. W. (1959). *The Sociological Imagination.* New York: Oxford University Press.

Online resources

The World Health Organisation (WHO) has explicit principles based on preventative, rather than reactive health. www.who.int/en/

Indigenous Health: Many nations report explicitly on Indigenous people's health, because this has been impacted seriously by the effects of colonisation. https://ama.com.au/system/tdf/documents/2017%20Report%20Card%20on%20Indigenous%20Health.pdf?file=1&type=node&id=47575

Health Promoting School Framework. https://gdhr.wa.gov.au/-/health-promoting-schools-framework

Further reading

Broom, D. H. (1991). *Damned if we do: Contradictions in women's health care.* North Sydney, NSW, Australia: Allen & Unwin.

St Leger, L., & Young, I. (2009). Creating the document 'Promoting health in schools: From evidence to action'. *Global Public Health, 16*(4), 69–71.

World Health Organisation (1948). Constitution of WHO: Principles. Retrieved from www.who.int/about/mission/en/

5 Child wellbeing – contested views

Figure 5.1
Source: Yarrow Andrew, with thanks to Flinders University Childcare Centre

Questions for consideration
- The terms health and wellbeing are often used interchangeably, but are they the same? And does the difference matter?
- How have we come to our current understandings and definitions of child wellbeing? Whose voices might be missing?

Vignette from practice

As a Year 1 school teacher in Canada, Jenn was expected to take part in a national survey called the Early Development Index (see breakout box). This required teachers to complete a healthy development checklist for every child in their class during their first year of school. Jenn can remember diligently filling out the more than ninety questions in the questionnaire based on her assessment of each of her students' development, including their physical health and wellbeing, trying her best to record an accurate answer for each of the questions. Though she felt she was a caring and engaged educator who knew her students and families well, this was still a difficult thing to do. She felt many of the questions were highly subjective, and not easy for a classroom teacher to make a definitive statement about. The researchers and creators of the original instrument chose to use a teacher-completed survey to measure and assess children's development and to justify this decision through the claim that 'young children's limited cognitive and language skills and attention spans' make young children's contribution to the survey unnecessary, impractical or even impossible. Jenn found filling out the surveys discomforting. Not only did the children she was assessing have no say in their assessment, there was also no input from young children about what was important to assess in relation to their development. It made her question, given the inherently subjective nature of wellbeing, how useful a tool to assess children's wellbeing can be, if we don't know how young children experience being well.

Introduction: Wellbeing – contested terrain

In early childhood contexts and in society in general, we often hear the terms health and wellbeing used as one concept to denote a broad definition of health, or used interchangeably. However, health and wellbeing are fundamentally different concepts, which are understood, measured and supported in different ways. Chapter 5 will explore the concept of wellbeing as distinct from health and how current understandings of health and wellbeing inform and impact upon our work as early childhood educators.

The fundamental difference between the concepts of health and wellbeing are the way in which they are (or can be) measured. Health can be measured with varying degrees of objectivity or externally, which means standardised measurements or assessments can be developed to assess people's health. Examples of this include medical tests and diagnostics, life expectancy, health behaviour assessments and so on. Wellbeing, on the other hand, includes elements that can only be measured subjectively or internally from the individual's perspective such as happiness and quality of life.

Early Development Instrument (EDI)

The EDI was developed in Canada and first implemented in 2000. The instrument has been adapted for international use in North and South America, Asia, Europe and Australia. Australia was the first country to use the EDI at a

> national level and has created an Australian adaptation called the Australian Early Development Census (AEDC). In Australia, the de-identified data is collected and aggregated at a local (suburb and council area) level, state level and national level to report on trends in child development across Australia and is available to the public.

The new sociology of childhood

The need to include children's understandings and perspectives in current conceptualisations of children and childhood have come from a number of disciplines including early childhood education, children's rights discourses (stemming from the UNCRC) and the new sociology of childhood (see also Chapter 1). The *new sociology of childhood* is a specific sociological sub-discipline that has sought to redress the almost complete absence of studies on children in mainstream sociology, at the time this work began. Alan Prout and Alison James (James, Jenks, & Prout, 1998; Prout, 2005), professors of sociology and pioneers of the new sociology of childhood movement, characterise this research as being presented with two key tasks. The first is to create a space for childhood within sociological discourses, and the second to confront the complexity and ambiguity of current constructions of childhood. In thinking through the complexity and ambiguity of how childhood is currently positioned, Prout presents the following dichotomies:

(1) Children as agents **versus** childhood as a social structure
(2) Childhood as a social construct **versus** childhood as natural (see chapter 6)
(3) Childhood as being **versus** childhood as becoming

Due to this ambiguity, and from a sociological understanding, an arbitrary distinction has been created between adults and children with 'different versions of child or adult, including the very distinction between them, emerg[ing] from the complex interplay, networking and orchestration of different natural, discursive, collective discourses' (Prout, 2005). What this means, in practice, is that young children are most often positioned as incapable or as lacking sufficient agency to contribute to knowledge. This deficit approach has led to their almost complete exclusion in the construction of knowledge of childhood. The new sociology of childhood instead argues that while differences between adults and children should be acknowledged, they are simply that, differences. Sometimes these differences do matter when it comes to participation and autonomy, such as a child needing to have adult supervision until they reach an age where they can stay home alone, for example. However, other differences, such as intelligence, creativity, lived experiences are differences that are not hierarchical, rather they are fluid throughout one's life and should not act as a barrier to participation and negotiated autonomy. This second group of differences are simply ones that must be taken into account when carrying out research, not as a basis to exclude a group's participation. This is the essence of the participatory research movements, that the group being researched should play an active role in contributing to knowledge (see breakout box).

Participatory research

Participatory research encompasses a range of approaches and techniques with the objective of handing power during the research process from the researcher to research participants. Within participatory research, participants are partners in the research process with agency and control over the research process. Most importantly, research participants play an integral role in analysing and reflecting on the knowledge and information uncovered, contributing actively to the findings and conclusions of the research process.

When we consider the highly subjective nature of wellbeing, the almost complete exclusion of young children from current knowledge and understandings of child wellbeing raises questions about how trustworthy and useful our current constructions and operationalisations are. Encouragingly, the lack of children's participation in knowledge about child wellbeing has been challenged by a number of research studies from research disciplines such as public health, children's rights, sociology and early childhood education.

Unpacking wellbeing

Despite the widespread use of the term wellbeing it is not easily defined, nor is there pervasive agreement on a definition. To muddy the waters further, the term wellness is often used synonymously with wellbeing, making the distinction between the concepts murkier still. While wellbeing and wellness do have different origins (see Foster & Keller, 2007 for further information) they are generally both used to denote an individual's feelings and perceptions of their state of being at a particular time. In their synthesis of wellbeing theorisation and research across disciplinary lines, Ethan McMahan and David Estes (2011) define wellbeing as optimal functioning and experiences, or 'the good life'. Wellbeing is most often understood as the combination of two distinct but related philosophies: hedonism and eudaimonism.

A hedonic understanding equates wellbeing with pleasure and happiness, whereas a eudaimonic view conceptualises wellbeing in relation to an individual's cultivation of personal strengths and contribution to the greater good in relation to their value system. Shelly Kagan (1992) summarises this distinction further through identifying the focus of each approach to wellbeing. As such, the hedonic approach focuses on a subjective determination of one's positive mental state, and the eudaimonic approach focuses on experiences that are objectively good for an individual.

An important aspect to highlight in the discussion of wellbeing is that while there are many elements that have large-scale agreement across disciplines, there is not one agreed-upon or definitive definition. Due to its popular use across a variety of contexts and platforms, wellbeing remains a contested and 'fuzzy' concept.

For us as early childhood educators, however, what is likely to be most important to understand is not the philosophy and theoretical work behind the concept of wellbeing. Rather it is how wellbeing is currently conceptualised and how it relates to our work with young children and families. The next section will explore how current conceptualisations of wellbeing impact upon our work and children's lives, and how wellbeing has become operationalized within education and care contexts.

Wellbeing: Measurable and malleable

Despite the subjective nature of wellbeing (see breakout box), the concept of wellbeing has been operationalized to make it a measurable and useful construct. This means that researchers from a wide variety of disciplines, such as psychology, social sciences, health and education have attempted to identify individual aspects of wellbeing so that the wellbeing of an individual or population group can be measured and assessed.

Objective and subjective measurement

In some areas, the difference between an objective measurement tool and subjective measurement tool is clear. An example of this is in judging sport. When judging who has won a 100 metre race, the competitors are timed and the fastest finisher is the winner. As time is a standard unit of measurement that can be consistently applied, this can be considered an objective measurement. Contrast sprinting with martial arts or gymnastics, which are judged based on criteria such as performance and style evaluated by a judging panel, we can see that these are more subjective, relying as they do on different people's assessment of complex events.

When it comes to health and wellbeing, the line between objective and subjective becomes less clear. While health can be measured more objectively than wellbeing because it is generally an external assessment based on standardised checklists and assessment tools, there are still varying level of subjectivity needed in completing and assessing with the tools used. So while there are significant differences in the levels of objectivity and subjectivity between health and wellbeing, there are no truly objective measurements for such complex constructs.

The purpose of operationalising wellbeing is to identify ways to support, enhance or protect the wellbeing of individuals or populations. As critical educators we know that our work and how it impacts upon the wellbeing of individuals in our classrooms must be contextualised within our sociological understanding of the reality of children's lives. There are likely impacts for children's wellbeing in being members of particular populations, such as those defined by gender or race (see chapter 1) and many of the social determinants of health (see chapter 4) will also be relevant here. There have been many different types of tools and instruments created to identify and measure individual aspects of wellbeing, each with their strengths and weakness depending on the theoretical or philosophical approach and design. Current research trends have seen the use of social indicators as the most popular measure for wellbeing. Social indicators are an identified variable, or multiple variables of wellbeing that contribute to an individual, population group or community's overall wellbeing. From a sociological viewpoint, social indicators are variables used to monitor social systems (patterned networks of relationships between individuals, groups and institutions) which can be used to guide interventions and support positive social change (Ferriss, 1988).

The past two decades have seen the use of social indicators extended to the assessment and measurement of child wellbeing, replacing the previous measure of child mortality. This has been an important shift as child mortality rates have fallen substantively and remain low in most countries in the world necessitating more in-depth and critical measurement tools to assess quality of life, rather than simply life itself. Asher Ben-Arieh & Ivar Frønes (2007, 2011) are leading researchers in the area of child wellbeing research and highlight the importance of childhood wellbeing as a key indicator of lifelong wellbeing, education attainment, fulfilment and productivity. There is general agreement that child wellbeing encompasses multidimensional and ecological aspects including a child's economic, social, psychological and environmental realities and experiences. As such, the social indicators associated with child wellbeing generally revolve around concepts such as health, safety, feeling loved and happy, successful social relationships, opportunities for learning and development, and material basics. There are a number of different tools and instruments that use social indicators to define, measure and assess child wellbeing. Table 5.1 below explores a few sociological definitions of child wellbeing from Australia and internationally.

Reading through the definitions you likely noticed that each one encompassed a range of social indicators. Table 5.2 explores how the social indicators used in various definitions overlap and gives us an idea of current conceptualisations of child wellbeing.

These definitions demonstrate that while there is consensus about the utility of social indicators to identify individual components of child wellbeing, there is still little consensus on what combination of indicators should be used. You will also note that the definitions and chosen indicators run the spectrum from a biomedical view of health (e.g. a focus on physical health and the absence of

Table 5.1 Child wellbeing and development constructions

	Source	Definition
A	**Report Card: The Wellbeing of Young Australians** (Australian Reasearch Alliance for Children and Youth, 2013)	Wellbeing is expressed as 'the good life', defined by the successful attainment of positive outcomes in the five key result areas: feeling loved and safe, being healthy, opportunities for learning, material basics and community participation
B	**Australian Institute of Family Studies – Growing up in Australia Longitudinal study** (Australian Institute of Family Studies, 2014)	Wellbeing is appraised through the vehicle of how children spend their time, stating that 'children's construction and use of time and participation in positive activities are indicators of health's positive development … particularly in the attainment and development of skills'
C	**Early Development Instrument (EDI) / Australian Early Development Instrument (AEDI) / Australian Early Development Census (AEDC)** (Guhn, Zumbo, Janus, & Hertzman, 2001; Goldfeld, Sayers, Brinkman, Silburn, & Oberklaid, 2009).	The instrument provides information on the five domains of children's early development: physical health and wellbeing, social competence, emotional maturity, language and cognitive skills (school-based), and communication skills and general knowledge.
D	**UNICEF – Child poverty in perspective: An overview of child well-being in rich countries** (UNICEF, 2007)	Wellbeing is measured and assessed under six different headings or dimensions: material well-being, health and safety, education, peer and family relationships, behaviours and risks, and young people's own subjective sense of well-being
E	**CWI – Child and Youth Well-being Index** (Land, Lamb, Meadows, & Taylor, 2007)	Wellbeing expressed as seven quality of life domains; family economic wellbeing; health; safety/behavioural concerns; educational attainment (productive activity); community connectedness (participation in schooling or work institutions); social relationships (with family and peers); and emotional/spiritual wellbeing

disease and injury) to a social view of health (such as access to services and education and social participation), which we explored in chapter 4. For example, consider the UNICEF definition (row D) that focuses on aspects – behaviours and risks, health and safety, and material wellbeing – that are largely objective, individual and more easily measured. This is in stark contrast to the ARACY definition (row A) which in addition to material wellbeing focuses on more subjective aspects such as feeling loved and safe and community participation.

Table 5.2 Child wellbeing indicators derived from the five selected child wellbeing/development constructions

	Indicator 1 – Feeling Happy, Loved & Safe	Indicator 2 – Being Physically Healthy	Indicator 3 – Opportunities for Learning	Indicator 4 – Material Wellbeing	Indicator 5 – Social Participation	Indicator 6 – Relationships
A	Loved and safe	Being healthy	Opportunities for learning	Material basics	Community participation	
B			Development of skills Construction and use of time		Participation in positive activities	
C		Physical health and wellbeing	Language and cognitive skills		Social competence	Emotional maturity; communication skills
D	Subjective wellbeing & behaviours and risks	Health and safety	Education	Material wellbeing		Peer and family relationships
E	Emotional & spiritual wellbeing. Safety & behavioural concerns	Health	Educational attainment	Family economic wellbeing	Community connectedness	Social relationships

Regardless of definition, a key aspect to take away from this discussion of the use of social indicators in relation to child wellbeing is that the purpose of operationalising wellbeing for young children is to identify areas of need and risk in order to support children's healthy development. One example is the EDI and AEDC, introduced in this chapter's opening vignette. This instrument uses social indicators to assess the areas and levels of risk (poor health and development outcomes as defined by the instrument) in communities, to ascertain where and what interventions may be needed. Using this information, local and state/provincial governments can decide how to use funding in the development of programmes, services and infrastructure to support identified areas of need.

A significant tension between the use of social indicators and early childhood education philosophy, however, is the heavy focus on children's future health and development, rather than their current experiences. The significant focus in public health discourses on children's future wellbeing is often expressed as their wellbecoming, to highlight the distinction. While we do not argue that children's wellbecoming is not a key concern for educators, we do strongly argue that children's current wellbeing is of primary importance and should be the driving force in our work with children.

Wellbeing or wellbecoming

Instruments or scales that use social indicators to measure or assess child wellbeing, such as the EDI and AEDC, are designed to produce a 'point in time snapshot' of children's health and development at an agreed upon point in time (generally age or a significant life event such as school entry). However, when we consider current conceptualisations of wellbeing as per the definitions in table 5.1, we can see that the constructions of wellbeing, in many ways, equally focus on children's wellbecoming. Language such as 'successful obtainment of positive outcomes', 'attainment and development of skills' and 'educational attainment' demonstrates the value placed on children's futures within wellbeing constructions, in addition to their current state of eudaimonia.

This lack of conceptual clarity between children's wellbeing and wellbecoming is problematic as it has impacts on how information about children's wellbeing (or wellbecoming) can and should be obtained. In the next section we will explore how we know what we currently know about children's wellbeing, and whose voices have informed our knowledge.

Child wellbeing: Whose opinion counts?

A systematic review of young children's wellbeing in 2016 uncovered over 80 different tools, instruments and scales that have been developed to measure at least one aspect of young children's wellbeing. Despite the vast amounts of research that went into creating these tools, none of these instruments or scales used children's experiences or understandings of wellbeing to inform their

88 *Child wellbeing – contested views*

creation. Current definitions and assessments of children's wellbeing have been developed through the lens of what adults think is important to young children, or what adults think young children need. The lack of young children's input into matters that affect them is troubling, as this is an essential tenet of the United Nations Convention on the Rights of the Child (1990).

Missing perspectives

The current state of child wellbeing constructions is a key contributor to the focus on children's wellbecoming and their future obtainment and development of skills and education. Not only because these are important aspects, but also because these aspects of wellbeing are most easily measured and assessed. Therefore there has been a substantive focus on standardised assessments and large-scale quantitative measures of child wellbeing to assess the state of young children's wellbeing and inform knowledge, practice and policy in relation to children's early development. The information gathered by these tools is meaningful, however it is also reflective of ageism at work. The exclusive use of adult-derived measures has implicitly and explicitly positioned and reinforced the idea that young children lack the skills to participate in the construction of knowledge surrounding child wellbeing (see breakout box).

As early childhood educators we know and understand young children to be capable and competent individuals that are knowledgeable about their own experiences. Yet, they have been excluded from current understandings of child wellbeing due to the challenges, or perceived challenges of involving young children in the creation of knowledge within childhood research. There have been and continue to be challenges to the belief that young children do not have the ability to inform and extend current understandings of childhood. Some of these challenges have come from theoretical perspectives within sociology, others from research methods used in a variety of disciplines interested in childhood. The next section will explore social movements that are challenging this status quo.

Figure 5.2 Joyful group activities are always a good way to encourage physical activity in children, and these can happen indoors or outside.

> **Case study: Engaging children in wellbeing research**
>
> Of the 85 instruments designed to measure child wellbeing (the EDI/AEDC being one of them) none have been informed by children through participatory research or consultation. This is due to the pervasive (and ageist) belief that it is too difficult or unnecessary to engage young children in the research process, and it is therefore more feasible to ask parents or educators to speak on behalf of children.
>
> This failure formed the basis of a research project by one of your authors investigating whether young children understand and experience wellbeing in the ways that adults have currently defined (Fane *et al.*, 2018). Drawing on a tradition of visual research methods in participatory research with children (such as drawing and photography) this study pilots the use of emoji with children to explore how they conceptualise being well.
>
> Throughout the focus groups in each centre, the children demonstrated complex and nuanced understandings of emotions, relationships, agency and autonomy, with the emoji enriching these conversations. Young children are capable partners in any knowledge-making process that affects them, and when given opportunities to participate meaningfully will make valuable contributions to interrogating childhood wellbeing.

Child wellbeing and child protection

This chapter has so far explored current constructions of wellbeing and how, due to the subjective nature of wellbeing, it is a highly contested construct that continues to evolve. This is an essential knowledge for our work with children because a key aspect of children's wellbeing which impacts the work of early childhood educators is our duty of care in preventing long-term damage to children from abuse and neglect. When it comes to responding and reporting abuse and neglect there is significant subjectivity in certain situations as to what constitutes abuse or neglect, and what the best action is to take – such as the decision to remove a child from their home. This section will explore how child protection is framed and understood in Australia and internationally, and how this impacts our work as educators.

Child protection internationally

A report by the Australian Institute of Family Studies (2014) outlines broad categories of approaches to child protection internationally in Minority World countries. The first is a 'child protection' orientation used in countries such as

Table 5.3 Child protection orientations

	Child protection orientation	Family service orientation
Stance	Children need to be protected from harm	Abuse results from family conflict or dysfunction caused by social, economic, structural, and psychological issues
Service model	Single entry point through third party notification	A range of entry points and services exist
Service approach	Standardised procedures, rigid timeline adherence	Flexibility in systems to meet client needs
Service location	Separate from family support services	Embedded within broad child welfare or public health services
Accessibility	Resources and support focused on 'at risk' families or families where abuse or neglect has been identified	Resources available to a wider variety of families as a preventative measure

Australia, New Zealand, Canada, the United States and the United Kingdom. The second is a 'family service' orientation approach which is used in many European countries such as Denmark, Belgium and Sweden. Table 5.3 outlines the two orientations and their marked points of difference. When reading through the table, think back to the discussion of biomedical versus social approaches to health in chapter 4.

In exploring the orientations, you may have noted that the 'child protection' orientation has similarities to the biomedical approach where the focus is on the individual and reactionary in nature to instances of abuse and neglect. Conversely, the 'family service' orientation fits within a social (and sociological) view of health which recognises the structures that impact on individuals and is proactive in its approach to supporting families to prevent abuse or neglect. Using a sociological lens to address child protection means that the wider issues at play which impact on child abuse and neglect, such as poverty, discrimination, marginalisation and exclusion, are recognised and responded to as part of the strategy to keep children safe.

These two orientations are broad approaches that many Minority World countries have adopted as a response to child protection. Yet, there are marked differences in how individual countries respond to child abuse and neglect and the structures in place to support children and families, even within these two orientations. Each of the countries listed has published documents, at either the national or state/provincial/territorial level which outline structure, mechanisms, protocols and foci for child protection. Examples include the National Framework for Protecting Australia's Children, Child Protection Policy (New Zealand), National Framework for Child Protection learning and development in Scotland, and the Danish Child Protection Policy. These can be worth exploring if you are interested, as an educator, about other models and challenging the orientation of the systems around child protection in your country.

Mandatory reporting

As early childhood educators, it is essential to be familiar with the relevant child protection policies and procedures, as in most national contexts, all educators are subject to some form of mandatory reporting. This means that we are legally and ethically required to report suspected cases of child abuse and neglect to the relevant authorities. To ensure an adequate understanding of these ethical responsibilities some countries, such as Australia, require educators and other professionals who work with child populations to undergo specific training. Preservice educators must hold a completion certificate in order to complete placements or be employed in schools and childcare settings.

What constitutes abuse or neglect can become murky when we understand that people from different cultures, upbringing and social classes have varied views and understandings of parenting, children, behaviour management and safety. This means that it can be very difficult to decide if it is appropriate to report a suspicion of child abuse or neglect, especially if you are unsure if there is abuse or neglect happening. For example, parents from a variety of cultural backgrounds may be comfortable with forms of corporal punishment, such as smacking, whereas this is now considered abusive, or potentially so, in many countries.

The key thing to remember when deciding whether or not to make a report is that the only decision that you as an educator will be making is whether or not a report must be made, not whether there will be an investigation or if a specific course of action (such as a child being removed from the home) will happen. When an educator makes a report to their state/territory reporting authority, the information is reviewed by a case worker at the reporting authority and the decision of whether to act or not at that time rests with them. It is often valuable as an educator to make a report because having a conversation about the issue with someone from this authority may help you gain a better understanding of your concerns.

Depending on the nature of the reported suspicion, it may not be until several reports regarding the same child or family situation are made that further action will be taken. As an educator, it is your duty to report any reasonable suspicion or belief of abuse or neglect in relation to a child in your care. What happens afterwards is a decision made by someone trained in the area of child protection. In Australia, recent research has shown that anywhere between 5 and 23 per cent of children experience abuse, neglect or family violence. As such, it is essential that possible instances of abuse or neglect are reported so that necessary preventions and supports are put in place to protect all children.

Child protection and curriculum

Concepts relating to child protection and the prevention of child abuse, such as relationships, sexuality and sexual health, consent or cyber-safety are found embedded internationally in curricula across Minority World countries. For school-age children, these concepts are generally taught within the health or physical education learning area, targeted to the concerns, awareness and increasing independence of children as they age. Concepts such as relationships, consent and sexual health education, when carefully scaffolded to support young children's needs and understandings as they grow, are as pertinent to preschool-age children as they are school-aged children. However, for children prior to school these concepts are often encompassed in early years frameworks such as the Early Years Learning Framework or Te Whāriki, through concepts such as safety, communication and relationships. This is due to powerful discourses about the need to 'protect' young children from information or knowledge that could challenge their perceived innocence. These discourses, which are strongly held in many Minority World countries and educational systems, assume that children should be shielded from information or lack the capacity to understand complex and challenging ideas. See the 'Activities for teachers' section at the end of this chapter for examples of where the debate on 'how much' young children should know about child protection related concepts is a frequent theme in the media and public sphere.

Recently, a government education department in the state of South Australia has received international recognition for their work in the creation of a Child Protection Curriculum which is in current use both within Australia and internationally in schools and early years settings (Department of Education and Child Protection, 2015). This has been mapped alongside the current National Curriculum in Australia and the associated Early Years Learning Framework (for prior to school settings) to ensure that children are learning key concepts in relation to preventing and responding to abuse and neglect. This Child Protection Curriculum, called *Keeping Safe*, identifies four key focus areas for child protection: the right to feel safe, relationships, recognising and reporting abuse, and protective strategies. You may notice from previous discussion in earlier chapters that these focus areas parallel the articles in the UNCRC on the Rights of the Child. These areas are linked to specific curricular outcomes to ensure that the content is designed and delivered suitably for children from preschool age through to Year 10. To ensure that all teachers and educators understand the Keeping Safe curriculum and how to embed these concepts into their classrooms, all teachers and educators employed by Department of Education schools and preschools must undertake training on the child protection curriculum. This is an innovative approach which seeks to incorporate some preventative measures into a system that is largely reactive to child abuse and neglect.

Pedagogies and practices that support young children's wellbeing

In addition to ensuring young children have access to education and information to keep themselves safe, and adhering to the duty of care protocols in your context, another key role educators play in developing and sustaining children's wellbeing is ensuring the classroom and learning environments are supportive spaces for all the children in our care.

As this book explores the social lives of children and their learning and wellbeing needs broadly, you will find that that many of the pedagogies and practices mentioned here are also discussed in other chapters, as educational practice that supports children's social and relational and overall wellbeing does not know 'subject' boundaries. Below are some key strategies for supporting young children's wellbeing, and how they link across children's educational experiences and chapters in this book.

Supporting children's wellbeing through giving children agency

As explored in the emoji case study, the reasoning behind children's exclusion from knowledge making is based on the assumption that children cannot participate in childhood research. However, we can see in the findings of the study that, given the opportunity to participate with tools that supported their participation, young children were engaged and ready participants whose voices contributed new understandings to child wellbeing. Through this example we can see how essential it is to respect children's agency and autonomy within educational contexts and children's lives. In this way, it is clear how the concepts of agency and resistance discussed in chapter 3 impact upon children's overall experiences of wellbeing during their schooling experiences.

Supporting children's wellbeing through respecting diversity

The children in our classrooms come from diverse family backgrounds, countries, cultural groups and experiences. While we cannot as educators be experts on the lived experience of all our children, we have a lot of power as to how welcoming our classrooms are to families (especially from minority groups) and taken for granted assumptions of what is 'normal' and how families should operate or support their children. This complex and difficult work is essential to children's wellbeing, as we know that feelings of inclusion, social participation and safety are integral to wellbeing. Chapter 10 will continue to explore the challenges and joys of working with diverse families in early childhood settings, and how we as educators can ensure our classrooms are safe and welcoming for all.

Building relationships

Building from respecting and encouraging diversity is the added element of building meaningful and supportive relationships with the children in our care and their families. Relationships that support openness and trust are essential for developing a classroom climate that encourages children and families to connect with you, fellow educators and one another. Building on from the discussion in chapter 2, some of the ways you might know that you have built strong and sustaining relationships that support children's wellbeing are if children share

94 Child wellbeing – contested views

Figure 5.3 Small Worlds play helps children make sense of their social relationships, and can help build a sense of emotional wellbeing.
Source: Yarrow Andrew, with thanks to Flinders University Childcare Centre

their ideas, concerns and challenges with you or if parents and careers feel confident in approaching you to discuss their children and their learning, social and emotional needs. These relationships foster wellbeing in the classroom and support children and families through difficult times.

Supporting children in identifying and communicating their needs and emotions

A final key aspect to supporting children's wellbeing in the classroom is supporting children in using and developing tools and strategies that allow children the opportunities to freely communicate their needs and emotions in positive ways that support their wellbeing. Emoji are an example of an open-ended tool that can give children a variety of options in expressing and discussing their feelings and emotions, both verbally and pictorially. Pictorial representation options are particularly important for children from minority language groups, or children with specials needs who may often be excluded from verbal conversations and activities. Tools to support children's wellbeing can also include having items and spaces that allow children to remove themselves from overly stimulating environments or self-soothe. These can include quiet areas or sensory rooms, or items such as weighted blankets or vests or manipulatives. Chapter 6 will explore emotions and responses to children's feelings further.

Concluding remarks

In this chapter we have looked at the critical area of wellbeing, and how we can support children's wellbeing through empowering them, and through forming respectful relationships with all children. These are important themes throughout the book, but we will address them especially in chapters 6 and 9. In looking at wellbeing, we have also looked at the serious issue of protecting children from abuse, and the role we can play as educators. Abuse and other forms of trauma seriously damage children's capacity to engage in their educational settings. As we begin to intervene more thoughtfully and effectively in children's lives, we are engaging in a form of preventative educational work, which saves much effort and heartache later on in education, in trying to deal with children's pain remedially.

As educators we know how much our own wellbeing, on a given day, can impact on our ability and focus in the classroom. Feeling physically and mentally well gives us the strength and energy to deal with disputes, accidents and challenging attitudes with creativity and kindness. A focus on children's wellbeing helps us to realise that children's lives are not so different. When we understand the significance of feeling well (with all that can include), then we will be better able to support children, and they will be happier, more energised and more willing to resolve disputes peacefully.

Questions for reflection

- In the case study explored, emoji are used as a way to elicit young children's experiences and understandings. What other strategies might you use with young children to help them share their opinions?
- What are some ways to support children in engaging with key concepts of child protection curricula?
- Reflect on an experience you have had when working with children which you believed supported children in enacting agency. What were the key elements that facilitated this (think about pedagogical practice, attitudes, environment)? What are the challenges in letting children enact agency within early childhood settings?

Activities for educators

- In the case study, emoji were used as an example of a tool that could support children in identifying aspects of wellbeing important to them and communicating their feelings, emotions, and understandings of the world. Select or create materials to create your own resource that could be used to support children's wellbeing in early education and care settings. Write some guidelines for how this resource could be used for a specific group of children, so you could share it with others.
- The UNCRC is clear on a child's right to information and knowledge in relation to matters that affect them, such as consent, safety and education. However, what children 'should' learn at a particular age inspires heated debate across the world. Below are two examples where children (and young children specifically) are portrayed as innocent being who must be protected from information which is believed by some to be 'corrupting', 'inappropriate' or 'explicit'.

The below links explores opinions on child protection issues that differ from those presented in this book. As you read through, think about what some counter arguments to these claims might be as explored in this and earlier chapters.

> Case study 1 – Teaching consent to 2–5 year olds in Scotland – 2017
> www.pressreader.com/uk/the-scotsman/20171125/281633895547600
> Case study 2 – 'Safe Schools' in Australia 2016
> http://youreteachingourchildrenwhat.org/safe-schools-coalition/

Key readings

Australian Research Alliance for Children and Youth (2013). *Report Card: The Wellbeing of Young Australians*. Canberra: ARACY.
Ben-Arieh, A., & Frønes, I. (2007). Indicators of children's well being: What should be measured and why? *Social Indicators Research, 84*(3), 249–250.
Department for Education South Australia. Child protection curriculum. Retrieved from www.education.sa.gov.au/teaching/curriculum-and-teaching/keeping-safe-child-protection-curriculum/about-keeping-safe-child.
Goldfeld, S., Sayers, M, Brinkman, S., Silburn, S., & Oberklaid, F. (2009). The process and policy challenges of adapting and implementing the early development instrument in Australia. *Early Education and Development, 20*(6), 978–991. doi: 10.1080/10409280903375800
Guhn, M., Janus, M., & Hertzman, C. (2007). The early development instrument: Translating school readiness assessment into community actions and policy planning. *Early Education and Development, 18*(3), 369–374. doi: 10.1080/10409280701610622
James, A., Jenks, C., & Prout, A. (1998). *Theorizing Childhood*. New York: Teachers College Press.
Land, K. C., Lamb, V. L., Meadows, S. O., & Taylor, A. (2007). Measuring Trends in Child Well-Being: An Evidence-Based Approach. *Social Indicators Research, 80*(1), 105–132.

Prout, A. (2005). *The Future of Childhood: Towards the Interdisciplinary Study of Children*. Abingdon: RoutledgeFalmer.
UNICEF (2007). *Child Poverty in Perspective: An Overview of Child Well-Being in Rich Countries*. Paris: UNICEF.

Online resources

Australian Early Development Index www.aedc.gov.au/about-the-aedc
Kids Matter: Australian Early Childhood Mental Health Initiative www.kidsmatter.edu.au/early-childhood

Further reading

Australian Institute of Family Studies (2014). International approaches to child protection. Retrieved from https://aifs.gov.au/cfca/publications/international-approaches-child-protection/different-orientations
Ben-Arieh, A., & Frønes, I. (2011). Taxonomy for child well-being indicators: A framework for the analysis of the well-being of children. *Childhood, 18*(4), 460–476.
Department for Education South Australia. Child protection curriculum. Retrieved from www.education.sa.gov.au/teaching/curriculum-and-teaching/keeping-safe-child-protection-curriculum/about-keeping-safe-child
Fane, J., MacDougall, C., Jovanovic, J., Redmond, G., & Gibbs, L. (2018). Exploring the use of emoji as a visual research method for eliciting young children's voices in childhood research. *Early Child Development and Care, 188*(3), 359–374.
Ferriss, A. (1988). The uses of social indicators. *Social Forces, 66*(3), 601–617.
Foster, L., & Keller, P. (2007). Defining wellness and its determinants. In L. Foster, J. Boomer, & P. Keller (Eds), *The British Columbia Atlas of Wellness* (pp. 9–19). Victoria, BC: Western Geographical Press.
Goldfeld, S., Sayers, M, Brinkman, S., Silburn, S., & Oberklaid, F. (2009). The process and policy challenges of adapting and implementing the early development instrument in Australia. *Early Education and Development, 20*(6), 978-991. doi: 10.1080/10409280903375800
Guhn, M., Janus, M., & Hertzman, C. (2007). The early development instrument: Translating school readiness assessment into community actions and policy planning. *Early Education and Development, 18*(3), 369-374. doi: 10.1080/10409280701610622
Kagan, S. (1992). The limits of well-being. In E. Paul, F. Miller, & J. Paul (Eds), *The Good Life and the Human Good* (pp. 149–168). Cambridge: Cambridge University Press.
Land, Kenneth C., Lamb, Vicki L., Meadows, Sarah O., & Taylor, Ashley. (2007). Measuring Trends in Child Well-Being: An Evidence-Based Approach. *Social Indicators Research, 80*(1), 105-132.
McMahan, E., & Estes, D. (2011). Hedonic versus eudaimonic conceptions of well-being: Evidence of differential associations with self-reported well-being. *Social Indicators Research, 103*(1), 93–108.
United Nations (1990). *Convention on the Rights of the Child*. Paris: UN General Assembly.

6 Understanding emotions in context

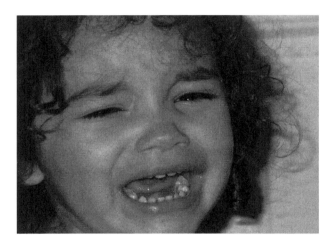

Figure 6.1
Source: Pxhere. Licence: Creative Commons CC0

Questions for consideration

- Are emotional skills and understanding always necessary for early childhood educators?
- What do you believe about emotional learning? How much is innate, and how much is acquired throughout life?
- Can we agree, across cultures and communities, about acceptable ways to respond emotionally to others, such as how we express anger?

Vignette from practice

At a neighbourhood playground, a parent is sitting watching his children playing. This is a familiar spot for this family, and it is a safe spot and a sunny day, so everyone is relaxed. There are a number of other children at the playground, and one of them has brought along a ball to kick. A small group of children start to play a free-floating game of football, running in and out of the play equipment, with lots of joyful shouting and boisterous enthusiasm. Though hesitant at first, because these children are a bit older, the son Cody joins in and is soon accepted into the game.

The daughter, Janie, has waited patiently for a swing, deciding today that she doesn't want a push, and will swing herself. She is soon swinging high in the air, squealing when the swing gives a lurch at the end of each arc, as it attempts to defy the laws of gravity.

Meanwhile, the ball game heads in the direction of the swings, and Dad half calls out, knowing that children often overlook just how far a swing can reach. Before he can finish his thought, it happens, and his son is the one who gets knocked off his feet, sprawling face first into the grass. But the game must go on, and the other children keep chasing the ball, while Cody looks like he is about to cry. Janie has slowed on the swing, feeling bad for her younger brother, and wonders whether she should go and help. Their Dad calls out from where he is standing, 'Cody, hop up, be a brave soldier!' Slowly, with some reluctance, Cody gets up, brushes off his hands and sets off after the others.

Janie's glance follows her brother, and then she resumes her swinging, and not long afterwards, starts experimenting with her latest trick, which is to jump off the swing while it is moving. She does this successfully twice, only once falling to her knees, but the next time, her hand catches on a rough part of the welded swing strut, scratching it painfully. Janie looks at the long scratch, and as blood starts to well up, begins to feel a bit wobbly. She runs over to her Dad, who looks at it, and says, 'you'll be okay, don't worry. Does it hurt? Do you need a bandaid?' Janie nods, with a trembling lip, and Dad fishes one out of the bottom of his bag. 'Would you like to sit here with me for a bit?' says Dad, and Janie snuggles into his side, her breathing slowing as she stops thinking about the scratch on her hand, now covered with a dressing.

Introduction: The world of emotions

In the previous chapter we looked at children's wellbeing, and examined some of the physical, mental and social impacts on this wellbeing. In this chapter we will be taking a closer look at emotions, and how critical they are for understanding educational settings. We usually think of educational institutions as places where people think, but often our most basic reactions in these places are about feeling.

Sociological understandings of emotion

Arlie Hochschild's work has been hugely influential in how sociology views emotions and the ways these are expressed and managed. Her research has primarily explored how those whose jobs involve significant contact with people put in considerable effort and energy to manage their own emotions and how their behaviour will impact on others. She looked initially at the lives of workers such as flight attendants and bill collectors, to understand what behaviours are expected in these jobs, and the emotions that accompany these (Hochschild,

1983). Hochschild makes a distinction between emotion work and emotional labour. For Hochschild, emotion work is what everyone does in their everyday lives, which is the unpaid work associated with understanding emotions and projecting feeling appropriate to that occasion in their own culture. As she notes, this is done more by some than others because, like other work, some people are expected to do more than their fair share. In most cultures, emotions are seen as something that women do better. As a consequence, women do more of this emotion work, and in a more intensive way. A similar phenomenon is true for social class, with those who have less economic privilege being expected to do more, when around those who have a higher status or wealth. Emotional labour constitutes all the types of emotion work that people must do as part of their paid employment, and we will look at this more closely in the next section.

Another important aspect of emotions within sociology is that people make normative judgements about others, and the phenomenon they witness, as a result of the emotions they feel at that time. Andrew Sayer (2005) argues that emotions are a form of complex evaluative judgement that allow human beings to make spontaneous decisions, based on their prior history of experiences with similar situations, which themselves generated particular emotions. For example, when a person feels angry, this is an evaluation at a bodily level that something may be wrong or threatening in that situation and the body mobilises to respond to this threat. The intuitive nature of emotions and their reactions makes these very useful for quick judgements about situations, although these judgements are not always correct and the reactions people choose may not always be the most useful.

Understanding that emotions are one of the ways we make decisions is important for educators, because we will often find that situations in our workplaces with colleagues, children or parents will push our 'emotional buttons'. Learning to observe your own processes and getting a better understanding of these emotional triggers and responses in yourself is a necessary tool for you in your work. The point is not that you should avoid feeling or expressing emotions – in fact your job requires you to act in a warm and responsive fashion to those around you. The point is that the work of an educator requires a large amount of emotional labour.

Emotional labour

When an educator wakes up in the morning, they may be feeling a whole range of things, from joy, to anxiety, to depression, to excitement. These feelings may impact on those in their household, and people often do emotion work to spare the feelings of those they live with. When that educator gets to the workplace (or even beforehand if they happen to bump into someone connected with work) they will need to access a range of skills concerned with displaying and enacting particular emotions considered suitable for the workplace. Whatever they are feeling they will need to make a conscious choice to manifest the sort of calm, professional demeanour that most families expect of early childhood educators. Hochschild distinguishes between this sort of emotional labour and the emotion work done in people's private lives because she argues that part of what people are paid for, and what their employers expect from them, are particular forms of emotional display and not others. Someone who is unable to do these forms of emotional labour at least most of the time will not last long in the early childhood workplace, because effective emotional management is a key requirement of this work.

Emotional capital

Like all forms of work, we get better at emotional labour the more we practise it. We develop a sense of what does and does not work in particular situations, in terms of emotional response and facial expression. We can build on the sorts of emotional skills we have in our private lives and add to them by developing the sorts of skills that are useful in the situations we encounter at work. This accumulated knowledge of emotional labour can be called *emotional capital* (Andrew, 2015). This builds on Bourdieu's metaphor of capitals which we looked at in chapter 2, seeing emotional competencies as another type of personal resource, in addition to cultural, social or economic capital. This is a form of practical wisdom which is built up through regular practice, rather than being learnt through a book such as this one. One of the resources of an experienced educator is this emotional capital, because it gives them the confidence to step into any educational setting and confidently manage their own feelings, as well as the feelings and experiences of those around them. One of the reasons early childhood education is taught through practicum experiences is because we learn these skills by watching more experienced people demonstrate them, and trying to put those lessons into practice ourselves. The reason these skills accumulate slowly over time is because no two

> ### Essentialism and social constructionism
>
> When we talk about *essentialism*, this is a broad way to discuss the assumptions that get made about certain qualities being innate – present from birth. It derives from the idea in very early philosophy that every entity has a fundamental form or *essence*. Sociologists tend to dislike essentialist ideas, because they encourage people to fall into mental traps, believing that their own or others' behaviour is 'natural' or unable to be changed. In contrast the discipline of sociology is based on *social constructionism*, the idea that our social selves and behaviours are constructed based on our experiences, and the constraints and opportunities present in our environments. Belief that human behaviours can be changed is necessary for those who hope for a better and more equal world.

people are the same, and no two situations you encounter in education will be identical. Our emotional capital reflects the accumulated wisdom of thousands of encounters, to help us automatically reach for a suitable-enough response to a new situation. As Marci Cottingham (2016) argues, it is important not to fall into the trap of assuming that emotional skills are inherently easier for some people than others – a form of emotional *essentialism*. All humans are capable of acquiring emotional capital, and it is an important part of everyday life. However not everybody acquires equal amounts of this resource, because some do more emotional labour than others, usually because others expect this of them.

Emotions and gender

Learning and modelling of emotions and emotional skills does not happen in a vacuum, and there are very different expectations about what feeling states are suitable for particular sorts of people. This is particularly true around gender, where we see caregivers having clearly different responses to emotions expressed by children, depending on the assumptions they are making about a child's gender. Traditionally, feeling states like sadness and fear have been considered more acceptable for girls, and more energising and volatile emotions such as anger are considered more suitable for boys (Root & Denham, 2010). It is not that these emotions are more likely to be felt by particular gendered bodies, but that adults themselves have been brought up to have particular emotional repertoires limited by gender, and so they tend to reinforce these social expectations through conversation and ongoing behaviour guidance. We saw this clearly in the vignette at the start of the chapter, where the father had different responses to the injuries experienced by his daughter and son. He cares about both children, and certainly there will be times when he will comfort his son, or when he expects his daughter to be a bit more stoic. Nonetheless, over time, children learn messages about what emotions others around them are most comfortable with them expressing, and will learn alternate ways of expressing or repressing those emotions that are seen as less desirable. Boys may learn to express their feelings of fear through anger, as this feels safer and more powerful, whereas girls might learn to internalise their anger, feeling resentful instead, and then acting this out through passive resistance to others' demands. Transgender children will tend to try and adopt the emotional repertoire of their affirmed gender, but may find themselves experiencing anger or sadness when others do not accept their gendered sense of who they are.

Gender is the one dimension of inequality where differing emotional scripts are very obvious. However other forms of inequality will also shape people's emotional lives, constraining or allowing particular emotions and emotional responses, depending on family and community cultures. Social class can also impact on emotional expression, such as when particular working-class neighbourhoods may encourage stoicism and toughness among both women and men, privileging emotions such as anger over others that express more vulnerability, such as sadness (Hochschild, 1979). Race and ethnic background may also influence this, so that, for example, Japanese culture encourages a more community-minded culture of self-control, for both women and men, leading to less noticeable or demonstrative emotional performances (Kitayama, Markus, & Kurokawa, 2000).

Working with emotions in early childhood settings

As Hochschild (1979) has explained, feelings and their expression are shaped by particular rules, which depend both on the immediate context, but also on the society and cultural groups within which this context is set. These are not set in stone, but describe the sorts of feelings that others will expect of us in that context, and that we will probably expect of ourselves. For example, at a funeral, most people are expected to act in a serious or sombre way, and may even be expected to show grief openly, such as through tears or wailing. Most occasions will have accompanying expectations around feelings and the ways these should be expressed. Part of our social and emotional learning throughout life is to become familiar with these rules in our culture and communities, and express these successfully enough to feel like capable human beings.

Think back to chapters 2 and 3, noticing both these *structural* aspects of emotion, but also that people always have agency about how they respond to the expectations of others in regard to emotion. One of the things many people enjoy about being with young children is the extent to which they express their emotions more freely than adults. We enjoy this when children get excited about quite ordinary events ('this is the best day EVER!'), but are more troubled when children express other feelings strongly ('I hate you!'). Part of children's learning as they move through the early years is to learn to moderate their emotional intensity somewhat to match the emotional levels of those around them.

Managing our emotions as educators

Careful expression of feeling is vital for those who are teaching, and there is a very tightly defined set of feeling rules, accompanied by clear expectations about how educators should act around young children. These rules are not documented, but are part of what 'everyone knows' (or should know) about being an educator. They will vary slightly, depending on your context, but will probably express ideas such as:

- Educators should be cheerful.
- Educators should be calm and unflappable, even when others around them are chaotic.
- Educators should be patient.
- Educators should not be angry, but should deal with this themselves, without troubling the children.

Notice that these are quite difficult behaviours to maintain for long periods, particularly given the stresses of many educational jobs, hence the need for emotional labour and the exhaustion that many educators feel at the end of a day of teaching.

You are expected to follow these feeling rules every single day that you are working with children. This is true, despite the likelihood that there will be many days where you feel anything *but* calm, cheerful or patient. All educators will experience difficult times in their life, such as grief over the death of a family member, separation from a life-partner or other profoundly unsettling events. Some educators will be experiencing temporary or ongoing issues around their mental health, and will need to be managing these effectively while in the classroom.

The important thing to know is that while this is often challenging, these are skills that we are called on to use throughout our lives. The more we practise them, the easier it will be to maintain them. Young children usually need and expect our support throughout the day, and part of doing our job well is to be able to be *present* for children, and engaged with their concerns at that moment. There will be days when you cannot do this, and any reasonable employer will understand that sometimes staff need time off to deal with unbearable emotional loads. On more ordinary days, this is about developing good habits when getting ready for work, to give yourself the best chance possible to be an emotionally competent educator (Elfer, 2015).

The most important of these is getting enough sleep. In the twenty-first century, with ever-present media-connected devices, many people are existing on far less sleep than is ideal. Doctors currently agree that even for adults seven to eight hours sleep per night is ideal. Making time for rest is a good way to prioritise your wellbeing as an educator. If there are things preventing you from sleeping, this can often be a key sign that there are stresses in your life that will need dealing with.

Stress can have a huge impact on the lives of both children and adults. Managing your own sources of stress, and finding ways to deal with these on an ongoing basis, will be vital for your ability to engage successfully with children, without excessive emotional management. This might involve changing aspects of your life so that they are less stressful or making time for regular self-care. This could be walking the dog, going for a swim, gardening, watching television or whatever works best for you, in relaxing, and 'turning off' from the demands of work or your daily life.

Even what we eat can have an impact on our emotions, not least because of all the conflicting messages there are in society about eating and making 'good' food choices. Finding a diet that is right for you, that reflects your cultural background, your dietary preferences or that gives you a greater sense of wellbeing, is often an important part of preparing yourself for the demanding work of being an educator. However we know that some aspects of this are out of your control in the workplace, with some foods prohibited due to child allergies, or timetables that don't allow you to eat when this would be best for you. Educators will benefit from building resilience to survive and thrive in the demanding work days of early education (Andrew, 2015).

As beginning educators you would be wise to find supportive and experienced colleagues, either within or outside of your workplace, whom you can ask for advice. Some workplaces will have structures which support this, but in others you may have to seek out these people yourself. As well as mentors, consider linking up with other early career educators, as their concerns will often be similar to your own. An important part of this is to enable you to discuss openly any mistakes you feel you have made (and you will make them) and to celebrate those beautiful moments in the classroom, where your planning runs smoothly and children are excited and engaged.

Helping children manage emotions

One of our most important roles as educators is to help children manage their own emotions. All human beings are born with the capacity to feel, although people seem to vary somewhat in how they embody these human capacities. So, for example, people on the autism spectrum may not interpret or express emotions in the same way as most other people do, or may find some emotions more accessible than others (Kouo & Egel, 2016). These variations in how emotions are experienced at an individual level are useful to know more about, but are not essential. All children can be helped by learning guidelines about expressing their emotions respectfully and safely. While psychology has tended to view emotion as located within individuals, as particular feeling states, sociology tends to view emotions as evolving responses to social situations. As critical psychologists acknowledge, understanding the interpersonal nature of emotions is necessary for a full picture of the world, in addition to individual experience (Main *et al.*, 2017).

Naming emotions

One of the first things we hope educators will do is give children language to name what they are feeling. While it seems that most feelings are interpretations of particular signalling molecules in our bodies produced by different glands, we do not talk about feelings in this way. We do not say to those we are feeling close to, 'I am getting an oxytocin spike right now', even if this may be what is happening. Instead we might say, 'I am feeling happy' or 'I am overwhelmed by love'. As babies we have the capacity to feel many things, but no language with which to talk about them or think about them.

As an educator it is helpful to develop the habit of naming emotions when you see them expressed in children, or are feeling them yourself, so that young children learn to associate particular internal feelings or external behaviours (such as crying) with particular words. This can be challenging for those who have, as educators, been treating the illusion of calmness as actual reality. Your work may require more honesty with children about the actual emotions you feel during the course of the day. We know that this will benefit children, as

106 Understanding emotions in context

Figure 6.2 All children need skills at naming emotions, and we need to name positive emotions as often as more negative ones. This child is excited to be swinging – a favourite activity.
Source: Pixabay. Licence: Creative Commons CC0

they will realise that you are a person who feels things, because adults can sometimes appear super-human to children! More importantly, they will learn it is possible to communicate respectfully even when in the grip of strong emotions.

A common feeling for young children is anger, as their lives are often constrained by others, or they feel overlooked or mistreated by their peers. It is really useful for children to have this named as 'anger', or perhaps one of its closely related feelings, such as 'frustration', or 'irritation'. Older children may already be able to name this feeling, but there will be a wide variation in how well even older children are able to recognise it within themselves when caught up in the heat of the moment. That is why is it useful to accompany the naming of the emotion, with some description of what you are seeing, as well as checking in with the child about whether you are correct, giving them symbolic power over their own bodies and feelings.

You might say, 'it looks like you may be feeling frustrated at the moment, or angry. Is that right? I am saying this because I can see you clenching your jaw and your voice sounds different – you are speaking more loudly than you usually do. Can you tell me what you are feeling at the moment?' The child may well say that they are not angry, knowing that this is often considered a socially unacceptable emotion within some cultures or for some people. Insisting that they are angry – which they may well be – is not going to be helpful, as this will simply reinforce their feelings of frustration, and is about you exercising very familiar forms of adult power. Instead see this as an invitation to have a longer conversation about what they might be feeling instead, how they would name this, and where in their body this feeling seems to be located. For some children it might help to suggest that they try and draw this feeling, act it out symbolically or try and represent it with modelling clay.

Pre-verbal children will not have the language to be able to do this, or to be able to contest your suggestions about their emotional state, and this requires more attentiveness on your part. Perhaps they may be able to show you where they were or what they were doing, when they started feeling this way (e.g. sad, angry), or maybe they can point to a person or object that to them seems to be the cause of this feeling. In that way you may be able to get some sense of what is going on for that child, particularly when you know them better, and have some sense of what usually makes them happy or unhappy. Don't be afraid to offer a variety of suggestions for what may be causing this feeling episode for the child. When and if you manage to guess correctly you will usually see the child relax in some way, because they realise you have understood what to them feels like the problem. As with adults, children are frequently frustrated or upset when they cannot do something, or cannot do it as well as they thought they could, and it is worth being attuned to this common catalyst for upset feelings. Note that children who are being raised as bilingual or multilingual may be used to articulating their emotions in their home language, and it is worth talking with their parents or caregivers about useful words they might respond to, particularly if they regularly have emotional upsets.

Making choices about our responses

One of the things many adults have not realised is that we are not captive to our emotional responses, and can moderate these over time. Most folk theories of emotion see our reactions as unconscious and often overwhelming, with little room to alter these responses. However sociological theories of emotion explain that these reaction patterns are laid down over time, and are shaped by discourses we are immersed in, based on our cultural backgrounds, our gender and our age, among other things. Knowing that these are patterns formed over time can be empowering, because we can choose to change them. When our reactions in the classroom have felt unhelpful, we can think critically about them, exploring how we might do them differently in the future. Emotions are performative, formed in similar ways to other gendered scripts (see chapter 2). Note that you as an educator are highly likely to be reinforcing gendered emotional scripts with children, whether conscious or not, and taking time to discuss this with colleagues can help you critically evaluate these reactions. The good news is that young children are still building up their emotional repertoires, and your influence as an educator can help them shape responses that are less extreme, and that will be more helpful in the long term.

As we saw in the last section about naming emotions, the key to changing these responses is noticing and understanding what is going on in our bodies. Whenever you witness children struggling with strong feelings – and this will happen multiple times a day in most early childhood settings – you have a chance to help them understand and reframe these feelings more positively. Most often you will do this with a calm tone of voice, using simple language that explains what you think may be going on for that child, as we saw earlier. At other times you will need to reinforce this with some form of respectful touch, such as a hug around the shoulders, or putting your hand on their forearm, to let them know you are present and willing to support them in these difficult feelings.

Children can and will learn from your guidance around their emotional reactions. You will not always see this learning immediately, but you are building emotional capital by doing this pedagogical work, and will come to trust that their emotional patterns are changing, even when you cannot see them. Part of this is continuing to model responsible emotional reactions yourself. When something makes you upset in the classroom, it is a chance to explain this to those around you, staying calm, but explaining what might have led to you feeling this way, and what you are going to do about it. You might even say, 'I am going to walk away and take some deep breaths, and then I will be able to think about this more clearly'. Children, even quite young children, will know when something has upset you, even if they do not necessarily have a name for what is troubling them about this situation and your response. Being explicit about this helps to make these experiences of emotion less scary for all the children close by, and helps give them models for how they might learn to behave in future.

Embodied learning – practice makes perfect

As you can imagine, this emotional learning is slow work, even for those who are very motivated to learn. It takes time and effort to change the ways we respond, and this is probably related in part to how entrenched we are in our habitual responses, as Sayer's (2005) work explains. It is important to do this work with young children, because their emotional patterns have not had as long to get established as older children or adults. Nonetheless, if you want to have an impact on the emotional reactions of an individual or group of children, then this will require consistent long-term guidance around the sorts of responses you would like to be seeing.

For example, the most common problem encountered by educators is children who are angry, sometimes extremely angry. There could be many good reasons for this, including that most children have had no choice about being put into this educational setting, nor about the length of time they spend there. In addition they are expected to learn, and much of this learning can be difficult and may make them feel inadequate or uncertain. The adults and children around them may seem really unreasonable, doing things that are disturbing to this child's equilibrium.

Many educators will want to know *why* a child is angry when they notice a child's posture, tone of voice or behaviour indicating such a feeling. While this can sometimes be a helpful guide to your possible response, many young children will not have the skills yet to pinpoint why they are feeling the way that they do. Indeed, most adults will struggle with this relatively often as well. Fortunately, we do not need to know why someone is feeling a particular way to suggest some good responses, as we will see below. In the case of anger, there are many suggestions you could make to help the child deal with these difficult feelings. One of our roles as educators is to scaffold children's skills in this area, with the ultimate goal of helping them to learn to manage these independently.

Emotional capital is fundamentally an embodied skill — that resides in our habitual external and internal responses to challenging situations. Your goal as an educator is to keep making connections between the different elements of such situations, so that over time children learn to make these connections themselves, and become competent emotional subjects. Children need to be able to recognise, first, the sorts of situations that cause them most distress (e.g. loud noises, losing a game, making a mistake in skip-counting). Secondly, they will need to recognise and name the emotions that this situation tends to provoke. Lastly, they will need access to at least one reliable strategy for moderating that emotional response and getting a handle on it. Over time, with your support, and that of others in their life, young children will learn to be able to regulate their responses themselves, and develop the sorts of self-discipline that will enable them to flourish in all their educational settings, as well as the world beyond the classroom door.

Key emotions and pedagogical responses

In this section we will look briefly at how to respond to feelings on an individual level, and in very general terms. In chapter 9 we will look in more depth at how educators can explore feelings at a whole group level, and manage behaviour within learning communities.

Anger and frustration

Anger is often accompanied by an excess of energy, which often needs to be expressed verbally or physically, to get back to a calm or relaxed state. For some children who feel angry easily or often, this need can get quite extreme, and it is worth having a variety of suggestions that are suitable for your site and your group of children.

You might suggest that children

- scream into a cushion,
- run up and down the outdoor space (if there is one available),
- jump up and down like fairytale character Rumpelstiltskin,

- squeeze a stress ball, or work vigorously with a material like clay that offers resistance,
- take deep breaths along with you, and roll their shoulders forwards and backwards, to release tension.

Tantrums

These are an expression of very strong emotion in young (and sometimes older) children, when they are frustrated about not getting something they want. They tend to decrease with age if well-managed, because they are a behaviour which children learn to control when they see that others' response is not meeting their needs. Darla Miller (2016) recommends staying calm as an effective response to tantrums, and removing yourself from the situation, while reminding the child you will talk with them once they have calmed down. This reminder helps give them an incentive to get their reactions under control, because what they most want is your engagement. The only intervention you may need to do is to ensure there is nothing nearby that the child might injure themselves on, and that other children stay out of the way, allowing the child to process their feelings without further irritation from others.

It can be useful to explain to the group as a whole that tantrums are a common reaction, if not a particularly helpful one. One way to do this is to use a book as a conversation starter. Choose a picture book that depicts a tantrum situation as part of the narrative, such as *Saturday is Pattyday* (Newman & Hegel, 1993). Books such as this can be useful in enabling collective understanding of this issue among peers, without shaming the child directly by discussing their particular frustrations.

Sadness and grief

Most sadness for children is quite short-term, and may be resolved with a cuddle or a comforting ritual, such as a favourite storybook. It is always worth encouraging the child to share their feelings with you in whatever way they are able to do this, and simply reflect back to them what you believe they are telling you. As noted earlier, you will feel a sense of 'letting go' in children when they feel they have successfully connected with you about what they are feeling.

However you should be aware that even very young children can experience quite long-term grief, particularly on the death of a parent or a much-loved family animal. In those cases, it is worth discussing the situation with the child's family, and see if you can work out some ongoing method of self-soothing, which will help the child calm themselves, while not being teased by their peers. At times a particular ritual may be helpful for a child, such as having a special object they can spend time holding for some of the day, which connects them to the person they are grieving. Children can even connect unexpectedly to moments of grief that happened some time ago, if these are brought to mind by something. Patient listening to them, or a conversation with their caregivers, may help to solve some of these mysteries.

Fear and anxiety

Many children feel some anxiety particularly when in public settings such as schools or preschools. Educators should always remember the potential stress of this experience for any and every child. It is easy to forget that children are still learning to manage the complexity of social dynamics beyond their immediate family, and even small groups of children can feel socially overwhelming. Children have a high sense of respect for the knowledge and opinions of their peers – perhaps different from, but often more significant than that of adults – and can be devastated when they feel they are failing socially. Children can and will feel scared and self-conscious about a variety of things; speaking publicly in front of larger groups, being naked, feeling exposed emotionally or feeling laughed at.

As educators, one role we perform is as a social facilitator, helping ease awkward moments among groups of children. It will also involve preserving the dignity of children in vulnerable moments – particularly the dignity of those children who may feel like outsiders within the group due to class or racial disparities, or perhaps an impairment. Even a privileged child will need this at times, such as when they may have had a toileting accident or are unwell, and so feeling additionally sensitive as a result.

Some children will experience a heightened sense of anxiety at all times, compared to other children. These might be children who have stressful home lives, such as living with a violent parent, or children who have experienced earlier trauma, such as refugee children. Some of these children may benefit from specialist support if this is available. Within your group you can help them by creating safe spaces to retreat to, and providing comfort objects such as soft toys or blankets to ease anxious moments.

Joy and excitement

We do not usually think of 'positive' emotions as needing to be managed, as most adults find these less challenging than emotions like anger or fear. However children still need support to express these in ways that are suitable for the local culture and classroom guidelines. For example, a child who is very loud and exuberant when expressing joy may be scary for quieter peers, and need guidance about how to express this in a somewhat calmer fashion. Alternatively, their joy could be channelled into sharing an exuberant song, which all could

112 *Understanding emotions in context*

Figure 6.3 Hugging a friend can be a useful strategy for children to know, when they are feeling fearful or anxious.
Source: Pixabay. Licence: Creative Commons CC0

participate in but would be less scary for quieter children. A similar thing can be true for excitement, such as the thrill of an impending excursion. As an educator it is worth planning for these moments, thinking of ways to channel children's excess energy at these moments into productive channels. You might also make extra time to remind them of the ground rules when exuberance can be risky, such as crossing roads or when travelling on a bus.

Concluding remarks

We have seen in this chapter that emotions are something we learn as much as something we feel, and that we can build up particular skills in this area through doing various sorts of emotion work. As children grow up, they learn a variety of emotional repertoires appropriate to their own culture of origin and family context, as well as other environments they move through. These emotional repertoires may appear different, particularly in terms of gender, but we all have access to the same basic human capacities in terms of feeling and expression. As educators, we have a key role in helping children learn new emotional repertoires suitable for early childhood settings. We can help children find alternative ways of dealing with and expressing their emotions which are more respectful of those around them, as well as being more effective in getting their immediate emotional needs met.

Questions for reflection

- How easy do you find it as an educator to engage in conversations with children about their emotions, and to suggest ways of expressing these differently? What lessons did you learn about emotions growing up? Have these left you well-equipped to practise these skills with children?
- How could you engage more effectively with the gendered ways that children have been taught to express their emotions? Are you more comfortable with typically female or male scripts around emotions? Do you respond differently to identical emotional reactions when expressed by girls and boys? How might you challenge your own discomfort about expressing sadness, for example, in order to model this more effectively for children who struggle with this?

Activities for educators

- Think of a person you know who seems to manage their own emotions well. Make time to have an extended conversation with them about this, to understand their successful emotional performances and find out what these feel like for them 'from the inside'. What lessons can you take away from this? What advice do they have for you about learning how to manage emotions better over time?
- Write and draw an emotions chart, expressing your own understanding of the world of emotions. Note that there is no right or wrong way to do this, and this activity will help you access your own knowledge in this area. What connections do you see between particular feelings? Which seem easy to express or more challenging? Which are 'noisy' or 'quiet' emotions? Which ones would you show in public, and which only in private, with a close friend, or alone? What colours do you associate with particular feelings? Are there tastes or smells that you associate with any of them? Work hard at making this an interesting and useful guide to your own understanding of your emotional landscape.
- Breathing can be a good tool for self-awareness, as traditional practices like yoga have shown us. At its simplest, this is about tuning into your breathing patterns at different times of day, noticing when you are breathing deeply or lightly, slow or fast. Feel the air being drawn through your nostrils or mouth and into your lungs, and learn to see this as both a clue to your emotional state, but also a way to moderate your feelings at certain times. When we are distressed or anxious we tend to breathe more shallowly, and this can add to the feelings of distress. By slowing breathing and being conscious of it in those moments, it can help restore some of your calm, and help you make better decisions as an educator.

Key readings

Andrew, Y. (2015). What we feel and what we do: Emotional capital in early childhood work. *Early Years*, *35*(4), 351–365.

Cottingham, M. D. (2016). Theorizing emotional capital. *Theory and Society*, *45*(5), 451–470.

Elfer, P. (2015). Emotional aspects of nursery policy and practice – progress and prospect. *European Early Childhood Education Research Journal*, *23*(4), 497–511.

Hochschild, A. R. (1979). Emotion work, feeling rules and social structure. *American Journal of Sociology*, *85*(3), 551–575.

Sayer, A. (2005). *The Moral Significance of Class*. Cambridge: Cambridge University Press.

Online resources

TED talk from a critical psychologist, arguing for the constructedness of emotions within human society and experience. www.ted.com/talks/lisa_feldman_barrett_you_aren_t_at_the_mercy_of_your_emotions_your_brain_creates_them

The International Sociology Association have a 'junior sociologists' section, but this is only for young adults, not young children. Can a young child learn how to do sociology? www.isa-sociology.org/en/

RECE – Reconceptualising Early Childhood Education. This organisation of educators and early childhood academics dedicates itself to promoting early childhood education beyond the restricted lens of child development theories. www.receinternational.org/

Further reading

Hochschild, A. R. (1983). *The Managed Heart: Commercialization of Human Feeling* (2012 ed.). Berkeley, CA: University of California Press.

Kitayama, S., Markus, H. R., & Kurokawa, M. (2000). Culture, emotion, and well-being: Good feelings in Japan and the United States. *Cognition and Emotion*, *14*(1), 93–124. doi:10.1080/026999300379003

Kouo, J. L., & Egel, A. L. (2016). The effectiveness of interventions in teaching emotion recognition to children with autism spectrum disorder. *Review Journal of Autism and Developmental Disorders*, *3*(3), 254–265. 1

Main, A., Walle, E. A., Kho, C., & Halpern, J. (2017). The interpersonal functions of empathy: A relational perspective. *Emotion Review*, 1754073916669440.

Miller, D. (2016). *Positive Child Guidance* (8th ed.) Boston, MA: Cengage Learning.

Newman, L., & Hegel, A. (1993). *Saturday is Pattyday*. Hereford: New Victoria.

Root, A., & Denham, S. (2010). The role of gender in the socialization of emotion: Key concepts and critical issues. *New Directions for Child and Adolescent Development*, Summer (128), 1–9.

7 Learning environments

Figure 7.1
Source: Alyssa Bagley. Used with permission

Questions for consideration

- What makes any place feel welcoming to you? Which places and spaces in your own life make you feel happiest? Can you work out why?
- Even though education can take place anywhere, many early childhood settings can end up looking very similar – institutionalised and sterile. Why do you think this is?

Vignette from practice

> *My son was a four year old at preschool and he was eager to attend to play with friends. One day I arrived to collect him and noticed that the children had spent the day making Humpty Dumpty pastings with pre-cut pieces. The pastings were egg-shaped with two eyes, legs dangling freely, a hat and a belt. I surveyed the walls of the room and could not see one with my boy's name attached.*
>
> *I asked Jake where his was and he pulled it out of his bag, somewhat crumpled, and I could see why it was not on the wall for public exhibition. Humpty had eyes, legs, but the belt was clearly vertical, not horizontal, and I said,*
>
> *'Jake, tell me about your Humpty Dumpty?' and he said,*
>
> *'Well, mum, those are the eyes and they are the legs and that [the belt] is the Band-Aid holding him all together'.*
>
> (Hard, Press, & Gibson, 2013, 324)

Introduction

We believe that good early childhood education can happen in all sorts of physical environments, but well-designed and organised spaces can make our work so much more effective. Can you think back to your early childhood years, and remember the sorts of buildings and classrooms in which these were located? How did you feel, as a young person, walking into those places? Classrooms are not only physical spaces, but also social and cultural spaces, and both aspects reinforce each other. When a physical environment feels welcoming, then everyone in it feels more relaxed, and this will support calm activity and good relationships.

In this chapter we will talk about all the important aspects of the spaces we create for children, and for ourselves, and how these will shape the experiences of everyone who spends time in those places. We will be picking up on key dimensions of inequality (see chapter 1) and asking whether the places we are creating are supportive of all children and families, not just the most privileged. As the vignette above shows, some environments are unwelcoming not because they are badly equipped, but because the pedagogical practices in those places are too narrow, with educators trying to control children's work too tightly. Jake was clearly engaged in the activity, despite the educator having pre-cut shapes so as to ensure a uniform 'product' from all children. However Jake made the 'mistake' of bringing his own ideas into the activity. Knowing the story of

Humpty Dumpty, a familiar nursery rhyme, he realised that a key element was the moment that Humpty gets broken. Jake knew what helped fix most of his own injuries, and compassionately decided to put a large bandaid onto Humpty, to help him keep his shell together.

When we fail to allow children to thrive in our settings by tightly controlling their actions, or by making spaces that are not conducive to learning, we are likely to destroy children's motivation for learning, or force them into acts of resistance (see chapter 3). This is not what any educator intends, but too often we see this dynamic playing out in early education settings. The formal curriculum Jake was being offered was about nursery rhymes, but in the hidden curriculum he was learning that adults are always right, and that creativity and initiative are wrong.

Colonialism and colonising practices

All of our early childhood services are located in particular places, all of them on one small blue-green planet, orbiting an unremarkable star, on a distant arm of a very ordinary spiral galaxy. We take this for granted every day, but in this chapter we want you to stop and think as broadly as possible about early childhood education. These particular places might be in wealthy neighbourhoods or poor ones. Some of these places will be recognised as Indigenous land, forcibly taken by colonisers in years gone by. They may be located in fertile lands, or harsher landscapes such as deserts or tundra. They may be peaceful places, or places disrupted by conflict and other forms of violence. Education is happening right across the planet, and it is shaped by the contexts in which it happens.

Alexander Sidorkin (2002) gives us this broad perspective, imagining what education would look like if viewed by aliens landing on earth. Sidorkin suggests that these aliens would think that human beings worship a god of useless things, because the small people in these 'schools' are set to work making things that are then just thrown in the bin, or otherwise go unused. He is not trying to be funny, but reminding us that much of education is likely to be mystifying to children. They are set tasks (like creating a Humpty Dumpty) that do not make much sense, and which do not teach what they are intended to. Sidorkin is also reminding us that education is a place for practising skills, over and over, and part of our challenge as educators is how to keep this process of repetition and reinforcement interesting.

The theoretical idea introduced in this chapter is postcolonial theory, and its critique of colonialism (Said, 1978). Looking at this small blue-green planet, we know that a variety of places in the world – Persia, China, Greece – developed early civilisations and many of these spread their cultural ideas and practices far beyond their original borders. The Persians, particularly, were determined colonisers, spreading their culture across much of what is now India, Pakistan, the Middle East and Turkey, from about 2500 years ago. In saying this, we want to remind you that colonisation can have a mixture of effects – it is often destructive of the cultures being colonised, but can produce unique hybrid cultures, valued by their citizens. It can sometimes produce unexpected benefits such as when technologies like writing spread across the world, allowing people's ideas to be recorded and stored rather than communicated only through oral traditions.

In the modern world the most aggressive colonisers of recent centuries have been the European powers, who travelled to Africa, Asia and the Americas, often occupying and brutally suppressing any native cultures. Postcolonial theory reminds us that almost nowhere in the world is unaffected by these colonial processes, and that we need to be aware of the effects this continues to have on societies around the globe. Colonising practices involve actual genocide, particularly of populations that resist, but also consist of cultural genocide, where the knowledge and cultural practices of particular communities are undermined or destroyed. As Edward Said (1978) famously argued, colonisers rewrite the story of the world's places and cultures, framing their own actions in a positive light, while tarnishing the cultures of the colonisers in racist ways, labelling them as primitive, savage or ignorant.

Postcolonialism and education

Most of the knowledge, and our fundamental understandings of the world, are rooted in a history of colonialism by Minority World countries. These colonial perspectives, which are largely white-privileged ways of thinking and acting, have become written into the governing structures of many colonised places. They continue to shape significant international institutions, such as the United Nations, and the many programmes that are run by these institutions. When we look at curriculum documents around the world, we need to remember that many of these may not reflect the authentic histories and practices of those places, but rather the legacy of colonial authorities.

As Gaile Cannella and Radhika Viruru (2004) have argued, our educational practices in early childhood need to be decolonised, in order to make space for a multiplicity of human perspectives, rather than the dominant discourses of the colonisers. For example, in Aotearoa/New Zealand, Māori people are the first inhabitants, whose culture has been disrupted by invasion and occupation by Great Britain since the 1840s. This occupation forced many Māori people off their ancestral lands, and has ongoing consequences right up into the present day, with many Māori people experiencing economic disadvantage, cultural marginalisation and other effects of colonisation. In more recent years, Māori people have realised the strategic power of education, in reclaiming their cultural power (*mana*), and have established early childhood services, schools and universities, which teach in Māori language, and from a Māori cultural perspective.

Colonisation processes have ongoing impacts, on both the colonisers and those who have been colonised. Those who have been privileged by this process – the descendants of the colonisers – must think hard about the ways they continue to benefit. This may mean being more likely to be employed as a teacher within the education system, through the processes of structural racism, or through finding that the histories told in their own education cast the actions of their ancestors in a positive light. For those who have been colonised, they may experience an education that silences their own cultural knowledge of the world, or actively presents people from their own cultural group in a negative light. Chana Teeger (2015) shows how these dynamics continue to play out in modern South Africa, with continuing denial by teachers about the ongoing effects of structural and interpersonal racism on Black students, and the ways this perpetuates the unequal effects of schooling. We want you to hold these colonising processes in mind, as we look more closely at how we shape our early childhood environments.

The art of place-making

This section explores the geographies of learning, and how to create environments whose elements reinforce the aims and practices of your service. The subject of geography looks at the physical and human aspects of space and place, asking deeper questions about why these places look like they do, and what this means for human life in that location. As educators there will be aspects of the places that you work that you do not have much control over, but there will be many that you can influence. Whether you can change them or not, we want you to be able to *notice* all the different components that go into making positive and socially equitable early childhood places.

Figure 7.2 Building on the existing mature tree as a landscape feature, this skilfully designed rocky mound and platform can be a cave, a castle, a mountain and more besides.

Source: Andrew Plaistow, with thanks to Alberton Primary School

Physical spaces

The most obvious aspect of any early childhood service is the physical structure in which it is located. In some cases, as with 'forest' school programmes, these physical structures may be very minimal, such as a hut for shelter in bad weather, given that most of the educational time happens outdoors. In wealthier countries or communities many early childhood buildings are purposefully designed for the needs of children, often by architects who specialise in these sorts of buildings. It is worth noting that these architects are not early childhood educators, and the buildings they design may look engaging but will not necessarily function as well for those who have to learn and teach in those spaces.

Building design and layout

In any early childhood service you visit, look around you. How old is the building? Was it designed specifically for education, or did it have other uses beforehand? Does it feel spacious or cramped? How well-maintained does it seem? These sorts of questions can help us evaluate the history of this service, and the intentions of those who create it. We want you to become curious about every aspect of the buildings you inhabit, and the implications for those of us teaching and learning in these spaces.

Sometimes, ironically, the best places for early childhood services are those which were not designed for children! That is because purpose-built services are often highly utilitarian in construction and design, making them feel like institutions and therefore less welcoming. When children's services are located in residential dwellings (either family childcare, or preschools located in converted residences) the building will have been designed to appeal to essential human needs, and the demands of family life. The materials it is constructed from are likely to be similar to other houses in the neighbourhood and the layout will feel more familiar to children.

Part of what our buildings do is create spaces of openness and of privacy. We are aware that educators in many contexts seem to feel uncomfortable with children being out of sight. This ignores the genuine stress that some children feel about long days in preschool without any moments of 'alone time'. When creating indoor and outdoor spaces, consider creating small locations where children can go to feel some sense of privacy, either by themselves or with one other child. We believe any issues that may be of concern for educators around lack of supervision are best addressed pedagogically, by discussing emerging problems with children, resolving problems within the group and building children's interpersonal skills in both assertiveness and care for others.

One aspect of this privacy is in the bathroom, and many of our toileting practices are designed for adult supervision (Foucault would call this *surveillance*). As we explained in chapter 2, when thinking about the practices pioneered by Emmi Pikler, young children flourish in conditions of respect and part of this is acknowledging their need for privacy. As an educator we hope you will continue to advocate for better practices around children's privacy needs. For those services which have open toilet stalls, why not include doors with a simple latch, which can be opened from either side, but allows the child to have some control over their privacy. Similarly, think about how change table arrangements can be adjusted to make these feel more secure for infants.

Regulations

In many countries, there are minimum regulations for early childhood services designed to support the overall quality of services. While these can be useful, their function as a minimum standard often means that services are built to these specifications, rather than taking account of the best interests of children. Stress levels are higher for children when the maximum legal amount of children are regularly in a particular classroom. It means more competition for resources and less possibility for quiet concentration. In these situations we believe the need for quiet or private spaces is even more important.

Frequently there are building regulations which regulate parameters like door heights and minimum ceiling heights. When we think about purpose-built centres, we note that these are often built to minimum specifications due to the cost pressures that exist in countries which have more marketised systems. Yet even a difference in ceiling height of 30 centimetres can make a huge difference to the perception of space in a room. Noise-absorbing materials or design are often more costly but can be vital for making early childhood classrooms more liveable, particularly for children who find excessive noise difficult, such as those with hearing impairments, some children with autism or children who may be hyper-vigilant due to past trauma.

Many of the above issues, including the need for privacy, are taken into account in the principles of Universal Design (see online resources). This resource – developed by architects for their field – helps everyone to think about what is needed to make buildings work for all of those who use them, whatever their size, age or levels of ability. While it is not easy to account for all possible needs, these principles provide the tools to maximise the possible use of any space. We are big supporters of these principles, which embody equity and social justice literally from the ground up.

Connections with the natural world

One of the most important physical features of any building, is its connection to the natural world. Those who work in services located in rural areas may take this for granted because they have good access to outdoor areas. However it is worth remembering that numbers of early childhood services are now located in high-rise buildings with little access to the outdoors. Many of these services must make do with 'active play zones' located in a particular part of the building, but without any access to soil, plants or the diversity of local ecosystems. Some services have tried to compensate for this lack of outdoor space by including

Figure 7.3 Whatever the climate in your area, you can make the outdoors accessible with the right clothing. 'Which pair will I choose today?'.
Source: Yarrow Andrew, with thanks to Flinders University Childcare Centre

generous (and well-fenced) balconies surrounding the rooms, in which various messy activities (such as sand play, or digging patches) can be accommodated. This also allows access to all-weather play, which is an important aspect of learning for children.

If a building does not have access to the outdoors, consider bringing nature indoors instead. Incorporating planter boxes or potted plants into the internal spaces of buildings has many benefits. These plants will make the room more beautiful and help to purify the indoor air, removing some pollutants that can build up in indoor environments. The organic growth of plants also constitutes an important part of the visual environment, contrasting with the straight lines and bright colours that are usually a feature of these spaces. There are many ways to draw these plants into your curriculum, such as making them part of 'still life' arrangements for art activities, or learning about plant biology.

One simple but critical feature of any building is its access to natural light. Windowless rooms lit by artificial light will feel claustrophobic, and most people feel better and learn better in rooms which have access to wider views. It is especially helpful if the windows in the room can be on different sides of the room, allowing a more even natural light across the space, which is better for art activities, and tends to feel more comfortable for most people (Alexander, 1977).

Social spaces

Perhaps the most critical aspect of any early childhood service is how our buildings and organisations function as social spaces rather than just physical spaces. Early childhood is a fundamentally relational field of education, with many close and warm connections built between children and between adults, both co-workers and the family members who use these services. We need our physical environments to help support this aspect of our work rather than hinder it. When laying out classrooms or front office areas we need to arrange them with an eye to who will be coming into them, and what they will see when they do. We want these spaces to feel welcoming, not just to those who are familiar with early childhood education but to anyone who comes in for the first time.

There are many things that can make a space feel welcoming, while still being functional, such as natural lighting, soft colours and objects like potted plants or artwork (children's artwork can be good) which help make visitors feel more at ease. Is it obvious where people can wait if they need to wait to speak to someone, and are there comfortable seats available? Many people will need information about your organisation, whether in their first visit or later on. It is good to think about where you might put this and how it will be organised. When you visit sites, notice what information is provided and how it makes the space feel.

Civil society

Increasingly with discourses of neoliberalism pushing the marketisation of society, many early childhood services, and indeed many schools, are starting to see themselves as businesses rather than educational institutions. This process is often reflected in the language being used, so that families become 'clients' or 'customers', and the focus may be on 'branding' their service (through staff uniforms or logos) rather than creating a welcoming place where learning and engagement will happen. These discourses, which came to prominence in the late twentieth century, see economic goals as the primary educational focus. This phenomenon has been talked about by Katrien van Laere (2017) as the 'heckmanisation' of early childhood, referencing well-known economics research by James Heckman, which argues for the long-term economic benefits of early childhood education to societies.

We believe that early childhood education is important, but do not agree that future economic benefits are the only possible rationale for our work. Instead we agree with Jill Blackmore (2006) that education should be seen as a public good, and that educational leadership should have social justice as its goal, rather than cost-benefit analyses. Our societies, our communities and individuals all benefit from greater knowledge and understanding. We believe this is true regardless of the costs of education or the likely outcomes. Throughout human history education has been a fundamental aspect of civil society, and its value does not depend on economic arguments.

Learning is an activity that most people find deeply satisfying, and contributes to the broader wellbeing of our communities. Looking back to a time before the dominance of neoliberal ideas, and before the widespread concern for child safety, Alexander and colleagues (1977) offered an intriguing vision of 'children's homes' (early childhood spaces) which were designed to be an integral part of civil society. In this vision there were public footpaths and cycle ways running through these children's spaces, to ensure that children remained connected to and actively engaged in the community. They were envisaged as places for children which they had a right to part of, rather than as services for parent-workers. This difference is important. Children have different desires for their own lives than parents have for them, and ensuring that our services address children's actual needs rather than those of adults or policy-makers remains an ongoing challenge.

Wanting our environments to support children's involvement in civil society is a vision only starting to be recognised, such as in the Scandinavian countries. Our environments can be constructed to support children in being active citizens connected to the world around them (see also chapter 12). As educators, you will be thinking about how your physical environments support the social relationships that children want to engage in. Your spaces should be set up to help children connect with each other meaningfully. Most traditional early childhood programmes are laid out to control children's movements, isolating them in particular rooms with peers of their same age, even when their friends or siblings are of different ages. We think multi-age grouping is an under-utilised model for early education, because it does not presume that all children pass through a particular stage of development in the same way or at the same time (see chapter 2). It allows children to become familiar with other children and adults and to be exposed to a wider range of personalities and abilities. At its best this way of working allows children to move freely throughout the physical spaces at the service – both indoor and outdoor – finding people, places and activities they wish to engage in, with adults offering flexible support to those who need it. This requires a different way of working for many educators, and some will be fearful of these changes. We feel this model expands possibilities for educators themselves, allowing more contact within the staff team, building adult relationships as well.

Just as we want the building to build relationships within its boundaries, we also want to think about its relationship with its neighbourhood. In our work as researchers and teacher-educators we often see schools and preschools with intimidatingly high fences, looking more like prisons than places of education, which is a materialisation of Foucault's (1977) theories about disciplining populations. These fences are usually justified as protecting children, but function symbolically to make services unwelcoming and disconnected from the communities around them. In some countries early childhood sites have only low fences, or marker poles establishing the boundaries (as forest schools do). These sorts of boundaries rely on educators trusting children to understand limits. These symbolic or human-scale boundary markers help to create different sorts of relationships with the world beyond the service, such that a neighbour might lean on the fence and chat to the children, building connections and creating opportunities for learning.

Cultural spaces

Lastly, we believe that it is important that early childhood services are cultural spaces, reflecting the deep values and beliefs of the communities in which they are situated. In an era of standardisation, when identical products are made available across the world, we think it is a mistake to apply this model to early childhood education. Every community will be different because the people who make it up and the variety of cultural backgrounds they come from will be different. Standardisation is often a relic of colonialism, and continues to reflect the values of former colonising cultures, rather than local communities. Honouring this specificity of place will mean educators will need to attune themselves to their context, and listen hard to the families who use that service. Chandra Mohanty, a feminist and postcolonial scholar, believes we need to create a world which is about 'mutuality, accountability, and the recognition of common interests as the basis for relationships among diverse communities' (2003, 7). This can be your aim in your own early childhood classroom.

The Commons

Picking up the earlier discussion about civil society, we wonder who should be responsible for early childhood education. Nowadays education is typically provided by commercial businesses (the market) or by governments (the state), as if these are the only choices. As Kate Raworth (2017) explains, in her reimagining of economic theory, this neglects two vital areas of economic life: the household and the commons. The origin of the word *economics* is derived from the word for household, as the original economic unit of life, because most economic activity was once household businesses (farms, smithies, weaving). Early childhood education also began in the home, and one of our current models of early childhood education is family childcare.

We think it is important to remember that the commons, Raworth's fourth sector of the economy, can also be a valuable model for early childhood provision. Indeed there are still many examples of community-run and managed services across the world, which reflect the communal values implicit in this sector. As Raworth (2017) explains – backed up by the Nobel prize-winning work of Elinor Rostrom who researched the economics of the commons – this is a significant area of human life and one deserving of greater attention. There is renewed attention to common resources as a result of climate change, because things like the seas, our atmosphere and our old-growth forests are all being put at risk by irresponsible development. Rostrom explained that common resources can work very effectively, but it is vital that they are controlled and carefully managed by those who will be using them. When this does not happen, many of these resources will be used at unsustainable rates, just as any business, state enterprise or classroom will fail without effective leadership and direction.

Whatever the typical early childhood service looks like in your locality, we think the commons offers a valuable and empowering model for education. When education is controlled by those who use it, it will reflect the values and ideals of that community, and will necessarily be well-supported and appreciated. This sort of common ownership can evolve from all sorts of origins. A commercial early childhood service, for example, could reimagine itself as a social business, whose articles of association and business philosophy were redirected from profit-making goals into social investments in the local community. Similarly, government-run schools or preschools could be made more genuinely democratic, by investing time in building up local governance structures (such as parent boards) with real power to influence the educational work in that site. Co-operative enterprises are organisations managed for the collective benefit of those who work in them or access their services. We believe this can be a valuable model for early childhood practice, and would offer a shared cultural space where educators and families could create and run a service that meets the needs of children and adults alike.

The services of Reggio Emilia

One of the most famous examples of cultural spaces is the early childhood services of Reggio Emilia, whose origins lie in a group of villagers' desire for a better world after the destruction of the Second World War (see also chapter 12). As a result of the organic processes by which these services first developed, they reflect the values of Italian people, which have now become literally built into the fabric of their services. For example, a long tradition in Italy is the *passeggiata*, an evening stroll with the family, and many towns have covered walkways to allow for this form of social and community interaction. Many early childhood services were built to include covered verandas to allow for these sorts of interactions, and to create comfortable spaces for learning with access to the outdoors. Similarly, Italy is famous for its artistic traditions, so that when these early childhood services were created, they included a key focus on art practices, often with a dedicated *atelierista* (art practitioner) to help build the children's skills in documenting their emerging thoughts and feelings through art.

Making inclusive environments

In talking about place-making above, we wanted to underline that the physical and cultural make-up of our services has significant impacts on the children and families who use them. When we say that our services embody cultural spaces, we are acknowledging that the dominant discourses within a particular country will shape the terrain of education, in terms of curriculum, physical environment, and pedagogical practices. When looking at the example of Reggio Emilia, we wonder how those services are perceived by families who are not from an Italian background, but who may have migrated from countries with different values and practices. For some families, the focus on art may seem frivolous, undermining a commitment to more valuable skills, such as reading and writing. We know that these services have a commitment to high-quality early education, but what if quality looks different to different communities?

Remember that digital spaces can be vital extensions of the physical spaces of our classrooms and services. Providing meaningful virtual resources can allow parents who work long hours or who have a chronic illness to engage in the life of your classroom, such as commenting on their children's work, or posting resources for other parents. There are increasing numbers of digital classroom resources, and many of them can help to extend the social and cultural spaces of the classroom, and help make partnerships with families more of a reality.

Depending on where you live and work, you might work in very culturally and linguistically diverse settings, or more monocultural ones. In all these settings, we encourage you to be attuned to the ways that families participate in your services. The advantage of services in multicultural communities is that they are more likely to be aware of the need to be sensitive to these issues, although this is no guarantee that they will be doing so effectively. For less diverse settings, we know it is easy to take particular aspects of education for granted, rather than be willing to evaluate all aspects of what you do on a regular basis.

Just as a service dominated by people from the dominant culture and shaped by those values can feel intimidating to those from differing backgrounds, so too can female-dominated environments feel intimidating to fathers or other male relatives involved in active care of their children, or any male staff members. As Nirmal Puwar (2004) has argued, anyone engaging in a setting where 'people like them' are not typical, will experience a variety of negative reactions, from incomprehension, to misunderstandings, to outright hostility. We are not suggesting that you 'bloke-up' your setting, or engage in stereotyping of any men who may be involved in your centre regularly. Remember that they may not be heavily invested in masculinity, and may not be heterosexual, so making these sorts of assumptions is unhelpful. However, we think it is important to make efforts to communicate actively with any male family members. Make sure you encourage them to spend time in the classroom on pick-up or drop-off, and specifically invite them to events like excursions or fundraisers.

In a similar way, settings that work with young children can often be places that feel very heteronormative, because the presumption for a long time has been that child-rearing is the prerogative of heterosexual couples. Therefore many services have not examined their practices, such as the design of their enrolment forms or the training of their staff, to be inclusive of same-sex families. Given the homophobia or transphobia that many LGBT+ parents have experienced in the past, many will be wary of being too open about their family lives until they know that your service can be trusted to treat them and their children respectfully. With most Minority World countries now working to eliminate discriminatory practices and legislation impacting on LGBT+

people, we know that children from same-sex families need similar effort and energy from early childhood educators (Newman, 2016).

Universal Design, mentioned earlier, allows buildings to be welcoming for people with different physical impairments or particular emotional or intellectual challenges. We hope that you are willing to evaluate critically all of your spaces to ensure they are accessible and welcoming, even in the absence of children or family members with specific disabilities. People will disabilities will notice and appreciate when educational settings are being proactive about how their spaces work for all children and families. Knowing that you are a welcoming environment will help parents with experience of disability to feel able to offer their own expertise about possible improvements to the functioning of spaces which you may not have considered. One way of being proactive is to employ staff with disabilities within your setting. As in other occupations, many early childhood roles are designed assuming that they will be filled by an able-bodied or able-minded person, without considering the possibility of employing someone with a disability. In employing staff with an inclusive mindset, we are forced to think about the design of all our processes and practices, not just those that impact on children or families. How might we reshape early childhood roles for someone with chronic fatigue, a visual impairment and so on? In advertising for positions with this diversity in mind, services are encouraged to open themselves up to new ways of educating.

Designing curricula, designing classrooms

A vital aspect of learning environments is, of course, the pedagogical strategies we use within them. The theoretical approaches of critical pedagogy ask us to move away from models of the child as passive recipients of knowledge and look at how knowledge is co-constructed. In their book, Peter Moss and Pat Petrie (2002) explore how practices in schools and children's spaces rely on these limiting discourses about children and childhood, and challenge educators to see education as about making meaning, with children, and in response to particular contexts and needs.

Many educators now work with formal curriculum frameworks within their national contexts, which may set some limits on how they can practise (see also chapter 5). As critical educators we can influence how such curricula are enacted, choosing to emphasise some elements and minimising others. In this way educators can remain responsive to their local environments, avoiding the universalising tendencies of many curriculum documents. As educators we want to teach children what they need to survive and thrive, and to teach this in ways that make sense to them. As Freire (2014 [1968]) realised in his work with marginalised adults, it is not that the aims of most curriculum are wrong, but that they fail to take into account the existing skills of those being educated. Whatever curriculum you are working with, there will be plenty of valuable knowledge within it that will be useful to the students you are working with. Your pedagogical skills allow you to take what you are learning from the relationships you are building with your students, and make connections with knowledge that will be relevant to their learning now.

The Generative Curriculum projects initiated by First Nations communities in Canada provides one model of this, building new forms of early childhood curriculum whose foundations are in community knowledge and experience, which are then brought into dialogue with other ways of seeing or engaging with children, such as colonial educational models (Dahlberg, Moss, & Pence, 1999, ch. 8). These projects were not just about the knowledge that would be passed on but also the ways that this knowledge was communicated, and the sorts of pedagogical processes which would enhance this for First Nations students themselves. These projects also highlighted that new forms of assessment and evaluation were needed to address the particular cultural values of these communities.

There are many useful resources to support you in this sort of work, and we hope that you will find like-minded critical educators within your own context to share their own stories. Having colleagues outside your immediate workplace with whom you can debate ideas and share difficulties is invaluable when trying to challenge existing discourses. There are many resources for evaluation, beyond the procedures of quality assurance schemes. These can be seen as pedagogical tools and used to think critically about the values and practices which inform your work. Remembering that they are tools, which may not be useful for the job at hand, helps keep us critically reflective of this evaluative process too, rather than adopting a new system wholesale. Change that works best is usually incremental, and responsive to the context in which it happens.

Material cultures

The materials we use daily are often expressive of our values as educators. The sorts of resources we use in our teaching might express our environmental values, such as not using plastic made from fossil fuel sources, or our political ones, if we choose not to source materials from certain countries or businesses, as part of a wider boycott to encourage a change in behaviour. As critical educators we may want to be explicit about these choices with the families we are working with, to help promote such practices further. Books and posters can be particularly influential materials, because of what they reveal about how human cultures are represented to children. What world is being created in children's minds by the materials you are using? Being strategic about what books you read or offer to children, or in the displays you create, can create a vision of the world that is inclusive of visual differences such as racial diversity or some disabilities.

Evaluating our environments

Having looked at what it means to make educational places that reflect our most fundamental needs as human beings, we will examine some ways we evaluate how they work. While evaluation can often be an intimidating word, because it suggests the many unhelpful forms of evaluation we may have encountered in schools and workplaces, we see this as a fundamental aspect of human life. The processes of inquiry-based learning involve praxis (action and reflection), and the reflective part of this cycle is where we evaluate the effectiveness of our actions.

No educational setting stays static, and no matter how well-designed or planned, the places we have created may not continue to meet the needs of those who use them. Some of the most effective early childhood settings evaluate their work authentically, by regularly surveying children and families about their experiences. By doing this regularly staff are less likely to get entrenched into patterns of behaviour and will be continuing to learn and grow as educators. For example, a school who had surveyed their families realised than many families actively used the school grounds on weekends, and found that their children asked them about school equipment which was locked up on weekends. The school negotiated to make some equipment accessible on weekends on a trial basis, and the school board agreed to assess the economic impacts from any loss or breakages at the end of the six-month trial. Parents have been asked to take photos of their children playing on the weekends, to allow for informal evaluation of this process during the week, and engage children in conversations about how to help this trial go smoothly.

Quality ratings systems

As well as the sorts of authentic local evaluation seen above, we know that many countries have developed systems to assess 'quality' in early education, including the learning environment. Many of these are embedded within quality improvement and assessment systems at the national level, either through governments or peak bodies (e.g. Australian Children's Education & Care Quality Authority, 2011; National Association for the Education of Young Children, 1984; Ofsted, 2016). Others, like the Early Childhood Environment Rating Scale, have been used since 1984 to assess early childhood spaces internationally (Harms, Clifford, & Cryer, 2014). Most of these systems have needed to be revised and updated as their original criteria and methods tend to replicate the cultural biases of the countries and research groups which created them.

Despite these revisions, sociologists remain concerned about the ongoing impacts of these quality improvement programmes. Any such programme is at risk of creating an arbitrary vision of 'good early education' which standardises and homogenises any early childhood services that come under its auspices. They can and do drive improvement in services, but this is improvement that does not come from local communities' own visions for their children, but from centralised authorities. This is a colonising practice, because it seeks to control the practices of educators and services, usually through coercive mechanisms such as regulation or funding practices (Miller, 2014). Italian early childhood services, as we saw above, are developed at a local level, and so are free to express the particular values of those communities in which they are established.

There have been many critiques of quality assurance programmes, and their disciplining and universalising functions. One of the most influential has been the exploration by Gunilla Dahlberg and colleagues (1999) of how 'quality' functions as a technology of normalisation, reducing all the possible ways to educate and care for children to specific techniques and practices delineated by these bureaucratic processes. In contrast, they argue, we need to understand evaluations of quality as a fundamentally political process, invariably subjective and dependent on context, and driven by values, even when these are not explicitly articulated (Moss & Dahlberg, 2008).

Concluding remarks

What we have asked you to consider in this chapter is not easy, because we are asking you, in many cases, to reimagine at the deepest level how we educate and care for our children. This is a form of practical wisdom, requiring attention paid to how our learning environments work over time, and for which people. We know that physical infrastructure is expensive to alter, and so slow to be changed, and many of you will not have the influence or the ability to be able to make big changes, at least in the short term. Even changing our spaces socially or culturally is hard, because these changes can be threatening to people's sense of how things have always been done. It might involve changing the power relations between adults and children, such as moving to multi-age grouping in which children's freedom to move reduces adult control. We must confront our own ageist assumptions, and learn to trust that children will use these new freedoms without endangering themselves or others. We have introduced you to postcolonial theories, because these processes require decolonisation – to move away from coercive control and from the systematic devaluation of some needs in favour of others.

We believe this reimagining of our environments can be transformative for our early childhood practices, and liberating for all within the early childhood community. When we build and use spaces differently, we must change in response, forming different relationships and learning new things. We know that young children become trustworthy by being trusted with new responsibilities and allowed to make mistakes. We hope you will be prepared to take risks with your own spaces, trusting that you will learn from mistakes. We encourage you to talk with your fellow-educators and ask how your settings could better reflect the most important cultural values of your country and locality. Who knows what might be possible?

Questions for reflection

- What sort of early childhood setting do you work in? Is it government-run, a commercial business or a community endeavour? What influences can you see on your service's practices and procedures from its management model?

How does it recognise your local community, and the cultural values of its users?
- Have you worked mostly in multi-age or single-age groups? Which of these have worked best for you? Which do you believe work best for those children? Why?
- What is your experience of quality assurance processes in early childhood education? Do they feel strengths-based, or do they seem like they operate from a deficit model? What have you found to be positive about them? What has been less helpful?

Activities for educators

- Think about the classroom you are working in, or the most recent one you have spent time in. Conduct a geographical audit, and spend time deliberately observing which areas in the space are used most intensively, and which spaces are neglected. If you have an outdoor area you use regularly, you might also want to do an audit of this space too. Think about the areas that are well-used, and those which are not, and what might be contributing to this. Some aspects you may want to analyse are: light levels (particularly natural light), noise levels, the physical materials (flooring, partitions, surfaces) and the levels of foot traffic nearby. Are there other factors that may make a difference in your setting, such as the relative privacy of a particular area, and the likelihood of educator supervision? While some aspects of your classroom may be hard to alter, such as availability of light, others are much easier to change, such as using rugs or other noise-absorbing materials to improve sound quality. Try and match the activities you want children to engage in with the qualities of each area, so that activities which need most concentration, or are considered most important, are located in the areas which are most beneficial.
- The curriculum documents we work with, whether local or national, often carry with them the legacy of colonial practices, such as the ways history is framed, or the validation of particular ways of knowing over others. Think about what you value most as an educator, and how you came to hold these beliefs? Some educators, for example, may believe that politeness is important for children, while others may think standing up for yourself is an important quality to encourage. Many of these values will privilege some children over others, and often will carry with them some historical legacies. For example, an emphasis on politeness has historically been a middle-class value, and so might feel frustrating or alien to children from less-privileged families. 'Standing up for yourself' might be read as a positive quality for white male children, fitting in with expectations of assertiveness and privilege, while the same behaviour may be read as defiance or opposition in an Indigenous child. Ask a colleague who is different from you, in terms of gender, ethnic background, or social class whether they will share with you their own values and understanding of curriculum. Notice how

your pedagogical positions are affected by your different experiences and identities. With your colleague, suggest one change the other person might try making in their practice, based on what you have each heard.

Key readings

Blackmore, J. (2006). Social justice and the study and practice of leadership in education: A feminist history. *Journal of Educational Administration and History, 38*(2), 185–200.
Cannella, G., & Viruru, R. (2004). *Childhood and Postcolonization: Power, Education and Contemporary Practice.* New York: RoutledgeFalmer.
Dahlberg, G., Moss, P., & Pence, A. (1999). *Beyond Quality in Early Childhood Education and Care: Postmodern Perspectives.* London: RoutledgeFalmer.
Moss, P., & Petrie, P. (2002). *From Children's Services to Children's Spaces: Public Policy, Children and Childhood.* London: RoutledgeFalmer.
Raworth, K. (2017). *Doughnut Economics: Seven Ways to Think like a 21st-Century Economist.* London: Random House.

Online resources

Universal design (UD) – These principle were created to help architects and designers make buildings that work for everyone, whatever their abilities. There are related principles in education, called UDE, dealing with curriculum and pedagogical practices. http://universaldesign.ie/What-is-Universal-Design/The-7-Principles/
This article looks at activism about the commons and communal ownership around the globe. www.onthecommons.org/magazine/tour-commons-activism-around-world
Interview with Professors Gunilla Dahlberg and Susan Neumann, about inclusion and participation in early childhood education. www.youtube.com/watch?v=1AWOEOrP26k

Further reading

Alexander, C. (1977). *A Pattern Language: Towns, Buildings, Construction.* Oxford: Oxford University Press.
Australian Children's Education & Care Quality Authority (2011). *Guide to the Education and Care Services National Law and the Education and Care Services National Regulations 2011.* Canberra: Commonwealth of Australia Retrieved from http://acecqa.gov.au/links-and-resources/national-quality-framework-resources/
Foucault, M. (1977). *Discipline and Punish: The Birth of the Prison [Surveiller et punir: Naissance de la prison]* (A. Sheridan, Trans. English ed.). London: Penguin.
Freire, P. (2014 [1968]). *Pedagogy of the Oppressed [Pedagogia do Oprimido]* (M. Ramos, Trans.). New York: Bloomsbury.
Hard, L., Press, F., & Gibson, M. (2013). 'Doing' social justice in early childhood: The potential of leadership. *Contemporary Issues in Early Childhood, 14*(4), 324–334.
Harms, T., Clifford, R. M., & Cryer, D. (2014). *Early Childhood Environment Rating Scale.* New York: Teachers College Press.
Miller, M. (2014). Productive and inclusive? How documentation concealed racialising practices in a diversity project. *Early Years, 34*(2), 146–160.
Mohanty, C. T. (2003). *Feminism without Borders.* Durham, NC: Duke University Press.

Moss, P., & Dahlberg, G. (2008). Beyond quality in early childhood education and care: Languages of evaluation. *New Zealand Journal of Teachers' Work, 5*(1), 3–12.

National Association for the Education of Young Children (1984). *Early Learning Program Accreditation*. Washington, DC. Retrieved from www.naeyc.org/accreditation.

Newman, B. (2016). Mother Goose goes to Mardi Gras: Connecting with LGBT+ families and children. In R. R. Scarlet (Ed.), *The Anti-Bias Approach in Early Childhood* (3rd ed., pp. 51–69). Sydney: Multiverse.

Ofsted (2016). *Ofsted Inspections of Early Years and Childcare Providers*. London: UK Government. Retrieved from www.gov.uk/government/collections/ofsteds-inspection-of-early-years-providers.

Puwar, N. (2004). *Space Invaders: Race, Gender and Bodies Out of Place*. Oxford: Berg.

Said, E. (1978). *Orientalism*. New York: Random House.

Sidorkin, A. (2002). *Learning Relations: Impure Education, Deschooled Schools, and Dialogue with Evil*. New York: Peter Lang.

Teeger, C. (2015). Ruptures in the rainbow nation: How desegregated South African schools deal with interpersonal and structural racism. *Sociology of Education, 88*(3), 226–243.

van Laere, K. (2017). The social and political potential of educare. Exploring perspectives of parents and preschool staff. Paper presented at the European Early Childhood Education Research Association conference, Bologna, Italy.

8 Spirituality and young children

Figure 8.1
Source: US Department of Agriculture. Licence: Creative Commons
Attribution 4.0 International License

Questions for consideration

- What spiritual beliefs do you have, if any? How do you think these beliefs impact on your values and pedagogical practice?
- What involvement have you had with organised religion during your life? Perhaps you attended a religious school, or were expected to attend religious services as a child? How do you think your experiences, both positive and negative, will impact on the relationships you form with families and co-workers?

Vignette from practice

Working in a babies room in a university-based early education setting, Sam was building many close relationships with parents, most of whom were first-time parents, and so worried about their babies' first experiences outside parental care. This had its challenges but it was also a privilege to get to know these parents at a deeper level, as they revealed their vulnerable feelings in regard to their children's wellbeing.

Although most of the families in the group were from European backgrounds, two families were from Iran, having come across to work and study at the University. Sam knew a little about Islam at the beginning of the year, but was glad of the opportunity to learn more about what Zhaleh and Jahan's parents wanted for their infant children, in an unfamiliar setting. Sam and Viola, the staff in the room, had been working hard to build relationships with Zhaleh and Jahan, and it helped that they were uncomplicated babies, who had settled easily and now eagerly embraced the social relationships and activities within the room.

Both families got on well with each other, and with the other parents, but presented quite differently, as Zhaleh's mum wore a hijab, while Jahan's mum did not. Sam had wondered if this meant that one family was more conservative, and had been cautious initially about raising issues that might be sensitive. Both families were very engaged politically, and always eager to discuss local political issues, as well as the political situation back home in Iran. Seeing the Iranian situation through their eyes was a good reminder that any society represents a tug of war between different groups with divergent opinions, and Iran sounded no different from anywhere else in this regard. Religion was one area of difference, but so too were education levels, as well as location, with urban dwellers likely to be more progressive and politically engaged. During the year, Sam got to know Mirza best, Zhaleh's dad, because he spent most time at the centre, playing with his daughter. Mirza was very comfortable chatting to Sam and Viola or any other parents who happened to be there.

It was clear that Mirza loved being a father, and was thrilled to have this opportunity to be the main caregiver for his daughter. While sitting playing with Zhaleh, or feeding her mashed banana (her favourite) there was plenty of time to talk about his hopes for her future, as well as laugh about the mistakes you make as a parent or an educator. Mirza loved to laugh, and the other babies were drawn to him, because of his easy-going personality. Sam was not brave enough to ask about what Mirza's family and friends thought of his role as a stay-at-home father, but loved having a dad so actively involved in what was usually a female-dominated environment. Most of all, Sam realised that human beings can never be easily pigeonholed, and that religious identities do not dictate political or social realities, any more than wealth or education do.

Introduction

Most of us have some experience of religion, either personally through being raised in one, or through the experiences of friends or colleagues. Usually though we only know one religion well, with few people changing religion in the course of their life spans. As educators, therefore, we are often unfamiliar with others' experiences or beliefs, and it is best not to make assumptions about these.

Sam and Viola learnt an important lesson from their involvement with the two families of Jahan and Zhaleh, in the vignette above. They came to realise that ethnic background, country of origin, religious belief or apparent conservatism reveal little about other aspects of someone's life, such as familial gender roles or parenting styles. We are all a complex mixture of influences, which change over the life course and the result is the incredible diversity of human cultures. We also move through different contexts in which particular discourses may be dominant, and this also affects our behaviours as we adjust to the norms of those around us.

In this chapter we will look broadly at how human existence is shaped by our philosophical beliefs, our spiritual practices and our religious affiliations. Many countries have a dominant religion which continues to influence government decision-making processes. For example, the United States has a secular public educational tradition but continues to have a significant proportion of the population who attend Christian churches. This can cause conflicts for parents who might want a religious education, and for political decision-makers seeking to influence the field of education.

Foucault and disciplinary power

In drawing upon theory to understand people's spiritual practices, we think that Foucault's ideas of disciplinary power are useful. These draw on his work around the rise of institutions, such as education or the prison system, in the last couple of hundred years. This type of power functions through influencing the bodies and minds of individuals, so that direct power never needs to be exerted (Foucault, 1977). In this way, governments and ruling bodies no longer need to exercise power directly but do so through people's own internalisation of the rules and regulations that guide those institutions.

Religious institutions have existed for much longer than modern systems of government, but many do appear to mobilise these forms of disciplinary power in shaping the lives of their adherents. They are one of the key social structures in society, as you will remember from chapter 2. Jennifer Gore (1995) writes about how specific techniques of disciplinary power function in educational settings, and her ideas are helpful in thinking through some of the possible effects of religious and spiritual beliefs on people's lives. Three techniques of particular relevance are *normalisation*, *individualisation* and *regulation*.

Societies where one particular religion is dominant will usually have co-opted these practices into the normative expectations for citizens in those cultures, whether or not they belong to the religious groups in question. As a result, most people will feel like they must subscribe to the basic ethical norms of those religions as well as honouring cultural aspects of these dominant religions, such as religious holidays (e.g. Eid al-Fitr, Christmas). This is a process of *normalisation*, where those who ascribe to such values and practices will feel affirmed while those who do not may be censured, by friends and family, or even by strangers. Within educational institutions, the dominant religious holidays of your own country are likely to be included in a taken-for-granted way within the school year, including the sorts of cultural events and practices which surround them.

Individualisation is a key technique of modern liberal societies because it expects that each person will take personal responsibility for their actions, and measure their own actions against the norms that they perceive in their communities. Even in secular systems, people are assessed on their personal ethics, and may be judged harshly if they fail to live up to normative standards (such as politeness). Within education this tradition is strong, and testing regimes rely on judging educational sites, teachers and students, as if each of these is uniquely responsible for the educational outcomes they achieve, despite the sorts of wider effects (family background, community economic circumstances, historic disadvantage or trauma) which are likely to impact significantly on those 'individual' outcomes.

Lastly, religious practices all draw on techniques of *regulation*, which rely on circumscribing the possible actions of people, usually through the judgements of others. Such regulatory regimes often exceed or diverge from the core precepts of those religious systems, as temporary or local prohibitions on particular practices become taken up as usual aspects of those religions. Educational institutions can function in a similar way, with issues such as school uniforms taking on great significance, despite their irrelevance to any learning in those settings.

In discussing disciplinary power from a poststructuralist perspective we do not want to suggest that such power is wrong or unnecessary, and certainly not that religious beliefs are wrong in being enforced through such practices. These techniques are part of all human societies, and are worth understanding to become aware of the ways educators are using these tools to control our own and others' behaviour. This behaviour change can be desirable, such as when we are contributing to creating more peaceful communities, or undesirable, when people are encouraged to become fearful of or hostile towards others, simply because they are different.

Religious and spiritual traditions

In this section, we will cover some basic information about the major world religions. There are more religions than these mentioned below, and many varying practices even within these religions. In addition, most major religions include different schools of thought, and these schools often have separate hierarchical organisations and places of worship. Included within this list is secularism, which encompasses a large variety of different practices and attitudes.

By including what seems like an absence of religion alongside other faith traditions, we want you to recognise that all religious systems are attempts to manage the gap between what we know, and what we still do not know. The idea of Socratic wisdom, which originates with stories attributed to the Greek philosopher Socrates, who lived around 2500 years ago, is that the greatest wisdom comes with understanding the limitations of what you know. Similar ideas are present in other cultural traditions, such as the Taoist saying, 'knowing is the way of fools' (Miller, 2006, 11). Religious belief systems are wide-ranging and pervasive human practices, present in most cultures and throughout history, and with many consequences for the power relationships within human communities (King, 2006). Many people who espouse no religion put their faith in science and the scientific method, in choosing to believe that science will at some point reveal answers to the world's mysteries. However there are many mysteries to which the answers may never be known, such as what happens to our consciousness after death, or whether life exists elsewhere in the universe other than this small planet.

In each paragraph we include an approximation of the number of adherents to these beliefs, based on the combined work of multiple researchers. These numbers do not try to distinguish between sincere or enthusiastic believers, but include all those who identify themselves with a particular religion, even if this is about basic cultural practices, or familial allegiance (Pew Research Center, 2017). The other major difference worth noting with religions is that some are scattered more widely across the world's nations, while others, such as Hinduism, or Shintoism, are concentrated much more narrowly in particular countries and cultures. We will try and offer a basic guide to key tenets of each religion, noting that any misunderstandings are unintentional, given the divergent beliefs even of co-religionists. As educators we hope these descriptions will orient you to possible belief systems held by families or co-workers, without presuming that these can capture the experience of any specific believer, as our vignette showed.

Buddhism (500 million)

This set of religious practices began around the time of Socrates, around 500 years before the current era (BCE). Buddhists are followers of the Buddha, Siddharta Gautama, who grew up in what is now Nepal. Gautama is said to have been moved by the continuous suffering of those around him and sought to find a way out of this, eventually achieving a state of enlightenment (*nirvana*), through meditative practices and asceticism. There are two major branches of Buddhism, Mahayana and Theraveda, with some believing Tibetan Buddhism represents a third type. Buddhist traditions tend towards an individual form of practice, including cultivating loving-kindness, wisdom and compassion, in order to reach a state of enlightenment such as Buddha achieved. Buddhists believe in reincarnation, meaning that this progress towards an enlightened state may be the work not just of the current lifetime, but many to come.

Christianity (2.4 billion)

This religion, along with Islam and Judaism, is classed as one of the *Abrahamic* religions, because all share some similar origins and beliefs, including stories about early prophets within those faiths, such as Abraham. All of these faiths believe in a single god-figure, although the Christian tradition views this god as having three aspects – called the trinity, one of which is Jesus, a person believed to have lived and flourished around the beginning of the current era in the region of Palestine. Current Western Christian practice is split into two major divisions, Catholic and Protestant, although the Orthodox traditions (Coptic, Russian, Greek) do not align neatly within this division. Protestantism itself is divided into many different divisions and practices. Most Christian traditions are guided primarily by a religious text, the *Bible*, a variety of manuscripts, mostly written by Jewish people, which were collected together in the first centuries of the current era. Most Christians, named after *Christ* (an honorific given to the person Jesus) believe in a form of personal salvation, often through *baptism* (literal or symbolic immersion in water), which ensures a place in an afterlife with god. Many Christians practise hospitality and care for the poor or suffering.

Hinduism (1.1 billion)

Strictly speaking Hinduism is not a single religion, but a way of life and common traditions shared by many people, particularly across South Asia. Arising in the Vedic period (3500 years ago) when civilisations flourished in the Indus valley (modern Pakistan), Hinduism has been called 'the eternal way' by its followers, because its origins are so hazy and predate many other religions. Buddha is believed to have learnt from Vedic teachers, and so Buddhism shares some understandings with the Hindu tradition. Hinduism is divided into four main traditions, Shaktism, Shaivism, Vaishnavism, and Smartism, each with their own sub-traditions. Most Hindu people worship a number of deities, such as Shiva, Lakshmi or Ganesha, although sometimes these deities are seen as aspects, or *avatars* of the supreme being Vishnu. This latter idea has something in common with the idea of unity/multiplicity represented by the Christian trinity. Many Hindu followers engage in religious rituals, expressing devotion to particular deities. Most aspire to values important within the Vedic traditions, such as *ahimsa* (non-violence, including to other life-forms), honesty and patience.

Indigenous spiritual traditions (400 million)

The most diverse religious tradition is that of the world's Indigenous peoples, and religions practised only by a particular ethnic group, which are often classed as folk religions. Some of these make a strong claim to be the oldest religious traditions in the world, stretching back to times when evidence for such beliefs can be hard to trace. For example, the stories of the Rainbow Serpent, one of the ancestral creatures of Australian Indigenous people, can be documented to 5000 years ago, and possibly as far back as the occupation of the Australian landmass 60 000 years ago. Many of these Indigenous religious traditions share a reverence for particular places (the idea of *country*), and have many rituals and practices associated with particular features in the landscape, or distinctive aspects of the environment, including seas and rivers. Some see these landscapes as being the originator of life, sometimes personified as a deity (e.g. Papatuānuku in Māori spiritual traditions). Most have religious affiliations with particular animals that are significant in those landscapes and within that culture, about which sacred stories are told, often as a form of education. Many Indigenous traditions see dancing as a sacred ritual, such as the grass dances of the Omaha-Ponca people, in North America. It is difficult to generalise about such diverse spiritual practices, but most share a reverence for life, and a keen interest in preserving intact ecosystems. Elders have a vital spiritual and leadership role within most Indigenous communities, and their input is always key in any engagement with a particular community.

Islam (1.8 billion)

People who follow Islam are described as Muslims, and represent another of the Abrahamic traditions. Worshipping a supreme god known as Allah, this religion grew out of the teachings of Mohammed, a prophet who lived and taught in the seventh century CE in Mecca (modern Saudi Arabia). These teachings are collected in a sacred text, the Quran, important to all Muslim people. Mecca is now a sacred place for most Muslims and most will try to visit it at least once in their lifetime, a pilgrimage known as *Hajj*. Islam, like other religions has different groupings, with the Sunni tradition being in the majority, and a smaller Shia tradition. The Islamic faith includes well-developed teachings around concepts such as economics and law, which continue to influence life in majority Muslim countries, such as the approach to banking systems. There are five important practices for most Muslim people, of which the Hajj pilgrimage is one, as well as daily prayer, fasting, the creed (core beliefs) and charity towards the less fortunate. This commitment to charitable giving by Muslims means that these donations have been estimated to exceed other humanitarian contributions across the globe from both individuals and governments. Some Muslims follow a mystical tradition within Islam called Sufism, which seeks a direct and emotional connection to Allah.

Judaism (17 million)

This religious faith is the third of the Abrahamic traditions, and also has its origins in ancient Palestine. Judaism has a sacred text, called the Torah, whose teachings are memorised and whose precepts have been debated extensively throughout Jewish history. Judaism's origins derive from the teachings of Moses and other prophets, perhaps around 4000 years ago. Jewish people do not make a great distinction between religion and ethnicity, and so those who follow Judaism are sometimes known as an ethno-religious group, with conversion to this faith also involving commitment to particular cultural practices, such as specific dietary restrictions. Family life and the importance of learning are important aspects of Jewish tradition, and many Jewish people orient their family lives around Shabbat, a weekly holy day, and particular religious festivals. As with other religious groups, there are different traditions within Judaism, reaching from liberal Judaism to more conservative Hasidic practices. Judaism has been impacted historically by considerable persecution particularly by followers of Christian traditions, and this has led to tightly knit and supportive communities, in reaction to traumatic events like *pogroms* or the Holocaust.

Secularism (1.2 billion)

For a significant proportion of the world's population the absence of religious belief, which we are calling *secularism*, is an important aspect of their worldview. The rise in secularism reflects the ongoing impact of the scientific revolution over the last 500 years, which has increasingly found answers to the questions which humans ask about their world, and which they might once have answered through religious faith. However, even when a person does not currently identify with a religious tradition, they may still be shaped by a familial or societal association with a particular religion. For example, a secular person in a Hindu majority country, such as India or Mauritius, is likely to share many of the values and practices of their family, friends and neighbours, even if they do not choose to spend time in religious practices. It is also worth noting that those who disavow religion may hold strongly to particular philosophical positions, in ways that can mirror the devoted belief of religious people. For example, some secularists may identify as *atheist* (literally 'no-god'), and can be quite vocal in trying to reduce the influence of religion in their particular cultural contexts. Many secularists hold passionately to a variety of ethical positions, and may be strong believers in concepts like social justice, or democratic values.

Sihkism (25 million)

One of the world's youngest religions, Sikhism arose in the fifteenth century CE, and follows the teaching of ten human gurus and a sacred text, called *Guru Granth Sahib*. Sihkism came into being in part as a response to religious conflict between Hindu and Muslim followers and draws on concepts from both of these traditions. Sihks tend to believe in reincarnation but also a single deity, even if this deity is expressed through multiple mystical aspects. Many of its followers live in the Punjab region of India, though like Judaism its followers also live right across the world. Sihks are strongly encouraged to spend their lives serving others and equality, including gender equality, is a feature of Sihk belief. The commitment to helping others means that all Sihk places of worship – gurdwaras – regularly provide free vegetarian meals to adherents of the faith and anyone else who needs a meal. Volunteers prepare and serve these meals and the equality of the community is demonstrated in the meal being shared together. As with other religions, there are various groupings within Sikhism.

Taoism (8 million)

The name of this religion is based on the word *Tao* (道, or *Dau*), a Chinese word meaning 'the way'. This set of philosophical principles has different schools of thought, but many Taoist beliefs draw on ideas of naturalness, such as simplicity, humility and frugality. One of the world's older religious practices, it began around the fourth century BCE, and originated among shamanic traditions in southern parts of China. Many well-known practices, such as traditional Chinese medicine, or *feng shui*, have their roots in Taoist thought. The main religious text, the *Tao Te Ching*, has been attributed to Laozi, a Chinese philosopher now consider a deity within Taoism. It has at times been the official religion in China, but now has adherents around the world. Taoists believe that by following the way they are becoming part of the flow of the universe, and so will embody *Te* (德), or virtue. Taoism has influenced other religions, most notably Zen Buddhism and Shintoism.

Religion and sociological thought

Most of us grow up in communities which have a dominant religious belief, even if this is a broad secularism and faith in the scientific method. As we saw in chapter 1, such belief systems constitute discourses (systems of power and knowledge combined) which influence practices and beliefs in the communities in which they circulate. Such dominant discourses enforce social norms, which privilege those who behave according to them and make others feel like outsiders. For example, as a Hindu in Gujurat in India you would feel like your life is unremarkable, and your neighbours and friends would expect you to take time out for spiritual devotions. Even if you did not practise your religion in any devout way, you would still find their *expectations* of such behaviours normal, and you would be familiar with justifying how your spiritual practices might differ from those around you.

Thinking back to our understanding of social structures, we would expect that institutions like the media, government or education would reflect these dominant religious discourses across countries and regions. One of the biggest differences between early childhood systems across different countries will be whether religious influences in education are normalised or discouraged. For example, in the UK many government-funded schools are run by Christian denominations (mostly Anglican) and the school day in these settings may start with morning prayers even if many families who use them are not Christian. In other countries, such as the US, there is an expectation that schools cannot teach religion of any sort, and that the system will be a secular one. The question of whether religion should be part of educational life is often contested within particular countries, and the rules for its inclusion or exclusion may be written into legislation in those places.

Whatever the formal curriculum suggests about religion, many educators themselves will have a religious affiliation, and this may influence how and what they teach in the classroom – the enacted curriculum. In a geography unit, for example, one educator might feel comfortable leading a discussion on the religious practices of the countries being studied, and how they compare to those where the school or early childhood service is located. Other educators might find this challenging given their own disagreements with religion and its related practices, and may focus instead on the political or physical features of those countries. We hope that educators will learn to talk about spiritual practices with children, understanding that these are an important part of life for the majority of the world's population, as seen from the population figures above. Young children are curious about the lives of others, and may want to talk with you about their family's religious beliefs as part of their emerging meaning-making about the world. Being able to do so in ways that are respectful to them while also honest about your own beliefs is important, and models for them the civil dialogue we need in our societies.

Working with different beliefs

It is inevitable in our work that we will be cooperating with people who hold different beliefs, such as co-workers or families. These may be people with different belief systems (such as from a different religion), or those with a similar belief system whose practices within this may be quite distinct from our own. Sociologists recognise the complex ways we engage with the discourses which surround us, and we contest some aspects of these while accepting many of them. Bourdieu's (1977) concept of habitus, which we introduced in chapter 3, describes the range of options which tend to be available to each person, depending on our location in social space, and the discourses which circulate in our society. As we saw in the vignette at the start of the chapter, this does not prevent people from expressing their own values, such as Mirza's embracing of the role of primary caregiver to his daughter, even if this is not a choice that was visible to him growing up as a boy in Iran. All cultures and religious systems change over time, reflecting the responses of their members to new understandings or interpretations of life. These new understandings might come from political change, from revolutions in scientific knowledge, from greater global interconnectivity or internal cultural changes (e.g. generational change or increased migration).

Respecting others' beliefs

One of our challenges as educators is to be aware of our own values, and be able to be honest with ourselves about the things in life which give us joy, distress us or feel irrelevant to our lives. In learning to work with others, we will particularly need to be aware of those aspects which may bother us about others' beliefs, so that we do not react towards them unconsciously in ways that are unhelpful. For example, an educator who is a Seventh Day Adventist (a Christian denomination), and has been vegetarian their whole life as a result, may struggle to understand and respect a parent who works as a butcher. This could be as simple as not knowing how to make conversation about their work, or might involve inner judgements about that parent's moral choices. Many religions have particular dietary prohibitions, and food choices can easily become a source of judgement because eating habits and cuisines are so strongly associated with our culture and family lives, and we become emotionally invested in particular food practices (Harris, 1985).

Whether the judgements we have are about dietary practices or about child-rearing issues such as behaviour guidance (another hot-button issue), it is important to keep in mind our shared goals. As educators, parents or extended family members, we have a shared interest in the wellbeing of each child. From each child's perspective, they need and want the adults around them to be able to relate to each other respectfully, and hopefully in a genuine and warm fashion. This will help them to feel secure in their relationships, and generate trust and self-confidence rather than anxiety. In chapter 10 we look more closely at working with families, and some of the useful practices, such as learning to listen, which will support your work in this area.

Spiritual beliefs and cultural practices

The conflicts we perceive as educators between the values present in our early childhood settings and those of particular families may be mostly in our own imagination. In taking time to explore with families (as sensitively as possible) how these dilemmas could be resolved you may find the 'problem' looks very different from their perspective. Most religious families using a secular system (or conversely, secular families enrolled in services auspiced by religious groups) have decided in advance that the benefits for their child outweigh the differences they may encounter, and will have anticipated the likely issues that would arise. Your willingness to talk about these issues and find acceptable compromises, if this is possible, will help these families to feel respected, while being honest about any differences in opinion that may exist. In those rare situations where families may be actively hostile, it is worth remembering that this may not be a problem you should be trying to resolve, as an educator or educational setting. In these situations it may be the best to suggest to this family any other educational options which may be suitable, if these exist in your local area.

It is useful for educators to learn to disentangle people's religious beliefs from the cultural practices that have built up around them. This may offer new perspectives on a particular relationship with a colleague or parent that is difficult. Many cultural practices with specific historical origins have become part of contemporary religious practices, without actually being necessary to those belief systems. For example, the Abrahamic faiths have often been antagonistic towards LGBT+ people, as a result of historically specific pressures on these faiths at the time they emerged. Even if these heterosexist attitudes have become ritualised within some faith traditions, such beliefs are not fundamental to those religions and most believers will not feel the need to be antagonistic about these issues in your educational setting.

Pedagogy, spirituality and young children

In this section, we want to help you think about ways you can honour a sense of spirituality with children, drawing on ideas and values from a variety of spiritual traditions. We think that engaging in these ways helps us to make sense of the world, including coping with the ordinary challenges that we face in life, such as grief, loss, uncertainty and trust. Whatever your own beliefs, being willing to talk about these things with children is valuable, creating space to engage meaningfully with painful or puzzling events.

Connectedness

One of the important ideas that comes out of many spiritual traditions is the idea of connectedness. This has a number of aspects. First, traditions like Taoism, Buddhism and Hinduism have developed many practices that help people feel connected to themselves, such as meditation or yoga, and many of these bodily practices can be useful pedagogically. Mindfulness practices have become popular within secular traditions, fulfilling a similar need. Secondly, traditions which practise charitable giving, such as Christianity or Islam, help us feel connected to others and build a sense of community. Much of our work in early childhood is about helping children connect with each other, as we build learning communities, or simply help children make friends and empathise with each other. Lastly, spiritual practices such as those from Indigenous cultures may help us feel connected at a deeper level to the places we live and the earth which is our shared home. This connection is often profound for children, and a vehicle for helping them to feel wonder, and explore the mysteries of the natural world, an idea we will pick up in chapter 11. These connections transcend any one religious practice or belief system and are part of many daily interactions. They can be built on within most educational settings to create richer, calmer and more settled learning environments.

Connecting to the self

There are many meditative practices which can be useful in the classroom when working with young children. Young children are still getting a handle on their bodily abilities and their relationships with others and tend to *react*, rather than choose how to act. These practices can help children gain a better understanding of themselves, which is useful for all aspects of their learning. Teaching young children to manage their reactions is an aspect of the disciplinary power we discussed at the start of the chapter, through helping them to conform to the expectations of their educational setting. As critical educators our aim in doing this should not be about making them docile beings, through individualisation and regulation. Instead we want them to learn the difference

Spirituality and young children 147

Figure 8.2 Many spiritual traditions have rituals connected with the seasons. Children enjoy an excursion to celebrate the leaf fall of deciduous trees in a local park.
Source: Hannah Chapman-Searle. Used with permission

between problems that concern their own unhelpful reactions to a situation, and ones which may be injustices that needs addressing.

Many educators have found doing yoga (a practice based on ancient Vedic traditions) with children to be valuable. Yoga techniques are a useful pedagogical tool, comprising forms of exercise which are good for the body, safe and can be performed at any level (Guber, Kalish, & Fatus, 2005). There are also poses which can be done with partners, helping children work joyfully and cooperatively with others. Most yoga poses are physically and intellectually interesting for young children, building their concentration and attentiveness. They can be helpful in calming your classroom down at noisy times, because they are done alone or with one other child, and require enjoyable challenge. Given its long history, most yoga was taught orally, and many poses have evocative names ('the cat', 'the tree'), making them engaging for children to learn. Perhaps most importantly, doing yoga helps children to feel present in their bodies at moments when they may be anxious or distracted, and some poses (such as the aptly named 'pose of the child') are specifically designed to help people calm their minds and bodies.

Silence and stillness are techniques used in meditative traditions from Buddhism to Christianity and beyond. While it might seem impossible that a young child could either be still or silent, it can be surprising how quickly they develop a feel for these practices, and learn to find them useful. For the youngest children, remaining silent and still for a minute might feel like a long time, while with older children five minutes can be a useful goal. As in many meditative techniques, it can be useful to have an aural or a visual focus while doing so, such as the sound of a Tibetan singing bowl, or the flame of a candle. In one Indigenous tradition, from the Malak malak people of Australia's Northern Territory, such deep listening (*dadirri*) is important for more profound understanding, and for generating meanings capable of connecting past, present and future (Clague *et al.*, 2017). Meditative practices can help us to learn the value of silence in other pedagogical moments. When children are distressed they may not be able to pay attention to words, but sitting side-by-side with them silently may be all that they need.

Silence is already part of our educational traditions, such as the use of *wait-times* when questioning (Rowe, 1986). As educators, when we ask children questions we need to be respectful and allow plenty of silence to give all children the chance to think and respond. Perhaps more importantly – but often overlooked – are the silences after a child has replied. Even a short silence at this point conveys thoughtful acceptance of the child's ideas, and communicates your own regard for two-way dialogue. Making time and space in your classrooms for these silences allows everyone (including you) more time to think deeply about the educational task at hand, and benefits all students, both the marginalised and those usually privileged within our systems. The pace of change in our worlds is increasingly fast, and the use of all forms of media, including social media, is increasing, among adults and even for young children. Using tools from spiritual traditions such as yoga or silence can be helpful in combating some of the negative effects of these changes on children's concentration and attention spans.

Connecting to others

In the same way as spiritual traditions offer guidance about connecting to a fuller sense of self, so too these traditions have many suggestions about ways that we can become more connected to each other. These are a useful resource for critical educators seeking ways to build supportive learning communities. One fundamental way that human beings connect to each other and to the world is through food, as noted earlier. Food and water are fundamental to life, and most religious traditions have rituals connected to food, such as Buddhist monks relying on food donations from believers, the charitable provision of meals within Sikhism or Indigenous traditions which honour the necessary death of food animals in various ways. Jane Bone (2005) has explored the ways in which food rituals can be an important part of early childhood communities, forming part of what she calls 'everyday spirituality'. When children bring food from home this is often a powerful reminder to other children of difference, as their households are shaped by different cultural food traditions, or by the constraints of economic circumstances. When we create rituals in our classrooms around the eating of food, we are helping to connect children with each other in larger circles than their birth families. These rituals might be around welcoming others to the table, by having some children take the time to set the table each day. It might be through speaking a short, non-religious grace (a thanks for the meal) at the start of any shared meal, or simply making a little time for communal silence. It might be around respect for the importance of food, by ensuring any waste is given back to the earth through composting, an insight into the circular processes of life which is strong in Indigenous religious systems.

Another important lesson about connectness is built when early childhood educators make space in their curriculum for non-human creatures, through keeping chickens or other working animals onsite, as school pets or wild creatures (such as allowing spiders to keep their homes on classroom ceiling). As educators helping to teach children how to be respectful of other creatures we are drawing on the tradition of *ahimsa* within the Hindu and Buddhist traditions, which is the principle of non-violence. Many children seem to feel this instinctively. By helping children to build compassion for other creatures we also help them build compassion for other people, and recognise that other beings may have needs very different from our own.

Many schools and some preschools are starting to recognise the importance of service activities, in helping their students connect to other people. This

Figure 8.3 Children can learn many good lessons through their connections with animals. This child is learning about connection, trust and confidence, in caring for this chicken.

Source: Pixabay. Licence: Creative Commons CC0

150 *Spirituality and young children*

Figure 8.4 Art can be a meditative process for young children, allowing them time and space to develop their ideas.
Source: Yarrow Andrew, with thanks to Flinders University Childcare Centre

might involve visiting elderly people in nursing homes, tree-planting or being part of national initiatives around environmental or social justice issues. This helps children to feel part of their local communities, and is a good reminder that education has broader purposes than just passing on academic skills.

Connecting to country

Lastly, our connectedness to others can be deepened to realise that we are connected not just to other creatures (human and non-human) but to the earth itself, and are enmeshed in complex living ecosystems which sustain and nurture us, in ways technologised cultures have often failed to recognise. Nancy Turner and her colleagues (2000) write about the traditional knowledge and wisdom of First Nations people in British Columbia, Canada. They show how the core of these beliefs rests on a spiritual understanding of the power inherent in all living beings, as well as a deep understanding of and connection to their ancestral lands, and the knowledge and practices that have grown out of this. This is rich knowledge, which includes stories, ceremonies and practical wisdom about seasonal change and the plants and animals that thrive locally. Such knowledge has enabled Indigenous people around the world to develop ways of living that honour the environments in which they are based, and sustain local ecosystems without damage.

As educators we can extend on this sense of connection through the sorts of geographical and Indigenous knowledges we include within our curriculum, as we will explore further in chapter 11. We can help children understand that soil is a form of community wealth, and that preserving and protecting this, through composting, mulching or resisting chemical fertilisers, is a way of honouring the fertility of the earth, and our reliance upon it for all our food needs. We can learn not just about individual animals (as often happens in early childhood) but engage children in deeper inquiry about how these animals live, their impacts on other systems (such as soil or plant life) and the things they eat, or what may eat them. This is complex knowledge, which is why much Indigenous traditional knowledge is taught through stories and metaphors. Yet it is vital knowledge if non-Indigenous people are going to learn, belatedly, about the interconnectedness of our own survival and that of the plants and animals around us.

Philosophy in the classroom

With older children, such as in the last year of preschool and the early school years, engaging intellectually with philosophical traditions can be valuable. This draws on secular traditions of knowledge construction, such as logic or ethics, which involve learning to think critically about what we know and how we know it (psychologists call this *metacognition*). While it was once thought that philosophical inquiry was too difficult for young children, increasingly such skills are being taught by critical educators, to help children to challenge and question what they are being taught (Haynes, 2008).

Philosophy can often provide an interesting perspective on religion and vice versa, and may allow educators who are uncomfortable with religion to engage with these ideas more meaningfully. One of the most famous ideas within European philosophy is the idea of a separation between mind and body, first articulated by Rene Descartes in his assertion, 'I think, therefore I am'. European philosophy has been built on many of these dualisms, which suggest a divide between nature and culture, between emotion and rationality, or between women and men (Peckruhn, 2017). While these separations can sometimes allow for conceptual clarity, they can also be dangerous in masking the fundamental connectedness between the binary terms being discussed.

Interestingly, a number of religions, particularly Buddhism, see one of the goals of enlightenment as achieving non-dualistic thinking, which erases the separation between such binaries. Non-dualistic thinking feels like a useful approach in a time of climate crisis, because it undermines the false distinction between nature and culture, and reminds us that cultures and cultural practices are intrinsically embedded in natural ecosystems. Non-dualistic thinking emphasises connectedness, rather than separation, across genders, across cultures and across the divide of species and experiences (Bone, Cullen, & Loveridge, 2007).

Art and spirituality

Many educators have picked up on the idea of mindfulness, as a useful practice to develop with children to help with their sense of focus in the classroom, and ability to concentrate for longer periods. There are many techniques which have been developed under the umbrella of mindfulness, and the practices of stillness and silence discussed above are some of these (Erwin et al., 2017). Art activities are an important feature of many early childhood programmes, and can be used to help children channel their attention.

The goal of mindfulness is always to keep children's awareness in the present moment, because this helps them not to worry about the past, or dread future events, but instead make the most of what is going on right now. Using art in this way in great for young children, because the movement involved, whether of the whole body in dance, the posture and lips in singing, or the arms in painting, becomes the focus for awareness. Focusing on this helps to remind children that it is the process of learning that matters, not the end result. Such process-based thinking helps children engage their creativity and imagination, through taking away the judgements they learn to expect from others about how 'good' their artistic products may be. Art practices such as these can be particularly helpful for children from marginalised race or class backgrounds, who may already have been given messages about being less capable in a school setting.

Concluding remarks: Spirituality and everyday life

As educators we think it is valuable to see spirituality as manifested in a variety of ways in our everyday lives, from specific religious practices, to the ethics of our relationships with others or the mindful attention to artistic work. By recognising the place of spirituality in extending knowledge beyond separate subject areas to an awareness of the multiple connections we make in life as embodied beings (Peckruhn, 2017), we can become more sympathetic to the varying child-rearing strategies of the families we are working with. Instead of finding these threatening or unfamiliar we might ask more generous questions, such as 'How do these religious practices support and affirm this family in their daily life?'

Martha Nussbaum (2003), in expounding on Amartya Sen's concept of capabilities and their relevance to social justice, reminds us that working towards human flourishing includes allowing for many ways of living. We need a concept of freedom which can allow for diversity while still expecting all communities to honour the full personhood of individuals within them, especially those who are not male, or are from historically outcast(e) groups. Religions have sometimes been tools for great divisiveness, but not always. As educators one of our roles is to build a sense of mutual respect in our classroom, creating understanding rather than division.

Attuning ourselves to the ways spirituality can connect us with ourselves, each other and the world has been a key insight within this chapter. Such attunement allows us to see how even apparently banal activities such as resetting an activity space for the next person can be viewed as a spiritual activity, offering a sense of welcome and care to those coming after us, as Bone and colleagues (2007) observed. In restoring a sense of order and beauty in our immediate environment we are reflecting at a small level some of our deepest and most important values, and this will have flow-on effects in our relationships and in our communities.

Questions for reflection

- What activities in your life give you a sense of purpose and joy? Are these activities you are able to be fully present within, and feel a sense of flow and ease? Can you extend this sense of presence to other activities you do, particularly your work as an educator?
- What activities in life make you most anxious, or stressed? Notice how your attention is taken away from the present moment, and into particular feelings in your body, or previous times when things have gone wrong. Try to notice at these times what you are learning, and note how you might do things differently next time.
- How comfortable are you with uncertainty and the unknown? How can you develop your pedagogical skills in supporting children in their uncertainty, allowing them to value their process of inquiry and ongoing learning?

Activities for educators

- Contemporary scientists are finding many ways in which the body and mind are more connected that previously realised, such as the large bundles of nerves that carry messages between our intestines and our brains. One simple practice within many religions that understands this connection is the use of breathing techniques. When animals, including human animals, become stressed, this initiates a 'fight or flight' response in our autonomic nervous systems, which sets off a number of hormonally mediated responses, including quickened breathing. By paying attention to our breath when we are anxious, we can notice when we are breathing quickly and shallowly, which makes our bodies feel more anxious. By choosing to slow and

deepen our breath, we cannot change the situation, but we can improve our ability to react to it in calmer and more reasonable ways.
- Making time to listen to others can be an important way to enhance a sense of connectness in your classroom. Consider making time each day or week for a talking time, where each person is listened to for a short but defined period (perhaps a minute). For those children who are shy, allow them to 'hold the floor' without speaking, and make sure that others listen to them respectfully, even when they are not speaking. Making time and space in this way will encourage all to feel valued, even when they do not know how to contribute, or feel less confident in the language of instruction in your classroom. Make sure that children with disabilities are included in this time as equal partners, including supporting their preferred communication modes where necessary. This activity can be supported as a ritual by having a particular object (e.g. a 'talking stick') to represent the person who currently holds the floor. You can add to this activity by building a layer of story-telling around it, either by writing a learning story about it yourself, or encouraging older children to write or draw their experiences of being listened to. This could build over time towards a class book, which could show children learning how to participate fully in this activity, and demonstrate its role in classroom life.

Key readings

Bone, J., Cullen, J., & Loveridge, J. (2007). Everyday spirituality: An aspect of the holistic curriculum in action. *Contemporary Issues in Early Childhood, 8*(4), 344–354.

Gore, J. (1995). On the continuity of power relations in pedagogy. *International Studies in Sociology of Education, 5*(2), 165–188.

Haynes, J. (2008). *Children as Philosophers: Learning through Enquiry and Dialogue in the Primary Classroom*. Abingdon: Routledge.

Miller, J. (2006). *Educating for Wisdom and Compassion: Creating Conditions for Timeless Learning*. Thousand Oaks, CA: Corwin Press.

Turner, N. J., Ignace, M. B., & Ignace, R. (2000). Traditional ecological knowledge and wisdom of Aboriginal peoples in British Columbia. *Ecological Applications, 10*(5), 1275–1287.

Online resources

This website offers a variety of moment-based activities to help educators improve children's attention and build cohesive classroom communities. www.gonoodle.com/

This news article describes a set of smartphone apps designed to teach children about the treasures of Columbia's many Indigenous cultures. www.theguardian.com/world/2018/jan/05/smartphone-games-colombia-indigenous-cultures-children?CMP=Share_iOSApp_Other

This video discusses the work being done by a school for Indigenous North American children and connecting their teaching to children's minds and hearts. www.youtube.com/watch?v=YsIoG7zFdmc

Further reading

Bone, J. (2005). Breaking bread: Spirituality, food and early childhood education. *International Journal of Children's Spirituality, 10*(3), 307–317.

Bourdieu, P. (1977). *Outline of a Theory of Practice* (R. Nice, Trans.). Cambridge: Cambridge University Press.

Clague, L., Harrison, N., Stewart, K., & Atkinson, C. (2017). Thinking outside the circle: Reflections on theory and methods for school-based garden research. *Australian Journal of Indigenous Education*, onlinefirst, 1–7.

Erwin, E., Robinson, K., McGrath, G., & Harney, C. (2017). 'It's like breathing in blue skies and breathing out stormy clouds': Mindfulness practices in early childhood. *Young Exceptional Children, 20*(2), 69–85.

Foucault, M. (1977). *Discipline and Punish: The Birth of the Prison [Surveiller et punir: Naissance de la prison]* (A. Sheridan, Trans. English ed.). London: Penguin.

Guber, T., Kalish, L., & Fatus, S. (2005). *Yoga Pretzels: 50 Fun Yoga Activities for Kids and Grownups.* Cambridge, MA: Barefoot Books.

Harris, M. (1985). *Good to Eat: Riddles of Food and Culture.* Long Grove, IL: Waveland Press.

King, U. (2006). Religion and gender: Embedded patterns, interwoven frameworks. In T. Meade & M. Wiesner-Hanks (Eds), *A Companion to Gender History* (pp. 70–85). Malden, MA: Blackwell

Nussbaum, M. (2003). Capabilities as fundamental entitlements: Sen and social justice. *Feminist Economics, 9*(2–3), 33–59.

Peckruhn, H. (2017). *Meaning in our Bodies: Sensory Experience as Constructive Theological Imagination.* New York: Oxford University Press.

Pew Research Center. (2017). The global religious landscape. Retrieved from www.pewforum.org/2012/12/18/global-religious-landscape-exec/

Rowe, M. (1986). Wait time: Slowing down may be a way of speeding up! *Journal of Teacher Education, 37*(1), 43–50.

9 Guiding behaviour in an unequal world

Figure 9.1
Source: Pixabay. Licence: Creative Commons CC0

Questions for consideration

- Does being fair mean treating each child exactly the same?
- Are we aiming to get every child to the same standard of behaviour, despite their unequal beginnings?
- What values are important to you, in helping to guide young children?

Vignette from practice

Jenni works at a small primary school on the urban fringe. Her school has been built very recently and has excellent facilities. Jenni feels lucky to have an interesting outdoor area specifically for use by her class, as well as access to the general playgrounds for the school. This outdoor area has many trees and lots of interesting natural materials.

One of the children in the foundation class, Brittany, is difficult to handle. She is a courageous child, but often gets into arguments with other children, and is not afraid to hit or scream at them when she is frustrated. She is known to have a difficult home life, and may have experienced a lot of violence in her life out of school. Her mother is not well connected into the school community.

The classroom teacher, Jenni, has worked hard to include Brittany in the classroom community, and because she can often be funny and engaging (sometimes especially when challenging adult authority) she has built up a good circle of friends. However Jenni has twice caught Brittany in the class's outdoor area, urinating behind a tree, in an area that is hard to supervise. When Jenni reminded Brittany where the toilets were, Brittany told her that at home she is allowed to go outside to the toilet, rather than coming inside to 'bother her mum'. On both occasions Jenni insisted she go inside to the bathroom, although realising this was unnecessary because Brittany's bladder was now empty. Brittany seemed grumpy about this but appeared to comply with the request.

Jenni hadn't thought any more about these incidents until one day in the staff room, when one of her colleagues – the deputy principal – told her that while supervising break-time in the general school playground they had caught Brittany showing two of her friends how to wee standing up, and encouraging them to have a try. This had necessitated two of them changing, and one did not have a change of shoes, which was very inconvenient.

Introduction

Guiding children's behaviour thoughtfully and effectively is never easy, as we can see in the incident above. While much of the time a solution will be obvious and easily implemented, there will be many occasions such as the one described above, where there is no simple or short-term answer. Children's lives can be complex, even those of very young children, and they will come into our classrooms with very different experiences. Some will have been given a great deal of love and attention, some will have had been provided with thoughtful limits around their behaviour by their parents or caregivers, whereas others, like Brittany, may have already experienced trauma, and may be trying to survive in what is a hazardous home environment.

In this chapter we will be exploring managing children's behaviour, a vital skill for all educators. In doing so we will confirm some of your existing strategies, and challenge you to rethink some of your ideas through some sociological provocations. Most importantly, we will be looking at the experiences children have, and how these may impact their behaviour. The things you have learnt so far about gender, social class, race and disability will help you to understand that your solution to any given situation will depend on the context, the child and your own creativity. These solutions will change from day to day, even with the same child, depending on their emotions on that day (see chapter 6) or other factors within your learning community. This involves practical wisdom, which takes time and experience – you will never stop learning new ways of handling challenging behaviours. Learning to do this effectively is one of the safest investments you will make as an educator, helping all children to have the best opportunities for learning in your classroom.

Important basic principles

We will start with theoretical foundations for behaviour guidance, as it will be valuable for you to understand the ethical basis for the decision you are making.

Children's rights

It is widely accepted today that children should be treated according to principles of human rights, as well as being given specific consideration because of their age. Many countries within the United Nations have ratified two international agreements – the Universal Declaration on Human Rights (1948) and the Convention on the Rights of the Child (1990). However, children's rights under the UDHR tend to be limited by ageism, in that children are presumed not to need particular rights. For example, Article 21 talks about the right to political representation, but children are excluded in almost all countries from voting in elections. Article 22 talks about the right to social security and Article 23 talks about the right to work, although children's access to both these rights are limited. Most people find children's economic dependence unremarkable, but this mindset also risks normalising children's powerlessness. What circumstances might there be where children should be allowed to work, or receive income directly from government payments?

The Convention on the Rights of the Child has protections specifically aimed at children, and some of these are very important, such as the rights to freedom of expression (Article 13) or freedom of conscience (Article 14). As educators, we should particularly be aware of Article 28 – the right to an education – although we would like this to advocate the right to early education as well. In thinking about behaviour guidance, Article 37 mandates that children must not be subject to inhumane or degrading treatment or deprived of liberty. While these may seem unlikely in early childhood services, we want our ways of guiding behaviour to honour these rights and interpret them as widely as possible. Do you consider a child being shamed about their behaviour in front of their peers as 'inhumane behaviour', for example?

Children's capabilities

One of the limitations of a human rights approach is that children, especially those of early childhood age, rarely have any power to enforce these rights and so are at the mercy of the adults around them. A right is only as useful as its ability to be enforced, and many children experience violations of their rights on a daily basis, in both wealthy and poorer nations. An alternative way to think about this issue is the 'capabilities approach', a set of principles and ideas which has been developed by Martha Nussbaum and Amartya Sen. This approach looks at what is needed for people to flourish, and how societies can be set up to maximise the wellbeing of all people. The emphasis is on people's freedom to do particular things, because it is believed that wellbeing is more than just health and access to sufficient resources, but also about being able to engage meaningfully in the world. The key difference between 'rights' and 'capabilities' is that the human rights approach looks at what is theoretically desirable, whereas the capabilities approach looks at a person's actual ability to achieve valued goals (Sen, 1993). It does not visualise a utopia of human rights, but the experiences of everyday life. It helps us examine how children's lives are constrained or enabled by educational spaces, including consulting with them in an ongoing way about their wellbeing and hopes for their lives. Under a capabilities approach we would ask, 'what matters most for these children?' and 'how able are they to achieve their desired aims?' What matters most will vary from group to group, across time and for different individuals. Not all aims can be met in the classroom, but children's sense of wellbeing will be improved when they can achieve their most important goals. In guiding behaviour we can ask whether what we are expecting of children may be in conflict with one of their primary goals, and whether there is a way to achieve what we want which honours those goals. For example, some children will highly value finding their own solutions to problems, and your attempts to help them may actually be deeply frustrating, causing rather than resolving conflict.

Participatory parity

One idea we believe is useful in guiding your pedagogical work is that of *participatory parity* (Fraser, 1999). Nancy Fraser is a political philosopher who has spent her career thinking about different forms of injustice, and how these can be connected under one overarching framework. For Fraser there are three main types of injustice. First, there is injustice through economic inequality, concerning the *distribution* of resources, in which poverty prevents many people from living a full life. Secondly there are inequalities due to *recognition*, such as discrimination against people due to the way they look (e.g. skin colour), the ways they act (e.g. LGBT+ people) or their abilities (those with bodily or mental impairments). Lastly, there are forms of inequality due to unequal legal frameworks – *political inequality* – such as denying children the right to vote, even though they are affected by the political decisions being made in their country (Fraser, 2007).

Fraser argues that one way to think about all of these forms of inequality is to think of them as barriers to equal participation in society. A lack of resources, of recognition or of political rights can all hamper this participation. 'Parity of participation' is a useful idea because it recognises that those who come into education may have a variety of barriers to equal participation. These children will need different sorts of support from us as educators to ensure their effective participation. This could involve practical support like suitable clothing or providing supplementary breakfast programmes, verbal support for children whose peers may be excluding them or advocacy (see chapter 12), such as using your influence to support children's participation in local community events.

Useful rules of thumb

These 'big picture' theoretical ideas are valuable in looking at the principles that can guide our pedagogical practices. However, they may seem too abstract to put into practice easily. Below we offer some practical tools you can use on a daily basis to help you make decisions about guiding young children. You will come across various statements of these principles in educational work, such as in the useful guidelines offer by Louise Porter (see breakout box).

Being respectful

In all our work with young children it is important to be respectful. We should be respectful verbally, but also physically in how we relate to children's bodies and personal space. As described in chapter 2, Pikler's work encourages adults to take infant's needs into account as part of everyday practice. These sorts of techniques communicate powerfully to babies and toddlers that their wishes and needs are respected. With older children this can be demonstrated through listening attentively, even when the day is busy, so that you do not miss the important things that might be going on for that child. Making a regular practice of listening carefully to children builds trust and lets them know that their views matter. Other forms of respect could involve including children in significant decision making or being honest with young children about difficult subjects that other adults tend to avoid (the null curriculum).

Basic principles of managing behaviour (Porter, 2008)

- **Reciprocal respect** between adults and children
- **Equal rights**: Children have the same rights as adults
- **Unconditionality:** Children deserve our affection, regardless of their behaviour
- **Individuation**: Acknowledging children's opinions and interests in your guidance
- **Considerateness**: Asking children to think how their behaviour affects others
- **Compassion**: Seeking to understand not judge the causes of children's actions
- **Leadership**: Wielding power wisely though considered decisions and insight

Avoiding harm or stigma

Doing no harm is an important part of many professional codes of ethics, especially those of various medical practitioners. For example, Principle 1.1 in the code of ethics of the US National Association for the Education of Young Children, begins, 'Above all we shall not harm children' (NAEYC, 2005). The code goes on to describe all the forms of harm that educators should aim to avoid, such as practices that are disrespectful, exploitative, degrading, emotionally harmful and so on.

While this may seem obvious, it is an important touchstone because we can identify harm to children through their body language, facial expressions or cries of distress. This is helpful in becoming aware of the impact our pedagogical decisions have on young children. This does not mean we should immediately change a chosen action simply because of a negative reaction from a child. Children will often be upset by decisions we make in response to their behaviour or our attempts to resolve a dispute. By noticing any negative reactions we can fine-tune those decisions, including taking the time to explain the reasons behind them. This can help to minimise the distress children may be feeling, or give them a chance to express themselves (Article 13 of the Convention on the Rights of the Child), reducing their sense of powerlessness or frustration.

The 'comparison test'

There is a simple way to check whether our actions are on the right path. This is to ask ourselves, 'Would I treat an adult in this way?'. Quite often, we unconsciously have double standards, and find that the ways we treat children are different from our behaviour towards adults. This is a form of ageism, because we are assuming that young children do not need to be treated as carefully or well as adults. This simple question can often help us work out what might be troubling about the particular action we are contemplating, and find ways to replace it with a more respectful solution. For example, when a child's nose is running with mucus from a cold it is common for adults to wipe the child's nose, without giving them any warning or asking for permission. We would not do this to an adult, even one that was incapacitated or infirm, and would consider whether they might want to do this themselves rather than having it done for them. By making this comparison we are forcing ourselves to take young children's own perspective, and making time to notice how this might feel for them.

Being consistent

There are a wide variety of opinions about being consistent, and how important it is in early childhood services (Porter, 2008). There are a number of different ways to think about consistency in regard to behaviour, and we may not agree with all of them, or any of them. We see three types of consistency being advocated across the sector, in regard to behaviour guidance. The first of these is consistency across a team of educators, the second of these is consistency in how we treat a range of children and the last is consistency over time.

Within a particular setting, it is often common to hear educators insisting on common behaviour guidance strategies across the team. We do not believe it is necessary to respond identically to children across a staff team, although it can be useful to understand each other's ways of resolving disputes, and to work from the same broad principles. One problem with this approach is that it is usually the least experienced or qualified members of a team who are asked to 'be consistent' with others' guidance strategies, replicating existing power dynamics within a workplace. This is likely even when those being asked to conform may be those most willing to be creative in their strategies, or have access to more recent ideas about positive ways to intervene with children. Children themselves do not need educators to respond identically, we believe. All children will experience different sorts of rules at home from those they encounter in the early childhood settings they attend, and they are generally very capable at mentally adjusting themselves to differing rules and frameworks. We believe your early childhood setting will be a richer experience for children if they can observe the adults around them coming to their own individual responses when needing to guide behaviour. It can be valuable for children to see educators discussing any differences of opinion in these areas respectfully to help them get a sense that there is no single right answer to any human conflict, and that differences of thought are inevitable.

From a sociological perspective, we certainly do not believe it is right to treat all children consistently, regardless of their backgrounds. The same sort of reaction (a firm reminder) may make an anxious child burst into tears, while being completely tuned out by another. Children need a response that is attuned to their particular needs while also being fair. We will look at some of the specific needs of children in the next section. The aim is always to achieve the same ability to participate, as advocated by Fraser, rather than identical treatment for children who are very different.

The last form of consistency is one we believe to be valuable, which is for educators to be personally consistent over time. Children will be watching you closely, wanting to build close relationships with you, and wondering whether to trust you fully. Part of having integrity and appearing trustworthy in children's eyes will be making decisions that make sense in relationship to your overall values and typical guidance strategies, and which are not arbitrary or capricious. Children are likely to spot patterns of unfairness very quickly if it is clear that some children are consistently treated better or more leniently than others. One useful strategy you might like to try is always to have a clear justification for your actions in any situation, and to reflect regularly and critically on whether your justifications are reasonable. Sometimes when we try to articulate our reasoning we realise we do not actually know why we are making a particular decision. This is an opportunity to think more deeply or discuss with your colleagues what a better response might look like.

Children's needs and experiences

Children enter our lives in some expected ways, such as local children enrolled well in advance, while others will arrive less conventionally, such as a child being placed by social services as a result of family difficulties. If we are in education for long enough we will encounter children from every walk of life, from many different cultural backgrounds and with a huge variety of coping skills. In this section we will look more closely at some of the children you may encounter, and what their needs might be.

The non-existent 'normal' child

Developmental psychology has been critiqued for creating an image of the universal child (Burman, 1994), when this image mostly represents only privileged children from Minority World countries, rather than the huge variety of childhoods that actually exist across the globe. Sociologists prefer to look at the diverse range of children that exist and how they differ, rather than seeing any particular behaviour as normal. Any normalising discourses mean that actual people and actual children become seen as difficult or problematic whenever they differ from this norm. Developmental checklists cause this problem for children, because every child is likely to have some abilities that do not match the expected standard. This then causes anxiety for parents or caregivers, when most children sit within a typical *range* of progress and will flourish if given the right sorts of support.

While such checklists can potentially be helpful in giving a general idea of what children may be capable of at a particular age, in practice they almost always lead to a deficit model of children, as we saw in chapter 2. Children are quick to pick up on this negative view of themselves, and may internalise a sense of failure, rather than the ability to learn and succeed. The capabilities approach outlined earlier helps acknowledge children's existing strengths and desires. As critical educators we know that all children are capable of a wide variety of learning and will flourish best when they feel valued within that setting. As sociologists, we know that the dominant discourses that circulate in society often function to privilege certain types of people, and make their success more likely, as Cordelia Fine (2010) demonstrates in her books about gendered myths. This means that some children will be much more likely to be considered 'in deficit' than others, simply because they are from more marginalised backgrounds.

Children from traumatic backgrounds

Many children will enter your classrooms having experienced some forms of trauma or disadvantage. Some of these are 'everyday' forms of trauma, such as having a parent die or coming from a very poor family. Other children may have a parent who is an addict or experiencing mental health issues, which can make their lives difficult. Others, such as those discussed below, may experience even more severe challenges. With traumatised children it is necessary that educators set aside their compassionate concern for this child so that these worries do not interfere with treating them in an ordinary way. Even when their reactions are extreme, you will want to model confidence that over time they will learn to manage their reactions more effectively. Other children may need to be reassured that the child's apparently extreme reactions are not something they need to be scared about.

For the child concerned, consider asking them whether they are okay for you to explain their situation to their peers, in order for others to understand them better. This should be explained in a way that is not shaming to them nor unnecessarily explicit for other children. Often what needs to be explained are the big or scary emotions that a child is feeling (see chapter 6) and tackling it from this angle is usually a good learning experience for everyone. With these simple explanations, other children can then be given strategies for how they can respond to this child when their reactions are extreme or unexpected, so that they feel more of a sense of agency in that situation. You will find other children learn to deal compassionately with their peers if given suitable strategies and sufficient information, demonstrating wisdom and sensitivity to the feelings of the traumatised child.

With some traumatised children, you may sometimes need to use *protective force* (Porter, 2016, 252–6), in which you must physically intervene in the violent or destructive behaviour of a child. This must be done with care and sensitivity to the child, even when it can feel like an intrusive and often scary way to have to intervene in a child's behaviour. When restraining a child, all of our fundamental guidance principles still apply, and it is helpful to stay focused on the reasons for your intervention, such as to prevent injury. You will be aiming to do no harm to the child, while avoiding harm to yourself and others as well. You will be treating the child respectfully, which may mean explaining calmly to them the reasons for your physical intervention, such as holding them around their wrists. Reporting your use of any protective force afterwards to your supervisor, other colleagues and to the child's parents or guardians, is absolutely vital. This protects you from any suspicion of using force coercively or cruelly, and helps others to understand why it happened and how to avoid the need for this sort of behaviour management in the future. Remember that this sort of physical intervention can be distressing to you as an educator, and you may need to debrief about it afterwards, within your workplace or with a supportive friend.

War zone refugees

Increasingly, given the violent conflicts taking places across the globe, such as in Syria or Sudan, there will be children in your services who have experienced very distressing early lives. They may have some post-traumatic stress responses, including re-experiencing the violence they have witnessed mentally. This may have been extreme, such as witnessing the killings of close family members. These are not events that most educators have any experience of, and may well be confronting for you in trying to work sensitively with this child. Children from these backgrounds may experience a range of impacts, from poor health due to malnutrition or lack of medical care, high rates of sexual and other forms of abuse (particularly for girls), or significant rates of physical injury and disability for those who have been child soldiers (Tamashiro, 2011).

Family violence

Young children who have witnessed violence at home, particularly between their parents or guardians, are likely to struggle when in their educational setting, due to the abnormally high levels of alertness (hypervigilance) they have needed to develop at home to keep themselves safe. As Sarah Horn and her colleagues (2017) suggest, most children in this situation will have difficulty concentrating for anything other than short periods, and may zone out or appear inattentive. They are also likely to over-react to noises, and may be sensitive even to quiet sounds. They may become stressed even when the sounds are not in any way threatening, such as other children's excitement. Children experiencing family violence are more likely to have tantrums or engage in destructive behaviour, and you might notice a visible adrenalin response, with quickened breathing or sweatiness in evidence.

Child abuse

Most educators will have had some mandated training in understanding the sorts of abuse that children sometimes experience, such as sexual or physical abuse, or neglect (see chapter 5). It is not always easy to identify children in these situations, and often those involved will actively work to conceal the abusive situations, out of shame or to be protective of the family or other siblings. Unexplained physical injuries are the most obvious sign of abuse, but more often such trauma is noticed in patterns of play or interactions that are not typical for children of that age. For example, while most children have some curiosity about sexuality and bodies, a typical child will not be fixated on these sorts of games, and will be happy to be redirected. A child who returns repeatedly to particular activities, especially genitally focused play or games involving penetration, should be considered at risk of having experienced sexual abuse. You should familiarise yourself with child abuse reporting protocols in your context, and discuss any concerns you have with colleagues or your principal or administrator, being mindful that children's safety is paramount and that other colleagues may sometimes try to avoid or minimise these issues out of a hope that such abuse is not occurring.

Children with disabilities

Children with disabilities are more likely to have experienced trauma, as they are more likely to have experienced institutional care, or because they are frequently treated by others as less capable, a form of discrimination (Salthouse & Frohmader, 2004). In getting to know this child, it will be important not only to make adjustments for their disability, but also to acknowledge the harms that may have resulted for some children from previous discrimination or rejection by others. For example, a child with a disability may be unable to do something not due to their disability but because they have been previously considered incapable of such tasks, and so not given the opportunity to learn skills in this area. It is always best to give every child the benefit of the doubt in these situations, and offer plenty of opportunities and encouragement in a wide range of activities. It is also important to understand the specific frustration that might exist for some children in comparing themselves with their peers, who may find a specific task easier or more accessible due to their lack of impairment. Being honest with children in responding to this frustration is important in helping them build resilience, and learning to find their own solutions to particular tasks. However it is important to remember that education itself needs to change if inclusion is to be meaningful, challenging taken-for-granted notions of 'competitiveness and biological completeness' (Whitburn, 2017, 494).

Class and racial backgrounds

One of the most common ways we might treat children differently is in response to their class or racial backgrounds. As educators we will not want to admit discriminatory behaviour to ourselves, but we will need to be honest with ourselves about this possibility. This is an effect of privilege and will impact primarily on those of us who are white or those of us who have come from economically privileged backgrounds. The most important thing to know is that, when we deny the possibility that this could happen, we also prevent ourselves from thinking about it, and learning how to do it better. Each day we work with children is a day when we can be more thoughtful about who we are, who they are and how equitably we guide their behaviour.

Stereotyping

There are many ways we may be doing an injustice to less privileged children in our class, and the most obvious way is through giving these children less attention or by being less patient with their learning journeys. Children are very attentive to the behaviour of adults who matter to them, and will tend to interpret this lack of attention as being about their own diminished worth. When we give children attention, it matters how we do this across the diversity of individuals in our classes. We are giving children signals about who is valued and valuable, in the world.

Stereotypes about particular sorts of children often drive this differential attention-giving. They are one of the ways that discourses shape human social life. Stereotypes reflect dominant discourses about the characteristics of particular social groups, and so make it more likely they will be treated differently as a result. It is useful for educators to be aware of common patterns of stereotyping to be able to resist these unhelpful thought patterns and respond with greater integrity. For example, stereotypes about teachers may mean that others assume you will always be extremely responsible in your private life as well as at work, whereas you may enjoy extreme sports, or other risky activities.

A common stereotype suggests that male children are less able to moderate their behaviours or are somehow 'naturally' predisposed to being more noisy, more aggressive or less settled in a classroom environment. As sociologists we know that gendered behaviours are strongly encouraged in young children from the beginnings of their lives, and that children themselves want to conform to these gendered beliefs, just as they are invested in learning how to be competent in other areas of their life (Fine, 2017). The problem for boys is that the assumed standard for their behaviour is very low, with most adults prepared to let them off the hook for any untoward actions, through common expressions such as 'boys will be boys'. In doing so adults model low expectations for boys, and they come to expect little from themselves. Knowing that these behaviours are part of how we are enculturated is vital knowledge, because it means that educators can expect just as much from every child that they work with.

Another pervasive stereotype accompanies children from working-class and poorer backgrounds, and researchers have shown how children from these families and communities tend to be labelled, unfairly, as less intelligent or less capable (David *et al.*, 1997). The same stereotype allows children from wealthier backgrounds to be perceived as more intelligent, despite most being children with average levels of ability. These assumptions seem to be made because of the classed habitus of children (see chapter 3), and the ways that privileged children are encouraged to speak up and ask questions, while those from poorer backgrounds are encouraged by their families to 'be good' at school and not to talk back to their teachers (Lareau, 2000).

There are many racially based stereotypes around and it is important to become aware of the sorts of assumptions we may be making about some children, simply because of their cultural or ethnic background. In many white-dominant cultures, young children with dark skin are presumed to be more poorly behaved, or less capable, and this stereotype is particularly damaging for young boys from African backgrounds (hooks, 2013). In Australia, such stereotypes impact negatively on Indigenous children, due to the long-term structural racism that has shaped the process of colonisation in recent centuries (Herbert, 2013). In some settings, children with Asian heritage may be presumed to be better behaved, or more intelligent. This may appear to be a positive stereotype, but it remains damaging because it prevents educators seeing the child for who they are, and their genuine skills and interests.

168 *Guiding behaviour in an unequal world*

Figure 9.2 This educator is taking time to talk through a minor dispute between these children, ensuring their feelings are honoured, and good solutions found.
Source: Nadine Quarello, with thanks to Emali Early Learning

Guiding children's behaviour

This chapter is not designed to give you lots of specific tips and tricks about managing children's behaviour. That level of detail is covered well in other books devoted to that purpose. Instead we will cover some key issues that reflect the underlying values of this book, and which support a sociological understanding of young children's lives.

Supporting children's problem-solving skills

As we discussed in chapter 1, power relations are one of the main issues sociology concerns itself with. These relationships of power are present in any guidance of behaviour within early childhood settings. Even the language we tend to use reflects this, with the language of 'punishment' and 'discipline' having being replaced in recent years by more benign words and concepts, as educationalists reimagine what discipline processes should look like. Whatever we call what we are doing we need to acknowledge the power we take up as adults in this process.

With any instance of 'problem behaviour' or in conflict situations, it is usually adults who decide what is worth taking into account and what actions should be taken in response. Some of this is inevitable, because we have ultimate responsibility for children's safety, wellbeing and learning processes within our classrooms. However when it is adults making all of these decisions then children are learning almost nothing, except perhaps that adults are in charge, again! This is particularly troubling, when educators are using their power to 'expect' children to apologise, even when they do not yet feel sorry. This is unhelpful because unless genuine it forces the child to be untruthful, and usually to resent the educator involved, or the child they feel forced to apologise to. We suggest it is more useful to explain to the child the consequences of their actions for the person harmed, and give them time and support to find their own solutions to this social dilemma.

We believe that your lives and children's lives will be vastly improved if you start to see behaviour guidance as an integral part of the learning processes of education. Framed like this, it is clear that what is most important is not children's immediate safety or the smooth running of the classroom, but what children are learning from each behavioural interaction. Are they learning that their needs are irrelevant? Are they learning that some children are always believed, whereas they are not? Are they being made to feel ashamed or stupid, rather than as someone who has made a mistake?

Fixing the problem

Viewing behaviour guidance as an opportunity for learning means including children in the process from the outset. This requires that educators take time to talk about ground rules and expectations, and encourage children's thoughts on what these should look like. Children in the early years of school will be able to offer many suggestions, and the process of discussion around these suggestions becomes valuable in itself, helping all those in the group to get a sense of each other's views and beliefs. With babies, they will not have the language to contribute in this way, but they will make their needs and desires known over time, and the educators who are working with them can reflect on what these small people are trying to communicate through their actions. We frequently see babies showing compassion towards other children's (or adults') sadness, or actively wanting to help out with the work being done by others (e.g. Hepach, Vaish, & Tomasello, 2013). These sorts of caring and proactive behaviours can be encouraged directly, but also taken as signs of the broader desires of that group of children.

Once children have acquired enough language to articulate their ideas, then we can begin to support them in providing solutions to problems themselves rather than having educators intervening and providing these. This is not always an easy process, but conflict is an inevitable part of human relationships and helping children to develop the skills to resolve their own conflicts is valuable (Church, Mashford-Scott, & Cohrssen, 2017). Often this takes more time for educators than a typical 'top-down' solution. We would argue that it is much more valuable and empowering for children to learn these skills, however difficult, than to have adults making decisions for them.

Interestingly, expectations about behaviour guidance appear to be strongly influenced by culture, with quite different norms being present in different places. In the video ethnography project undertaken by Tobin and colleagues (1989), participants from China and the USA were surprised to observe how much their Japanese colleagues in preschool settings allowed children to resolve their own conflicts. To an outside eye, it looked as if the Japanese teachers were being careless about quite serious disputes between children. However this practice – allowing children considerable freedom to resolve conflicts themselves – appears to pay off, with children in these preschools becoming more skilled at managing these situations than their peers in China or the USA. This common practice by educators in Japan appears to reflect a strong belief in community and social cohesiveness, and a willingness to allow children to learn and make mistakes while resolving conflict, as part of longer term goals about education and society.

Many Indigenous groups have differing perspectives on what effective behaviour guidance should look like, particularly given the effects of colonisation (see chapter 7). Catherine Savage and her colleagues (2014) have explored how this looks from *te ao Māori* (the Aotearoa/New Zealand Indigenous worldview), and the different values that underpin this. Many of their values resonate with sociological concerns about forms of discipline which focus on deficits, on punishing and on shaming. They advocate a form of culturally responsive pedagogy, built up at a whole of school or site level, which focuses on building on children's strengths, such as *manaakitanga* (empathy, caring for others).

Being creative

Our most common reaction as educators, when children are not on track or in the throes of conflict, is to deliver a lecture. As adults this helps us feel purposeful and authoritative and sometimes we might offer some useful perspective. In general, however, we suspect that this is not an effective intervention from children's own perspective, and potentially achieves little. Given that no two situations you encounter will be identical, and that the circumstances of any conflict and its participants will be different each time, we suggest that a good way to think about behaviour guidance is through the lens of creativity. To be creative is to try and enact a response that is different from previous responses, and that is suitable for this exact moment and the situation presenting itself. What could you do differently from your normal response? What are you feeling at this moment, and what emotions can you see the children revealing (see chapter 6)? What response would most help children's learning, about social interactions, about self-discipline or about empathy, in this situation? Instead of

Guiding behaviour in an unequal world 171

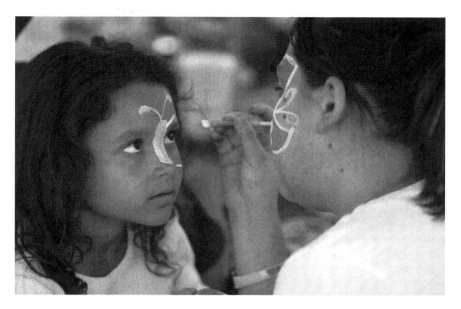

Figure 9.3 An older OSHC child paints the face of a younger one, building trust and community. Practising care for others builds empathy, which is a key to most effective dispute resolution strategies. Martin Egnash.

Source: Public domain

the lecture you were about to launch into, why not ask the children whether they *already* understand what went wrong here. If they agree that they do, then perhaps you could suggest they take one minute to think quietly about how they might manage this differently themselves the next time that this happens. They might want to tell you what they come up with, but that may not be necessary. What you have done is to demonstrate respect for their existing skills, and trust that they will work harder at this next time.

On another occasion you might think it is worth compromising your dignity as an educator just a little, and reflecting back to the children how you are seeing them behave. Perhaps you might pretend to have a tantrum, or to imitate how grumpy they look at this moment. This is not done to mock them but to lighten the mood, helping them to laugh at the thought of an adult behaving as open-heartedly as children often do. You might take the chance to explain what you think the child you are mirroring may be feeling, in looking grumpy or throwing a tantrum, and the uses that may have for them in releasing their anger or demonstrating their feelings. This will depend on whether you think extra words would be useful to those listening. Perhaps the demonstration (and the smile that accompanies it) is enough of a provocation to their own problem-solving than anything else you might say.

Being creative involves knowing that there are no hard-and-fast rules for guiding behaviour, except the basic principles of doing no harm and always modelling respect. Children anticipate the adults around them behaving in particular ways, and often rely on these habitual reactions when they are looking for particular sorts of attention. By modelling a wide variety of responses you are inviting the children to be more creative in their own social lives, and to explore what the possibilities and limits might be.

Working with parents and families

Before we finish this chapter, we will note how important it is to cooperate with families, in regard to guiding behaviour. We will be looking at this more in the next chapter, across a variety of issues. As observed earlier, in discussing consistency, children are used to different disciplinary strategies between home and their early childhood settings, or between different homes when they live with separated parents, or are cared for by multiple relatives. Some educators, we are aware, feel obliged to try and replicate familial guidance strategies when asked to by parents. We agree it is important to listen to such requests and to talk about the situation, including hearing their reasons for the request. At times you may come to agree with them, and be willing to support their suggestions. At other times you will need to insist that your educational values or your site's philosophy are different, and that you will not be able to do what they ask. Consider also the possibility of reminding parents of the rights that their child has within your setting to make their own choices and to build an independent self beyond their parents' expectations. These are not easy conversations, but they are critical ones if we want children to be recognised as more than 'possessions' of their families.

In taking time to understand the feelings or reasons behind this request, you and the family will get a better idea of why each setting is different. Knowing these reasons may help you to come up with an alternative strategy that might resonate better with your pedagogical values, while also supporting the aims of the family. As educators we do not often take the time to listen deeply to the views of the families we work with, but it is the process itself which helps communicate the respect you have for them, rather than what you ultimately do with that information.

Concluding remarks

Returning to the story of Brittany at the beginning of the chapter, we hope you will have a better sense of how you might handle this situation if you were Jenni. You might realise that your chances of engaging the mother in a meaningful conversation about this issue are going to be limited, and that what Brittany most needs is to feel valued and supported. You might channel her obvious leadership skills into more constructive challenges, while affirming how much you value her quirky ideas. You might realise that under her confident exterior Brittany is anxious, and try to engage with her about that, in the hope that she would open up about what is going on at home. You certainly might believe that keeping this child engaged and positive is more important than the less critical issue of hygiene in the outdoor areas. There are many possible 'right' ways to handle the situations you will encounter as an early childhood educator, and some less helpful ones. You will make mistakes – more often than you would like – and accepting these as good opportunities to learn and reflect is one more way you can model something useful for children.

Questions for reflection

- What do you think about Porter's seven principles for guiding behaviour, detailed earlier in the chapter? Which of these make most sense to you, and which do you struggle with? You may, for example, find the idea of 'leadership' challenging, if you do not see your educational role in this way. How could you take up each of these categories in turn, to help you reflect upon your own practices as an educator or parent?
- Are you a good problem-solver? In which situations do you find it easiest to apply this sort of mindset? Some have argued that problem-solving is a key aspect of intelligence, and something that can be practised and developed over time. Pick an issue you are having difficulties with at the moment, and list as many different possible solutions as you can, including those that might seem impossible. The point is to try to find as many ideas as possible, without judging them before you even write them down. How does this free you to think through the most practical possibilities?
- Do you remember a time when you were not respected as a child? What happened to make you notice this? Were your opinions ignored? Were decisions made without consulting you, even though they affected you deeply? Did you ever try and demand respect, but were refused this recognition by the adults around you?

Activities for educators

- What stereotypes are you holding onto about women? Men? People in wheelchairs? People with autism? People from China? People from Latin America? Elderly people? Preschoolers? People in poverty? Write down the stereotypes as clearly as you can, taking time to make them as explicit as possible. Sometimes getting them out of your head and onto paper can make you realise how ridiculous they seem. Once you have done this, think hard about people you have met in that category, and whether they all match that stereotype, and if so, to what extent. Next think of people you know who are not in that category (including perhaps yourself) and ask if that stereotype is true for others beyond that group. While some stereotypes contain a partial truth, they are mostly effects of perception, where we choose to notice particular things about those who seem different from us.
- When you are next working with young children, try this simple exercise. Rather than making an immediate decision in trying to guide children's

behaviour (except when you must prevent a child getting seriously hurt!) stop and watch for a couple of minutes how the children resolve it, remaining close by, but without active intervention. At the same time, consider how you might react differently from your normal response to this sort of situation. How does this extra time help you to make better decisions? What did the children achieve for themselves, and what did you notice about this, when you stepped back a little from more active interventions.
- Think of a child you have worked with who has a traumatic history. Find out more about the background to this child's situation, without being intrusive into their family life (perhaps you can ask others who know them for information, if this feels possible). Now go and do some research about this particular situation, such as investigating the recent history of a war-ravaged country that this child originates from, or exploring useful ways of relating to a child's particular disabling condition. How can this extra information help you develop more compassionate and engaged responses, in guiding this child's behaviour in future?

Key readings

Fine, C. (2010). *Delusions of Gender: How our Minds, Society, and Neurosexism Create Difference*. New York: Norton.

hooks, b. (2013). *Writing beyond Race: Living Theory and Practice*. New York: Routledge.

Lareau, A. (2000). *Home Advantage: Social Class and Parental Intervention in Elementary Education* (2nd ed.). Lanham: Rowman & Littlefield.

Porter, L. (2016). *Young Children's Behaviour: Guidance Approaches for Early Childhood Educators* (4th ed.). Sydney: Allen & Unwin.

Tobin, J., Wu, D., & Davidson, D. (1989). *Preschool in Three Cultures*. New Haven, CT: Yale University Press.

Online resources

Calmer Classrooms Guide – We recommend the general insights of this guide, and the suggestions about relationship-based classroom management in section 3. http://education.qld.gov.au/schools/healthy/pdfs/calmer-classrooms-guide.pdf

Raising feminist boys – This podcast is a comedic take on this important everyday intervention into gender politics. www.youtube.com/watch?v=IzWSnP5nOvQ

Restorative justice – This set of principles is starting to be used more in educational settings, and supports children and young people in finding their own solutions to social conflict. www.edutopia.org/blog/restorative-justice-resources-matt-davis

Further reading

Burman, E. (1994). *Deconstructing Developmental Psychology*. London: Routledge.

Church, A., Mashford-Scott, A., & Cohrssen, C. (2017). Supporting children to resolve disputes. *Journal of Early Childhood Research*, 1476718X17705414.

David, M., Davies, J., Edwards, R., Reay, D., & Standing, D. (1997). Choice within constraints: Mothers and schooling. *Gender and Education, 9*(4), 397–410.

Fine, C. (2017). *Testosterone Rex: Unmaking the Myths of our Gendered Minds*. London: Icon Books.

Fraser, N. (1999). Social justice in the age of identity politics: Redistribution, recognition and participation. In L. Ray & A. Sayer (Eds), *Culture and Economy After the Cultural Turn* (pp. 25–52). London: Sage.

Fraser, N. (2007). Re-framing justice in a globalizing world. In T. Lovell (Ed.), *(Mis)recognition, Social Inequality and Social Justice: Nancy Fraser and Pierre Bourdieu* (pp. 17–35). London: Routledge.

Hepach, R., Vaish, A., & Tomasello, M. (2013). A new look at children's prosocial motivation. *Infancy, 18*(1), 67–90.

Herbert, J. (2013). Interrogating social justice in early years education: How effectively do contemporary policies and practices create equitable learning environments for Indigenous Australian children. *Contemporary Issues in Early Childhood, 14*(4), 300–310.

Horn, S. R., Miller-Graff, L. E., Galano, M. M., & Graham-Bermann, S. A. (2017). Posttraumatic stress disorder in children exposed to intimate partner violence: The clinical picture of physiological arousal symptoms. *Child Care in Practice, 23*(1), 90–103.

NAEYC (2005). *Code of Ethical Conduct and Statement of Commitment*. Washington, DC: NAEYC.

Porter, L. (2008). *Young Children's Behaviour: Practical Approaches for Caregivers and Teachers*. Sydney: McLennan & Petty.

Salthouse, S., & Frohmader, C. (2004). Double the odds: Domestic violence and women with disabilities. Paper presented at the Home Truths Conference, Melbourne, Australia.

Savage, C., Macfarlane, S., Macfarlane, A., Fickel, L., & Te Hēmi, H. (2014). Huakina Mai: A Kaupapa māori approach to relationship and behaviour support. *Australian Journal of Indigenous Education, 43*(2), 165–174.

Sen, A. (1993). Capability and well-being. In M. Nussbaum & A. Sen (Eds), *The Quality of Life*. Oxford: Oxford University Press.

Tamashiro, T. (2011). Paper commissioned for the EFA *Global Monitoring Report* 2011: The hidden crisis: Armed conflict and education. Paris: UNESCO. Retrieved from http://unesdoc.unesco.org/images/0019/001907/190712e.pdf

United Nations (1948). *Universal Declaration of Human Rights*. Paris: UN General Assembly.

United Nations (1990). *Convention on the Rights of the Child*. Paris: UN General Assembly.

Whitburn, B. (2017). The subjectivities of 'included' students with disabilities in schools. *Discourse: Studies in the Cultural Politics of Education, 38*(4), 485–497.

10 Working with diverse families

Figure 10.1
Source: Yarrow Andrew, with thanks to Flinders University Childcare Centre

Questions for consideration
- What fears or hopes do you have about working with families? What skills do you think you personally bring to these particular adult relationships?
- What was your own experience of growing up in a family? What do you assume about 'normal' patterns of family life, based on your own experiences? How might you broaden your understanding to work more respectfully with others as an educator?

Vignette from practice

Finding the right primary school for your preschooler is not always an easy task, especially if there are a number of schools close by which might be suitable. Maeve and Steve were looking for a supportive school for their bright but anxious son, Sam. They wanted a school where children flourished, teachers were kind and the staff had experience of working with people with disabilities. Feeling a sense of belonging in a school community was very important for their son and themselves.

This was the first open day they had attended, and Maeve wasn't sure what she should be focusing on – the quality of the facilities, good leadership, an accessible location from their place or something else. They were just about to meet one of the teachers who would be teaching the new intake next year, and Sam was excited to see who might be there from preschool. Maeve remembered some of the challenges of school, and the need to feel included. She hoped that Sam would find this easier than Maeve herself had, as a person of short stature. Or rather, she thought to herself, 'as a dwarf', which is how most people had described it back in her day, as if any day now she might be heading off on a quest with elves and hobbits!

They went to the designated classroom, and caught the eye of another parent, Shoba, that they knew from their preschool. It would be great if there were other children Sam knew coming here, as that would help him feel happy and more settled. The teacher was doing the rounds of nervous parents and children – 'I'm sure that isn't an easy thing to do', thought Maeve.

When the teacher came up to them, Maeve introduced herself, Steve and Sam. The teacher looked at Sam and said, 'Well, you're a bit too tall for your first year of school, aren't you?'

Maeve was furious. There was an awkward silence. Maeve held Sam's hand and gave it a squeeze – the squeeze of solidarity.

They joined the tour. On leaving, when Sam was playing with friends, Steve said, 'Well clearly we're not putting Sam's name down here'.

'You bet we're not'.

Introduction

As educators we will end up working with many people over the course of our working lives. We will work not only with children, but their parents, guardians, grandparents, siblings, cousins and extended family. This can sometimes be an intimidating thought, especially if you are a young educator. You may feel much less experienced than some of the older family members you work with, some of whom may have high-powered jobs, or intimidating personalities. We don't want to say this is always easy – it isn't – but we do want to encourage you that there are many and diverse skills you will gain from the efforts you choose to make in this area.

You are becoming an expert in early childhood education, even if you don't quite believe that yet. You are spending time and effort learning about curriculum, pedagogy and sociological understandings of human relationships. Most parents will relate to your sense of doubt about your abilities, because many of them will feel similarly doubtful about their parenting skills, without the benefits of any training. Many of the skills needed to be a parent and to be an educator are similar, so collaborating with families will be useful for them, for you and for their child. These skills are the same because this is work that requires practical wisdom – ongoing face-to-face experimental learning – due to the complexities of human relationships (Sayer, 2011).

There is never 'one right answer' when it comes to working with people, because the situation changes, the individuals change and the feelings and views of each person involved will be different depending on the day. Practical wisdom is a kind of fuzzy logic, helping you to make good decisions despite the changing circumstances. It is a slow form of learning, built up through experience and learned in context. Most parents learn this wisdom, but in very specific ways and circumstances and mostly with their own children. Your involvement with much larger numbers of children, and changing groups of children, will see you picking up these skills at a much higher level (Hooks 2010). When parents say to you, 'I couldn't do what you do' (as they often do), they are probably more accurate than they realise!

The wide range of work with families

When picturing work with families, you may be thinking very narrowly about either the sorts of people you expect to work with, or the sort of workplace you intend to end up in. Yet your work as an early childhood educator will take you to a range of places, from work in small settings, such as family childcare, to speaking out in a public forum about the advantages of early childhood education. Along the way you will encounter many different sorts of families, and be interacting with them under a variety of circumstances. We will use a wide variety of words when talking about families in this chapter (such as caregiver, guardian, parent) to acknowledge the many adults who find themselves in parenting relationships with children, either intentionally or through unexpected circumstance.

Take a moment to imagine the everyday conversations that educators have with the caregivers of the children that they are working with. These conversations happen most often when working with babies, because of their greater care needs, but continue throughout the preschool years and on into the early years of school. This chapter will help you think about these fundamental daily conversations, and some ways to help them go smoothly.

There are many other circumstances in which you will encounter family members outside of your classroom. You may, for example, end up sitting on the management committee of a preschool or the governing council of a school, alongside family members – a very different type of relationship. You may have family members accompanying you on school trips, such as excursions to local wilderness areas, where you might see a different side of each other's skills.

Many will encounter the families they work with outside of work hours, at times when they are not expecting it. Learning to balance the professional and the personal as an educator is never simple, but this gets easier with practice.

Understanding families through theory

According to the work of Annette Lareau (2003), first seen in chapter 3, the assumptions we make about parents will be shaped by our own social class background, and experience of schooling. Early childhood education is built on particular assumptions about child-rearing, and mirrors what Lareau called 'concerted cultivation' (see breakout box). This middle-class value assumes that every moment is a teachable moment and that adults should always be seeking to 'improve' children. This will be taken for granted by some families you work with, whereas the main focus of others will simply be about whether their child is happy. It is also likely that family members who were raised working-class will be less likely to make demands about their children's needs, and may feel intimidated by the institutional atmosphere of your service, or when interacting with degree-qualified educators (Braun, Vincent, &

Concerted cultivation and the accomplishment of natural growth

Annette Lareau is a sociologist from the US, who has conducted extensive research with families around their attitudes to education. She studied families from a wide range of class and racial backgrounds, and concluded that there were only two basic patterns of parenting. These are 'concerted cultivation', where parents dedicate themselves to keeping their children occupied as much as possible with productive activities, such as sports, fitness activities, cultural activities (singing and dance lessons) and so on. This is an attempt to make sure that their children succeed in school and in life. This tends to be a middle-class or ruling-class pattern of parenting.

By contrast, there are other parents who believe in 'the accomplishment of natural growth'. These parents see their role as providing their child with love, shelter, food and guidance, but without needing to involve their child in extra activities beyond compulsory education. This tends to be a pattern seen more with working-class and poorer parents. Lareau was emphatic that all parents were doing what they believe to be best for their children. However the first strategy is often the type of parenting encouraged by early childhood educators and schools, while parents adopting the second strategy of parenting (Lareau called these different 'logics of parenting') are often judged by educators as not caring much about their child's education.

Ball, 2008). Some families, such as those from discriminated-against groups such as Roma people, may find it hard to trust educators, and will need you to demonstrate some basic cultural competence before they consider trusting you (White & Ottmann, 2016). This can be particularly true for children from Indigenous and First Nations families, for whom the ongoing injustices of colonisation (see chapter 7) may still have an impact, making them wary of educational sites and their connections with child removals and other colonial practices. Making time to engage with all families about what they want for their children, and doing so sincerely, will help break down some of these barriers.

Building intimacy

Although we don't often describe them in this way, our relationships with families are intimate ones, particularly when working with the youngest of children. As educators we are feeding children, putting them to sleep, responding to their strong emotions and even managing their toileting needs. These are intimate activities, and families must be willing to trust us with these tasks. Susan Murray (1998) captured well the complexities of early childhood work, and the intense emotions we may feel about it, as well as the need for educators to manage their emotions on behalf of others. Lynet Uttal (1996) showed the range of expectations parents have on their own side of this relationship, ranging anywhere from viewing educators as paid employees to seeing them as surrogate parents. The relationships you build with families must necessarily respond to these varying desires of parents, picking up on their expectations and trying to be respectful of the boundaries they are creating.

Even if you work in the early years of school, and so have less frequent contact with families, building these relationships is still invaluable. We often talk in early childhood about the importance of learning names, and how this can help build bridges to family members you may not know as well. It is a simple thing but also a profound one, because it communicates that you value the person enough to make some effort. Learning the names of the child's most significant contacts – whether a grandparent, a favourite aunt, the partner of a parent or a close family friend – will demonstrate to children that you recognise that their community is a vital part of their life. Be aware that among some cultures personal names are rarely used within families, and children grow up calling their relatives by their relational name (e.g. 'older brother', 'grandmother' and so on). In those cases you may be able to use this relational name with children instead, in their home language. Your efforts to connect with extended family may be vital if there is a crisis in the family. These connections can help you access supportive networks for that child to keep them engaged in their education. Such support will be most needed for children in your group from marginalised backgrounds, whose connection to education are more likely to become disrupted.

Ask, don't assume

The most important thing we hope you will remember in these relationships with parents is that you cannot assume you know what any particular parent or caregiver wants, or how their family works. Whenever you are not sure about something, ask questions! Approaching each parent with an open and curious disposition will help them realise that you want the best for their child, and for their family. A common point of tension occurs with parents of younger children about when and how long they might sleep during the day. Most educators know that children can get exhausted by the social complexities of preschool, and will often benefit from sleep or periods of structured quiet time. Some parents, however, worry that their child will be allowed to sleep for too long, meaning that they won't sleep well that night. This doesn't need to be stressful. Talk to these parents about the particular challenges they face with their child. It may be that their child suffers from night terrors, and that any change in sleep patterns has big impacts on the whole family, including their siblings, magnifying the stressful nature of this issue. In talking about these issues, you will build up your practical wisdom about the specific challenges of all caregiving relationships. You will also be less likely to fall into the trap of judging parents unfairly, without knowing what the experience is like from their point of view.

Making mistakes

You will make many mistakes in the course of building these relationships with parents. It is easy to feel like you know best for children because of the skills you are learning as an educator. Despite this you will frequently get it wrong, making a bad call in terms of how you manage a child's feelings or doing something that offends or upsets a parent or family member. Whatever you have done, or however annoyed or ashamed you may feel, it is your role to repair this relationship. This is your ethical and professional responsibility and not the responsibility of the family member involved. Learning to apologise sincerely for your part in a disagreement will help to rebuild the damage that has been done, and begin to repair the trust that will have been damaged in the process. Some educators struggle with this, feeling that it will undermine their position, or that no one will respect them. In contrast, we have found that it is only the most resilient and self-aware people who make a habit of apologising regularly, because they have seen the beneficial impacts of doing so across all aspects of their lives. This includes apologising when you forget names, rather than simply avoiding the issue. To do so humanises your relationship, helping families remember that you too are a fallible human being, but one who is always willing to keep trying. Children from families who have experienced trauma may feel the need to create conflicts, to help them feel in control of their lives, even if this means creating the stressful environments they have experienced most. Your willingness to work at repairing all the relationships among your classroom community offers a good model for these children about the possibility of a life that can be calm, not traumatic, and relationships that are safe, not scary.

Vital partnerships

These relationships with families are always important, but they become especially so when working with children with disabilities. Even if you are trained as a special educator, and so are familiar with a range of impairments, you will still encounter children with challenges that are unfamiliar to you. While their parents or caregivers might have felt equally bewildered when this child first came into their family, they have learnt fast and hard about the sorts of support their child needs to thrive, to communicate and to learn. Their knowledge is going to be vital in getting you started in thinking about ways to support their child's learning. Ideally this will lead to building a supportive partnership, where you can share ongoing stories about what works for this child. A child with a communicative disorder, for example, may not be able to tell you directly that strong smells bother them, but the parents are likely to know this already, and can spare you weeks of guesswork about the child's strong reaction to your favourite perfume. Many parents will have learnt the hard way that their child's needs will only get met if they advocate strongly on their behalf, so try not to be offended when parents are very explicit about the care needs of their child. This is a good chance to set your own knowledge aside for a moment, and listen behind the words for all the other things that a parent might also be communicating about the child's life up to that point. Listening well, and becoming known for doing so, will make your job easier in the long term, as you will be more trusted in your local community.

Although we tend to think most about children with disabilities, we forget that there will be parents or family members with disabilities, as we saw in the vignette at the start of the chapter. We don't know what the teacher was thinking in making her comment, but what she said touched a sore point in Maeve, through her experiences of past prejudice. If she had made Maeve and her family welcome from the outset, rather than the awkwardness that actually happened, this teacher would have had the chance to learn something new about the experience of those with disabilities within education. She lost the opportunity to engage in some rich curriculum in her classroom if Sam had enrolled, as Sam's classmates inevitably would ask questions about his mum, and why she looks like a grown-up just without so much 'up'. In many classrooms, talking honestly about impairments tends to become part of the null curriculum (see chapter 1), silenced by the awkwardness of the mostly able-bodied and able-minded people who become educators. Although this is not true for Maeve, it is worth remembering that some young children with a disabled parent undertake a caring role with that parent. This is a reminder that we all have interdependent relationships to some degree, and that educators and caregivers will at times need support ourselves (Tisdall, 2012).

Given the challenges faced by many children with disabilities in schooling in previous decades, it is probably not surprising that so few educators themselves have a significant disability, despite the valuable contribution they would make to any teaching team. However, it is worth remembering that nearly everyone experiences periods of impairment, such as through illness or ageing. Some of us will have extended periods when we are impacted by mental illness, which may require adjustments in work patterns. We definitely all have a wide variety of capabilities, and these can be used by critical educators to reflect on the sorts of skills or capacities that we value (or that we overlook) in our classrooms.

The gender dilemma

As sociologists we know that one of the dimensions of inequality that is particularly relevant when talking about engaging with families is gender. As you will be aware, the overwhelming majority of the early childhood workforce is female, or identifies in some way outside traditional ideas of masculinity. This is true right across the globe, with minor variations depending on the gendered cultures in particular countries. For example, in much of the Majority World the early education workforce is exclusively female because this role has for so long been identified with motherhood. In Minority World countries, where strenuous efforts have been made to attain a more gender-balanced workforce, it is still rare to find more than 10 per cent of the workforce being male, as is the case in Norway or Mexico. Even in Norway this statistic hides the fact that many of these men will be working with older children rather than infants or toddlers, with gendered divisions being present even within the early education workforce. This gender division is particularly strong for sectors like family childcare, where the work often combines mothering their own children with paid childcare work.

What is less often discussed is that the majority of the work in families whose children are in early education is undertaken by women as well. While men (fathers, grandfathers, step-parents) are increasingly engaged in dropping off or picking up children, they are less likely to engage in sustained conversations with educators and are certainly less likely to be drawn into volunteer work at the site or become a representative on the management committee. One consequence of this is that the majority of the conversations that occur and the relationships that are developed are between women.

Feminist researchers have identified some issues to which we need to pay attention. First, not only are most women with children in early education engaged in paid work, but they are still likely to be doing the majority of the domestic work as well, which is often called 'the second shift' (Hochschild & Machung, 1989). In reality there may also be a third shift for many mothers, who carry most of the responsibility for selecting a suitable preschool or school, and do most of the everyday management of their child's involvement, including worrying about their child's achievement or wellbeing (Reay, 2000). This tends to cut across social class boundaries, meaning that women's access to free time for leisure or self-care activities is severely constrained. When you are building relationships with mothers, as an educator, it is important to be aware of this triple shift and have sympathy for those parents whose emotions get frayed due to the stress of juggling so many responsibilities.

Secondly, be aware that when stressful conversations are needed with family members about a child's behaviour or ongoing learning it is almost always the mother (or primary female caregiver) who is contacted in the first instance. This is partly a response to the stereotypical patterns of family life just mentioned, but also understandable because a female parent is likely to be the person the educator knows best. This means that women on both sides of the educator–family relationship undertake the emotional labour of negotiating and defusing stressful interactions. When these are not successfully resolved, mothers and/or educators tend to be blamed for the problem and such resentment or hostility can persist for long periods, undermining the relationship. Feminists have long understood that structural problems (such as the over-representation of women as educators, or the expectation that mothers will do most of the educational negotiation work) are often misidentified as individual failings, which means that educators and mothers end up feeling responsible for the problem (Tronto, 1994). In working with families, ensure that you try and engage all parents or caregivers equally. Remember also that the stressful situation is usually not a personal one, but may be due to structural issues, including lack of funding or inadequate leadership.

Figure 10.2 There are many ways to communicate with families. An engaging story about classroom activities is positioned where family members usually wait, offering an invitation to become more involved.

Source: Yarrow Andrew, with thanks to Flinders University Childcare Centre

The particular expertise of early childhood educators

One persistent dilemma in early education has been the misunderstandings about the skills needed for parenting and for being early educators. It is common to hear young early childhood educators bemoaning the fact that they are not (yet) mothers because they feel they therefore lack some essential skill. As Joanne Ailwood (2008) explains, these misunderstandings reach back as far as Fröbel, who made the beginnings of the early kindergarten movement in the nineteenth century synonymous with the skills and emotions of motherhood.

In actuality – as anyone who has been both a mother and an educator would tell you – they have some skills in common, but it's like saying that paddling a canoe will prepare you for running a large passenger ferry! There are no regulatory or legal requirements in becoming a parent and still comparatively little scrutiny. It is done for free, which means you can do it as diligently or badly as you like, depending on the tolerance of your child and your ability to ignore the views of those around you. As an early childhood educator, by contrast, the world is always watching, and in most early education your work is highly regulated, and your funding will often be conditional on maintaining high standards.

The systemic undervaluing of early childhood work has left many educators apologetic about the skills of what they do, often describing themselves as 'just' an early childhood educator (Andrew, 2015). We think this does our field a disservice. Early educators need knowledge across a wide variety of disciplines, but they also need to be able to translate this knowledge clearly and effectively for beginning learners, in ways that will provide a strong foundation for what comes afterwards. As the children we work with are often having their first experience of formal education we need sophisticated pedagogical skills, because children are not habituated to schooling practices as they are in later years. This includes a range of respectful and inventive behaviour guidance techniques, driven by keen insights into the motivations of human beings. Our close connections with families means that we often need a range of social-work skills for supporting families, so their children will feel more settled. We often are required to have first aid training, including skills in asthma management and anaphylaxis responses, in order to keep young children safe and healthy. Perhaps most critically, we routinely work with large groups of children, often with disparate needs and abilities and very different backgrounds, and must draw them into positive, harmonious and creative learning communities.

All of these skills, as we mentioned earlier, take practical wisdom – the willingness to learn through daily experimentation, tweaking practices and fine-tuning them in response to the varying personalities involved in that moment. It is relational work, and emotional work, both of which tend to be undervalued in today's world; it is most definitely highly skilled work. Understanding what you have to offer the families you work with is vital, because it is at the heart of quality early education. Without understanding your own expertise, and being willing to defend what you are doing (and why), your work will be wasted. Those who have not examined their own values are simply going through the motions, and will be offering little to children and families.

Changing times, changing environments

Early childhood work has moved from the margins of education to become a central part of most educational systems. In most countries there have been large changes in the formal governance of early childhood systems, at national and regional levels. There have been significant increases in the numbers of children attending, particularly in the youngest ages, and much greater scrutiny of the nature of early childhood practices and the benefits they may be able to bring. Your work with families will vary greatly, depending on the type of setting you are in and the families you are working with, and below we will touch on some of the specific issues you will want to be aware of.

Institutional cultures and practices

Early childhood education and care encompasses an incredible range of workplaces, from forest schools and bush kindy, to kindergarten and junior primary classes in schools, and home-based childcare in both poor and wealthy countries. The role of an educator and the expectations of parents will be very different across this diverse range.

For example, in a *kōhanga reo* (language nest), you would be a Māori-speaking educator, working with children from local *whānau* (extended families), in close collaboration with parents and community elders. These are fairly intimate settings, and ones with shared bonds of language and culture. Kōhanga reo services have clear aims for nurturing cultural safety and resilience among children, and for building curriculum based on valued local knowledge, as well as wider knowledge. In this situation your role as an educator, and your cultural obligations, would be well understood by yourself and others in the community, and the biggest challenge might be dealing with the ongoing impacts of colonisation and racism on families, and the impact this could be having for children. Spiritual ties to country help to keep Māori communities cohesive, and the close involvement of Elders provides trusted leadership, and these are a source of resilience for many Indigenous communities worldwide (see also chapter 8).

In contrast, many educators will be working in larger institutions, such as primary schools or the large kindergarten services in countries such as China or Slovenia. In these settings it is impossible for educators to know all of the families, and you will be dealing with a much larger variety of families, from quite different economic backgrounds or varying religious beliefs. In this case your role as an educator is one of cultural mediator, understanding the standard secular curriculum in your country, and helping to make this meaningful to the diverse children in your classrooms. You will not be able to tailor your curriculum to a specific community, but will tend to be working from national or regional curriculum guidelines or the philosophy of your service. In doing so, your goal will be trying to build a shared sense of community among these parents, and an understanding of the secular goals of the education system. At best, when you get to know some families better, you may be able to see points of alignment between their hopes for their children and the wider curriculum. If you see that the curriculum material you are expected to work with does not meet the needs of the children in your community, then you may need to think about taking up an activist role, which we will explain more about in chapter 12.

Ethnicity, migration and belonging

We live in a global world, where there is increasing migration by families, either seeking a better life elsewhere or escaping war and persecution in their home country. Whatever the reason for migrating – and many refugees now find themselves experiencing discrimination or suspicion in their destination country – it means that your classrooms are more likely to have children from many backgrounds. Part of our work as early childhood educators is to honour children's home cultures. They will often feel strongly about these, both in feeling connected to them, but also experiencing a sense of ambivalence as they get older, in trying to negotiate their identity in relation to the dominant culture.

In thinking about culture, it is important to remember that you have one too, even if you belong to the dominant culture. It is a form of privilege to be able to pretend you don't have any cultural norms or values, and you have this privilege because your habits and values are the normative ones within your society. Becoming aware of these values will help you reflect critically on them, and the aspects of your own culture you cherish and the ones you may not. Remember also the complexities of culture for everybody. Each person has multiple identities, and our ethnicity can include things such as home language, religion, national identity, physical appearance and sometimes Indigenous status. Intersectionality, as we saw in chapter 1, means that these aspects of identity sometimes reinforce disadvantage, while at other times ameliorating it. For example, religious people will tend to have more conservative values around sexual expression, and these may be quite different from the sexual ethos of contemporary culture.

As an educator you will need to build your cultural competence, particularly in those cultures that you know are well-represented in your community. This does not mean that you should pretend to be an expert on other peoples' communities and values – of course not! What it means is trying to learn what things may (or may not, because culture is complicated) be important to families from particular cultures. For example, a family from a Muslim background may be very devout, or be very low-key about their faith. This may depend on the country they grew up in, because there are majority-Muslim nations in very different regions of the world, and with many different languages. Knowing that young girls are not required to wear hijab (usually a headscarf, but the word actually means a curtain or partition), but often do because they want to be like their mothers, can help you inquire respectfully about the expectations of the families you work with.

One noteworthy aspect of culture is how recent the family's experience of migration has been. You may believe someone is a migrant if you perceive them as being different to your own cultural background, whereas they may actually have a longer history in your country than you do. It may have been this child's grandparents or earlier ancestors who migrated, and the family may share many cultural values with you once you look past superficial differences. In modern multicultural societies – despite the structural racism that is still present in most of them – there is a tendency for views to converge around valued norms within that country. Education systems are often a part of this convergence, through giving all children a shared experience, with a particular language of instruction and a specific curriculum.

Recent migrants may feel nostalgic for their previous existence, whereas those whose families and lives are firmly entrenched within your community will often feel much less of this emotional connection to a former homeland. Some migrants will hold onto an image of their homeland and the customs they found comforting, and then experience a shock when they return years later to find that change has also happened there, making them feel like an outsider in their homeland too. Migration experiences are never easy, and remembering that will help you be sensitive to the feelings of the families you work with.

You should be aware of the increasing number of 'climate refugees' in the world, who have been forced to move as a result of famine or other impacts of climate change. This phenomenon is only going to get more serious as the effects of climate change take hold, and we will look in the next two chapters at how your work can be responsive to this situation. The significance of climate refugees is that their need to flee their homeland is a direct consequence of the resource-intensive lifestyles of those in the Minority World. We hope, therefore, that you will be prepared to take this into account when your own country is dealing with refugee challenges, and think about what you would do if your current life was made impossible by catastrophic climate impacts.

To be inclusive of all families requires a commitment from educators, and from the leadership of the service, to active communication with families whose cultures and backgrounds may be unfamiliar. We encourage you to build these sorts of deeper conversations into your introductory processes when settling children, so that parents and caregivers realise that you value their perspectives on your processes. One of the best ways to ensure your service reflects the diverse nature of your community is to employ staff members from cultural backgrounds that are well-represented in your local catchment area, including local Indigenous communities. These staff can act as cultural ambassadors for the service, providing culturally sensitive communication, and sometimes translation, in both directions. Building good relationships with the families at your

Figure 10.3 This community garden and outdoor pizza oven has been created with the school community to support the wide involvement of families in the life of the school.
Source: Andrew Plaistow, with thanks to Alberton Primary School

service is ongoing work, and will need to evolve and grow with the changing communities in your area.

Social parenting

In this section we explore *social parenting*, a term which reminds us that parenting is mostly about the social and emotional connections built up over time with children, rather than a biological connection. This is familiar to children who have grown up distant from a biological parent, through separation or adoption, and realise as adults how minimal a connection they feel with that person despite any shared genetic heritage.

For many years LGBT+ individuals and couples have raised children, and a wide variety of countries are now expanding marriage to include same-sex families. LGBT+ families have the same joys and challenges of other families, including divorce, sibling rivalry and so on. However they will often be part of queer communities as well, with distinct cultural values and community life. Respecting young children's experience of their community values is important to their wellbeing. Heterosexist ideas, such as the belief that having LGBT+ parents can be damaging to children, are increasingly being revealed as lacking evidence. Extensive reviews show that children flourish in situations where they are well-loved, and their essential needs are taken care of (Knight et al., 2017). Given the history of discrimination against LGBT+ individuals, some families will be protective of their privacy and may not immediately (or ever) share details about their personal lives or LGBT+ identities. However if they do you can accept this as a sign of trust, and belief that you will support their child within your classroom.

Some children you will work with may have become part of their family through adoption, either locally, or from another country. However don't assume that you can guess this adoption status from appearance. Children sometimes look very different from a parent, but this may just mean that their appearance is more similar to another parent you have not yet met. In fact, we advise educators to stop being concerned at all about whether children are biologically related to their current parents, as this is unlikely to be relevant to your work with them. It is a common topic of conversation within families and communities to talk about where a child inherited some particular physical feature or personal characteristic, but we urge you to be wary of such conversations. These can be confusing or hurtful to children who do not have a biological relationship to their parent but feel very strongly about their connections to that parent nonetheless.

What matter most are the child's social relationships (whom they feel most attached to in a parenting role), and their legal relationships (who has formal custody of this child). If you know this, then you can be confident that you are respecting the wishes of their legal guardians, as well as understanding their key emotional attachments. Adoptive families face many of the same challenges as any family, but there are some things to be aware of in working with them. Children who are adopted will often have been so when they were older, rather than as infants, and so will have memories of either a birth parent or a foster family. As a result, they may experience anxieties around belonging which cause them to react strongly at times when other children might be less troubled (such as a parent arriving for pick-up later than expected). Some adoptive parents describe their families as 'forever families' to help remind their children, at a visceral level, that they will be permanently loved and looked after. In some cases, adopted children may experience difficulties or impairments due to difficult early experiences, such as a severely drug-addicted birth-parent.

Lastly, be aware that you will work with children who end up in family situations that were not planned or intended, such as children being raised by a relative, a community member or a foster parent. This can happen for many reasons, such as the death of a parent, or because social services have removed a child they believed to be at risk in some way. The nature of social parenting means that some children may consider that adult to be a parent, even when that adult is resistant to the idea. This could happen when an accidental caregiver does not feel up to the responsibility or is still working through the decision to take on care of this child. Depending on your relationship with the child, you may decide to honour the child's feelings by referring to that person as a parent when talking with them in the classroom, even if you can't do so with that person present. There are times when we believe you should consider the child as your primary responsibility, and make decisions that affirm their wellbeing even when the family may disagree. For example, some educators allow children to dress in 'cross-gender' clothing, even when parents are known to disapprove of this. You may want to discuss these sorts of ethical dilemmas with colleagues, your principal or director, if you are not confident in taking this action on your own. You may, however, believe that it is your duty to support the child's rights, including rights such as the freedom of expression, as we discussed in chapter 9.

Concluding remarks

We do not believe working with parents needs to be difficult, but it does require thoughtfulness and attentiveness to the differing circumstances of others. Think about Maeve's experience in the vignette, and the ableism of the teacher in assuming someone's physical height was relevant to their learning. This educator created additional problems for a parent rather than offering support, by forcing her to explain to her child (not for the first time) that someone's efforts and attitudes are important, not their physical attributes. Knowing about the dimensions of inequality in society, and the multiple and intersecting ways they can impact on families, will help you form stronger relationships with families. These relationships will make your life as an educator easier, by reinforcing your connections to the children concerned.

Families are often our most profound connections, but also can be the source of anguish for some of us. Your role as an educator is both to support families, but also to be alert to any problems they may be facing, so that you can intervene productively on behalf of the child. Through being an educator we become an integral part of the support network of children, and often their families as well. We hope that what you have learnt in this chapter will help you to do so with tact and sensitivity.

Questions for reflection

- Which types of family do you feel most confident in working with? Why? Remember that your personal experiences may differ from others. Who do you feel less confident building relationships with? What might you do to educate yourself further about unfamiliar situations or life journeys? (Reading an autobiography, or watching a film focusing on a person's life can help you to understand different perspectives.)
- What skills will you need to be a more confident educator, in relationship to the diversity of families you will be working with? Could you practise being out of your comfort zone in your personal life, as practice for working with families? What could you do in a practical way to help you learn people's names or relationships as early as possible, or collect background information in respectful and open ways?

- What damaging assumptions might you be holding onto around gender and the sorts of attitudes and skills that people have? What have you learnt from people (of various gender identities) during your life about negotiating social relationships? How might you put those experiences into practice in your own life?

Activities for educators

- Think of a difficult situation you have been in with a parent, or a difficult conversation you have needed to have. If you still are a student, think of a conversation you hope you will never need to have, because it seems difficult. Ask a close friend to help you out, by engaging in a role-playing situation. You will be yourself, the educator, and you will explain to them the sort of situation and person you are having to deal with. Start the conversation as you would like to start it, and then have your friend respond, in ways you may not necessarily be anticipating. Be aware that this sort of role-playing can often activate emotions on both sides, despite the fact that you are 'pretending'. It can be helpful to have a third person willing to be a neutral observer, to mediate or offer additional feedback about the interaction.
- The next time you are in an educational environment, of whatever sort, take a moment to think how this might look to a parent, particularly one who is unfamiliar with education, or from outside the dominant culture. Write a list of things that might be unfamiliar or intimidating, or ways that the design or routines of the service are not clearly communicated. Now write another list, suggesting ways that these could be improved, and share it with colleagues or your site leadership. If you are currently working alone, such as in family childcare, write an action plan about how you will put these insights into practice in your own site.

Key readings

Ailwood, J. (2008). Mothers, teachers, maternalism and early childhood education and care: some historical connections. *Contemporary Issues in Early Childhood, 8*(2), 157–165.

Braun, A., Vincent, C., & Ball, S. (2008). 'I'm so much more myself now, coming back to work' – working class mothers, paid work and childcare. *Journal of Educational Policy, 23*(5), 533–548.

Lareau, A. (2003). *Unequal Childhoods: Class, Race and Family Life.* Berkeley, CA: UC Press.

Murray, S. (1998). Child care work: Intimacy in the shadows of family-life. *Qualitative Sociology, 21*(2), 149–168.

White, N., & Ottmann, J. (2016). Indigenous children, families, and early years education in Australia and Canada. In A. Farrell & I. Pramling Samuelsson (Eds), *Diversity in the Early Years: Intercultural Learning and Teaching* (pp. 102–129). South Melbourne: Oxford University Press.

Online resources

Diverse families – This article by Elizabeth Allen lists 30 children's picture books depicting a wide range of family life. https://bookriot.com/2017/04/20/theres-no-wrong-way-30-childrens-books-about-non-traditional-families/

Partnerships – This talk by Marion Wright Edelman, the founder of the Children's Defense Fund in the US, describes the importance of early childhood parent–educator partnerships. www.youtube.com/watch?v=kO4-pX6k4Cw

Resisting ableism – Short but powerful video by disabled people imagining a world as full citizens, not second-class ones. www.youtube.com/watch?v=USQeZsKEGs8&feature=youtu.be/

Further reading

Andrew, Y. (2015). Beyond professionalism: Classed and gendered capital in childcare work. *Contemporary Issues in Early Childhood, 16*(4), 305–321.

Hochschild, A. R., & Machung, A. (1989). *The Second Shift: Working Families and the Revolution at Home.* New York: Penguin.

hooks, b. (2010). *Teaching critical thinking: Practical wisdom.* New York: Routledge.

Knight, K., Stephenson, S., West, S., Delatycki, M., Jones, C., Little, M., … Oberklaid, F. (2017). The kids are OK: It is discrimination, not same-sex parents, that harms children. *Medical Journal of Australia, 9* (Onlinefirst).

Reay, D. (2000). A useful extension of Bourdieu's conceptual framework? Emotional capital as a way of understanding mothers' involvement in their children's education. *Sociological Review, 48*(4), 568–585.

Sayer, A. (2011). *Why Things Matter to People: Social Science, Values and Ethical Life.* Cambridge: Cambridge University Press.

Tisdall, E. K. M. (2012). The challenge and challenging of childhood studies? Learning from disability studies and research with disabled children. *Children and Society, 26*(3), 181–191.

Tronto, J. (1994). *Moral Boundaries: A Political Argument for an Ethic of Care.* New York: Routledge.

Uttal, L. (1996). Custodial care, surrogate care, and coordinated care: Employed mothers and the meaning of child care. *Gender and Society, 10*(3), 291–311.

11 Sustainable education for dangerous times

Figure 11.1
Source: Pixabay. Licence: Creative Commons CC0

Questions for consideration
- What do you know about climate change, and the ways human activities have accelerated this in the last century or two? How does this impact on you emotionally or spiritually?
- What environmental issues are most noticeable in your local community (pollution, habitat loss, coastal erosion, erratic weather, increasing drought, etc.)?
- What responsibility do you feel, as an educator, to develop an ecological mindset with young children?

Vignette from practice

Lukas, a preschooler in a rural kindergarten, borrowed one of the metal spades from the sandpit, to try digging up a patchy part of the grassed area near the fence, as part of a game about buried treasure. One of the educators noticed him doing this, and had a quick discussion with the other team members in the room.

'Should we allow this, and perhaps make a regular digging patch, or encourage him to dig elsewhere?' Rather than shutting it down, they decided this was a low-use part of the grassed area, and could be used in different ways.

As more children joined in, the hole got bigger and bigger, and one of the other children said, 'let's make a pond!'

This captured everyone's imagination. Why not make a pond? Over the coming days and weeks, with the help of various parents, and a particularly handy grandparent, the pond took shape. Given its depth, and the local play-space regulations, it was necessary to put a wide metal grille just under the surface of the pond, to avoid accidental drowning. This was fixed into the cement lining, constructed by adults, but with the children watching and giving suggestions. Eventually, after months of work, the pond was finally ready. It had a viewing platform reaching over the water, with a perspex panel for peeking below, lots of planting, and a solar-power pump, to keep the water aerated and circulating.

During all this time, there had been much discussion about who would live in the pond. While a shark would have been exciting, given all the 'pirate' play that had been going on, it was admitted that these would need saltwater, and perhaps a bit more space. Instead, some local native fish and two turtles were added, much to the excitement of the children. A pond-opening party was held, with all the families invited to witness the hard work that had been put it.

Introduction: Our own childhoods

Many of us experienced childhood in earlier decades, where climate change was not as widely spoken about. Most of us grew up in times when technologies such as smartphones were not yet a feature of everyday life. Usually our childhood days were less tightly monitored, and fears for our safety were less acute. As a result, our childhoods may have involved spending considerable time playing outdoors, unsupervised. Ideally, we developed some sense of connection to the natural world, perhaps being curious about bugs, growing vegetables or swimming in rivers or the ocean.

Childhood today, particularly in the Minority World, is often much more divorced from the natural world. The majority of the human population now lives in urban centres, often with little access to green space. With rising wealth, children have more commercial toys and games, reducing their desire to explore natural spaces. Some parents actively discourage their children from nature play, perceiving this as dirty, or not particularly educational.

We believe that there are many good reasons for early childhood educators to re-engage with the natural world. Aside from the valuable learning that

Figure 11.2 This young child is being given the opportunity to explore a local watercourse, and ponder the mysterious role of water in human life.
Source: Pamela Leach. Used with permission

occurs outdoors, there are health benefits from children becoming more active, and social benefits from developing a more thoughtful understanding of local ecosystems (Warden, 2015). Ultimately, we believe that children need to be taught that human beings are an integral part of the systems of the earth, for good or ill, and must manage our collective impacts accordingly. This chapter will help you think about how to do this.

The elephant in the room – global climate change

In ordinary times, we might see education for sustainability as a luxury, or an add-on to an otherwise flourishing educational setting. However these are not ordinary times. The world is facing the consequences of catastrophic climate alteration, with unknowable consequences for our ability to survive, to produce enough food or prevent the sorts of sea level rise that will make many cities uninhabitable. These are scary times. Inaction is no longer an option, which is why the majority of the world's countries have signed up to the Paris agreement (United Nations, 2015). This agreement attempts to limit the damage being done to planet's ecosystems by our transport, buildings and consumption, which emit more greenhouse gases (see breakout box) than the atmosphere can safely manage.

Greenhouses gases and the carbon budget

Greenhouse gases are those gases which accumulate in the atmosphere, trapping heat on earth more rapidly than ever in the geological past, and so increasing what is known as the greenhouse effect – global warming. The most well-known of these gases is carbon dioxide (CO_2), because it is the most abundant, and is produced by many of our human activities, such as burning fossil fuels for energy, or many of our industrial and agricultural processes. However there are other gases which also have an impact, such as methane (CH_4), nitrous oxide (N_2O) and even water vapour (H_2O). Some of these gases, although present in smaller quantities, trap heat more effectively and so need to be reduced urgently.

This simplest way to think about the challenge of climate change is through the idea of a carbon budget. Scientists can work out, with reasonable accuracy, the amount of carbon dioxide and other gases we think we can release into the atmosphere, without severely damaging the planetary life-support system. If we divide this total carbon budget for the earth by the total population (around seven and a half billion people, at the end of 2017) then we can come up with a personal carbon budget for each human being. This is the total amount of carbon dioxide you can generate, across all of your energy, water, food, travel and consumer purchases each year, without using up more than your fair share of our collective global safety net. At the moment this individual budget is 2300kg of CO_2 per year (Atmosfair, 2017). Most citizens of Minority World countries far exceed their carbon budgets, but the effects of climate change are felt unfairly by those who do not, particularly the global poor.

This is the elephant in the room because we cannot avoid it, but we want to. The reality is that most of us, particularly those in the Minority World, will need to change how we live and how we think about the world. The good news is educators are well-placed to make a difference, helping orient young children to ways of living in the world that are simpler, wiser and in line with the carrying capacity of the globe (Raworth, 2017). As we will see in chapter 12, there is always a need for activism and we know that most of you chose to become educators to have a positive impact in the world.

Managing change – thinking flexibly and creatively

One of our advantages, in the early childhood sector, is that the children we are working with are already creative and flexible thinkers, with a concern for fairness, and an intense curiosity about the world around them. They have all the right attitudes to help in the struggle to achieve a world of climate justice, and as educators we simply need to give them the tools to think and act differently from generations before them.

There are many changes happening as a result of global warming, including increasing health risks, which will impact disproportionately on young children. Warmer temperatures mean the increasing spread of infectious diseases through vectors such as greater mosquito activity, as well as the direct impacts of heat stress itself. We are concerned about public health, but we need to be worrying about planetary health, which underpins the health of all creatures. The impacts of climate change are exacerbated when children are living in poverty, as we will see in the next section. Julie Davis (2015) notes the tendency to question whether children of early childhood age really need to learn about these serious global issues, but her book explains clearly why this learning is needed, and what educators can do about this.

We will all need to embrace change, even those of us who appreciate routine and reliability. Fortunately, many of these changes will be good for everyone. A world that embraces climate justice will be more equal, will nurture natural environments, will value clean air and rivers, and will be a world where communities learn to work together rather than compete. This may be the world we have all been wanting but were not born into ourselves. We can make it happen, and we know what steps we need to take to make this happen (Monbiot, 2017).

Climate change and inequality

As sociologists, one of the most important things we need to understand about climate change is that its effects are already being felt around the world, and they impact hardest on those who have the least. As with other global issues such as pollution, the world's poorest communities tend to be exposed to the worst effects. One of the most useful theoretical ideas to understand this is Bourdieu's (1990) concept of *distance from necessity*. Those who can easily meet all their basic needs have the luxury of forgetting that they rely – just as much as anyone else – on the growing of food, the availability of clean water and adequate shelter. Most of those living in the Minority World have this distance from necessity, but this is not true in places like Bangladesh or Kiribati. Countries like these are particularly vulnerable to sea level rise, because much of their land is barely above sea level. Most of their populations have very little distance from necessity, and may already struggle to meet basic needs. Any changes, such as human-induced global warming, impact severely on their ability to survive and meet these fundamental needs.

One of the most visible impacts of climate change is the increasing intensity of storms around the world, which are a direct consequence of warmer sea temperatures. While Hurricane Katrina became well-known because it devastated a famous city (New Orleans) in a wealthy country (USA), there have been many similarly damaging storms, in places like Haiti and the Philippines, which have had severe consequences for local populations. For those Majority World countries, many poor people died or lost whatever security they had as a result of those storms, with long-term consequences for their lives. Poverty makes climate change a disaster, rather than an inconvenience. Even in New Orleans, the impacts of racial inequality meant that those whose lives were most affected were African-American people, especially those who were poorest. Any disadvantages, of race, of class and even gender (think of the many single mothers living on low incomes), make climate change a much greater threat. If we care about justice, then we cannot ignore climate change and its impacts (Hage, 2017). Similarly, if we care about the environment then we must take into account the differing capacities of people to cope with losses. People on low incomes cannot usually afford items like solar panels or better insulation, because of the importance of paying for absolute essentials like food or housing. We need to rethink our economic systems so that neither of these concerns are forgotten, as Kate Raworth (2017) explains so vividly and effectively.

Nurturing biophilia

As educators, one useful concept to think about is *biophilia*, a word which describes the love of nature. In educating for sustainability, this is where we can start. We can build on children's love of nature, and if necessary, counter any negative messages they may be receiving about the natural world being dangerous or dirty. Of course it sometimes can be, if you live near a polluted river or in a country with poisonous creatures, but the answer is not to avoid nature entirely. As educators we know these are all opportunities to learn more about how the natural world works, and to help children learn to manage the risks they may encounter in nature.

Nature play is increasingly recognised as a vital activity for children, and a rich contributor to their learning. One advantage of nature play is that it can be accessed at low cost. Any patch of dirt or waste land can offer opportunities for learning, if you know how to look for them. One rarely noticed aspect of the natural world is its complexity, and the irregularity and chaotic nature of outdoor spaces. As educators we want our children to learn how to deal with the unexpected, and this is always a possibility outside, with changes in the weather, and new insect and plant species to be encountered. The textures and sensory impact of materials indoors are fairly limited, but outdoors we can find a wide diversity of smells, textures, colours, sounds and even tastes. Given that we have the most nerve-endings in our hands, our feet and in our mouths, is it surprising that young children want to go barefoot, or put things into their mouth as part of their investigations? One of the saddest aspects of global warming is the loss of ecological diversity, as many species face extinction due to the encroachment of humans into their environments, or the speed of change making adaptation to warmer temperatures difficult. The earth is a rich environment, full of many marvels and wonders. There is good reason to want to preserve this complexity.

Young children do not have any difficulty feeling biophilia, and experience wonder at many things they encounter in the natural world, such as a crunchy autumn leaf. Children with disabilities are no different, but are often not included actively in nature play. We believe it is necessary to give children access to nature, and encouragement to engage with it, whatever their physical or mental abilities. While some things we want children to learn take effort, there is usually no need to persuade children of the appeal of the natural world. Most children have a sensitivity to other creatures, from a household pet to the insects that tend to wander into our classrooms. In helping nurture these connections we can help them to notice that these smaller creatures have lives all of their own, and that as much as possible we can observe them in their daily existence without interference or harm.

Thinking sustainably

For most of human history, the world has seemed so big, and its resources so inexhaustible, that people have been able to ignore questions about waste and resource use. In fact, as we are starting to realise, humans may have been influencing the climate for far longer than we imagined. As Jared Diamond (2005) explains, deforestation has been causing local climate change in places right across the globe and throughout history. Societies have collapsed, and some cultures have ceased to exist because they did not understand the connections between their actions and the response of their local ecosystems.

To think sustainably, we have to start to make the connections that many of our human ancestors have been ignoring. This is hard work and most of us would rather not do it. But without it we are risking all the beauty of the earth and the happiness of human beings. The stakes are high, but we know the way forward. First, we must hold in mind that 'everything comes from somewhere and everything goes somewhere', an aphorism which is as true for environmental flows as it is for economic ones (Godley & Lavoie, 2007). This is true for water, for food, for energy – for any resource we use on a daily basis. To think sustainably is to source these with the least impact, and make the most of them by minimising waste. This includes disposing of them in ways that allow them to contribute to a functioning ecosystem rather than damaging it.

The simplest example – and one that is fundamental to all our lives on this planet – is water. We must find potable water somewhere and this may come from a well, a river, a watertank or a reservoir. Do you know where your drinking water comes from? How can you make sure this water is kept free from contamination? For large-scale reservoirs, local authorities usually try to ensure they are surrounded by forests, which help slow run-off and the sediment that comes with it, as well as helping to purify the incoming groundwater. With a rainwater tank this might involve ensuring the roof areas which supply this tank are relatively free of leaf litter or bird droppings. In collecting this water for use, do we have suitable containers or pipes that will not pollute the water in unintended ways, as lead piping can do or certain sorts of plastics? If we move onto the second part of the aphorism, to where does this water go? Are there ways we can recycle our water use, to get multiple uses from it, such as using 'grey water' from washing or showers to water garden areas? Are we mindful of the sorts of contaminants that we may be adding, such as the products we use (dishwashing liquids, shampoos) or the materials we might be tempted to put into our sewer systems. With contaminated water (sometimes called 'black water'), are we able to treat this in ways that do not add to our environmental problems, and even purify it enough to make it safely drinkable? Composting toilets and reed-bed systems are accessible ways to manage human wastes at a local level, while returning fertility to the soil and maintaining the drinkability of groundwater. With rivers we need to think about how to manage agricultural or industrial uses upstream to ensure these do not contaminate water for those further down the river system that rely on this water for drinking. This is often a difficult issue when water sources cross national or state borders (as can be the case for rivers or underground aquifers) because this requires shared management of this valuable resource to ensure it is kept clean and shared fairly, as we saw in the discussion of *the commons* in chapter 7.

All of the things that we use, such as water, food, energy and air, can be subject to the same sort of analysis about their origins and destinations. For educators, each of these can be the subject of an inquiry unit or series of investigations with different levels of complexity. Even with babies we can be talking simply about elements of the water cycle, as they engage in water play, or as we pour them a drink of water. It is even better if these processes are visible at your service, such as installing a water tank which the children can see in operation and use water from.

Figure 11.3 This school aquaculture project raises fish and freshwater crayfish for food, with the polluted water cleaned up by filtering through an outdoor bed raising herbs for human consumption, before being recycled into the tanks.
Source: Andrew Plaistow, with thanks to Alberton Primary School

Pedagogies for sustainability

In this section, we will look at some of the tools you can use as an educator to build a rich set of sustainable practices within your service. Most of these are very accessible, and can be included immediately in any setting. We are confident that these practices will not just enrich children's lives but your own as well, and hopefully connect you more meaningfully to your local places and ecosystems.

Most of these draw on the traditions of *education for sustainability*, whose beginnings lie in events such as the UN Conference on Environment and Development held in Rio, in 1992. Section 36 of Agenda 21, which came out of this conference, focuses on education about environmental issues (United Nations, 1992). At the time it was optimistically assumed that knowing more about environmental issues would lead automatically to behaviour change. As sociologists we know that this is often not the case, and we need not just to teach *about* the environment and *in* the environment, but also *for* the environment (Davis, 2015, 24). We hope that you will work to include all three types of education for sustainability in your own classrooms and become activist educators, an idea we will pick up again in chapter 12. Sustainability needs to be a priority for all in society, from governments and policy-makers, to services and educators, and of course children and their families.

Nurturing ecological identities

Ann Pelo is an experienced early childhood educator who wanted to take a break from the intensities of teaching. She was going to do some non-teaching work, but then friends of hers needed a caregiver for their one-year-old child, and she decided that this was an interesting opportunity to spend some time educating outside her comfort zone. She asked her friends whether they would let her see whether it was possible to nurture their child's ecological identity very purposefully, by spending most of each day outdoors. Pelo's friends agreed, and the result was a life-changing year for both educator and young child, as they explored the natural world together.

Pelo brought all her teaching skills and experience to this task, helping the child to engage meaningfully with every aspect of the natural world, whatever the weather. In doing so she reflected critically on the sorts of practices that were most useful in developing this ecological sensitivity. There is much to be learnt from this year of exploration, some of which you might expect, and much which will surprise you. Pelo (2013) suggests that there are four key learning dispositions we must acquire as part of an ecological identity: being curious, paying attention, opening our hearts and being modest and humble. The last of these is particularly important and perhaps surprising, because it goes to the heart of the changes we need to make as a human species in response to our growing impacts on the planet. Being humble means acknowledging that we are not smart enough to know the full consequences of our interventions in the natural world. We must learn how to make minimal interventions to ensure that our interventions work with rather than against biological systems, such as developing composting systems which mimic effective natural processes. She also discusses a whole range of practices that are important in helping children connect with nature, whose details can be found in her book (Pelo, 2013). Some will be challenging to early childhood educators because they are not part of our usual repertoire of skills. For example she recommends practising silence, encouraging yourself and children to spend time observing and engaging without the need to provide explanations. These explanations may come later but often they work to short-circuit children's curiosity, and prevent them from making connections themselves, which is more valuable learning. Another interesting practice is the idea of creating rituals – regular activities that help you to engage meaningfully with the natural world, and to feel a deep connection to a particular place. They can be as simple as making a specific time each morning to be present with children in your outdoor areas. This could involve noticing what has changed since the previous day, perhaps keeping a diary or asking a child to make a drawing each day as part of the ritual.

There are those working in early childhood who will find this challenging, because they work in services that do not have access to outdoor areas or any tradition of including outdoor play in their programmes, such as services in countries like Singapore or Turkey. The specific histories of some early childhood systems have made indoor learning activities a priority, whereas in other places the pressure for land may be too great to make this possible. Wherever you are, it is still possible to do this, even in small ways. One great method is creating a 'bug garden' with the children. This can be done through finding or reusing an old fish tank or clear plastic container, and lining the base with gravel, some dirt, and whatever local weed or grass species you can uproot from a patch of waste ground. Children will be happy to bring in donations of weeds they have found. Once this is 'planted up', with perhaps a tiny dish of water included, and some form of netting stretched over the top, you are ready to find insects to include in this habitat. Children can bring these in as they find them, in their houses, on their route to your childcare setting or wherever. This set up, at minimal cost, can help children observe a great deal of insect behaviours up close, as well as developing skills at caring for other creatures. Can you, for example, have a discussion about how long it is fair to keep a particular creature in this restricted habitat, and whether they appear to be flourishing or suffering by being there? Do some creatures impact on others, and how do they do this? What inter-relationships are there in this mini-ecosystem that you can observe and learn more about? Just as children learned to solve human problems in chapter 9, how might they begin to learn how to resolve emerging problems they see within this habitat?

Joined up thinking

When we are thinking and educating sustainably, we need to be remembering that all our resources *come from somewhere*, and *go somewhere*. So if we want to teach with integrity in this area, we need everything we do to be giving the same message. This is most obvious when acquiring resources for your programme. You will need to ask where they come from, how they have been produced and what materials they are made from. Sustainability is also about *social sustainability*, and the longer lasting social connections created by places and objects.

> ### Thinking about materials in detail
>
> Whenever you source materials, it is important to investigate carefully the supply-chain for the material to try and be sure that its sustainability claims add up. We tend to assume wood is a sustainable material in that it is a renewable resource. It is better for this wood to come from sustainably managed mixed-species plantations, on land that is not useable for other purposes, rather than newly logged 'old growth' rainforests in less wealthy countries (Diamond, 2005). Similarly, while you might think it is best to avoid using plastic products, because the fossil fuels they are made from contribute to climate change, if you can find products which use a large proportion of recycled plastic, you are helping create a market for a more *closed loop* manufacturing process, in which the same material might be made into multiple products over its lifetime. This is a complex area, and we do not expect you to be able to investigate every material you use in detail. Nonetheless, the internet and social media allow us to research the environmental claims made by companies more easily, so we can support businesses which are working to minimise their environmental impacts.

You will need to think about the new acquisitions, and about how they might be used in your service, in multiple ways. For example, it is possible to buy small kits, mostly made of plastic and with a tiny solar panel, to demonstrate 'sustainable' energy. However, these are often expensive and very limited in their play-value. They are likely to be made out of 'new' plastic, a non-renewable resource, rather than using recycled materials. When they break or reach the end of their limited usefulness you will need to know if they can be separated easily into the different types of plastic for recycling, or be mended easily. Despite the 'ecological theme' of this resource, this might not be a useful item to acquire for your classroom.

Loose parts play

Simon Nicholson (1971) first articulated the idea and importance of loose parts, both in the wider community, but also specifically in children's play. He saw this as a means of making creativity accessible to everyone, and contributing to a more equal and enjoyable educational system. This is a useful idea, and even more useful in a time of resource constraint and environmental awareness. While loose parts play is possible with construction sets, these are limited because children cannot design or redesign the pieces themselves. Increasingly, to make them more toy-like, construction sets such as Lego are moving towards much less versatile and more highly structured pieces and thus limiting the creative input of children. A more useful loose parts play involves waste or repurposed materials, such as buttons, pieces of wood, strawbales, cardboard, fabric or almost anything you can think of, including materials like water or earth. The advantage with these is that they can be used in many different ways and in different contexts, forming an ever-developing palette of educational materials.

The advantage of loose parts, unlike conventional toys like puzzles or board games, is that it does not matter if parts get lost or broken. No one piece is vital to the whole play experience, and many are easily mended or reused in a different way. They also invite children's creativity and curiosity, causing them to wonder how they might be used, building on the dispositions of an ecological identity. They can be used in endlessly different ways, allowing children's increasingly sophisticated skills to develop along with the materials. Most of them are cheap or easily available, so there can be plenty of materials available, no matter how many children wish to use them or work with them, encouraging social play without conflict.

Loose parts play is an example of joined-up thinking, because it enables educators to consider the origins of our resources, by reusing and reimagining objects and materials. It minimises waste and expense because each part is not critical, and different sorts of materials can be combined to create new activities, models or art works. Lastly, loose parts play considers the waste stream, rescuing many items from this but also allowing for recycling or composting of materials at the end of their useful lives. From a sociological perspective this is an education strategy that is equitable, because it does not privilege wealthier children, who might have most access to technology or popular toys. It may advantage those children without economic privilege, who have generally needed to develop their creativity more strongly in response to less well-resourced home environments.

The turtle pond

In the vignette at the start of the chapter, we saw some other elements of joined up thinking. The children were allowed the agency to initiate a project, and included in most of the work and all the discussions about how this should be done. It was an environmental project, creating a richer ecosystem out of an unused patch of land, which was mostly compacted dirt. It allowed for a great deal of environmental learning, as the details of the pond and its inhabitants were discussed, investigated and then observed. Children were supported in their biophilia, being allowed to interact extensively with soil, water, plants and the creatures that lived in or visited the pond, including birds. It was made from largely sustainable local materials, such as earth, or wood. The concrete was a much more resource-intense material, and could have been compared with rubber pond-liner or bentonite clay lining, in evaluating its environmental impacts. The solar panel connected to the pond fountain directly, providing a direct and visible link to the sun's power, providing ongoing useful learning about renewable energy, as well as pond aeration for the inhabitants.

No project is perfect, and the pond was not situated in a naturally low spot which would have accumulated its own water, given its origins as a game of pirate treasure hunting. Building in a system to have the pond fill from rainfall on nearby roof surfaces might have helped build a clearer picture of the water cycle for children, particularly with ways to drain off excess water, perhaps through an often-dry stream bed. Although well-loved and respected by those children who made it, the pond ecosystem experienced an eco-catastrophe of its own, with a visiting child emptying a container of bubble mixture into the pond, killing the fish and many of the plants. This was a useful learning experience for the group in how much easier it is to destroy living systems than it is to create or nurture them.

Kitchen gardens

Gardens have a long history in early childhood, with Fröbel including gardening as one of the activities for children in his early kindergartens. Many schools and preschools have established food gardens with their children, including fruit trees and vegetable patches. The importance of these pedagogically is that children get to witness and be involved in the entire food cycle, from growing to eating to composting scraps, helping to them to understand this vital biological process. This activity helps nurture children's biophilia, particularly if the garden can encourage beneficial insect predators, though minimising the use of artificial fertilisers and other chemical products. Gardening is an activity familiar to many families you will work with, and you will easily find people able to volunteer time to help with this activity, including many with considerable expertise. Importantly, our kitchen gardens reflect our particular food cultures, as discussed in chapter 8. Gardens can be a non-threatening way to help families and children connect across cultures, through growing plants or fruit that are part of the traditional foods of families or cultural groups in your settings. (See Figure 11.4.)

Risk can be liberating

Many children love to embrace risks because this sort of play can be exhilarating, particularly in the company of other children. Children enjoy testing their limits, and are less weighed down by fear than many adults. One of the beautiful things about outdoor environments for young children is that they are not too tightly controlled, unlike indoors. There might be sharp objects, poisonous insects, steep inclines and other hazards – all very exciting! We now realise that an important part of children's learning involves experimenting with risk, and that something may be lost when we protect children too much. Helen Little (2012) and her colleagues explored the attitudes to risk of early

Figure 11.4 This childcare site is making the most of a generous yard by growing a range of fruit trees, as well as vegetables in raised beds. Children practise their gardening skills, and use the produce in their cooking activities.
Source: Yarrow Andrew, with thanks to Flinders University Childcare Centre

childhood educators from two contexts, Australia and Norway. They found that, although both groups of educators could see the value in this play, the differing discourses of child safety in each country impacted significantly on the support for risky play. These sorts of cultural differences, including the impact of over-zealous safety regulations, are likely to have ongoing impacts on children's experiences and attitudes in regard to risk.

Wherever you work, it is important to understand and evaluate the likely risks of children's activities. We want children to feel a sense of excitement in stretching themselves or exploring their fears, but we also have a professional responsibility to minimise unnecessary injury. Talking children through the activities they wish to try, and asking them to engage in problem-solving about risky endeavours, helps them to learn the skills they need to evaluate risks in and beyond the classroom. We believe risky play is particularly valuable for children with disabilities, whose lives are often unnecessarily restricted because of the worries of adults around them. A child who is blind, who uses a wheelchair or who has Down syndrome will be just as likely to learn from the thrills of risky play. Building their skills in risk awareness alongside their peers helps them to become resilient and get a sense of their own capabilities, whatever their level of impairment.

Forest schools and beyond

Drawing on the discussion about nurturing ecological identities and the idea of biophilia, we see the emerging movement of 'forest' schools and preschools as an educational response to this need. These educational experiments began in Norway, where there has been a long history of preserving existing forests, and of community access to these forests, even on private land (this is known as the 'right to roam'). This existing cultural attachment to *friluftsliv* (free air life) led to the establishment of schools and preschools which are situated in forests (Knight, 2013). Their main work is always conducted outdoors, with only minimal shelters for the worst weather or specific activities. These have proved to be very successful in nurturing children's adventurousness and their knowledge of wild spaces. These forest schools are being explored in other countries, often as add-ons to existing programmes. This means that children get the benefits of a day or an afternoon outdoors each week, with the potential to expand this further as the benefits become apparent.

We see these as offering a valuable challenge to educators working in settings where there is more restricted access to natural landscapes. It is incredibly valuable for children to be in places which are conspicuously not 'for humans' but are the habitat of plants, animals and insects whose lives and purposes may be mysterious to us. Rich ecosystems encourage children to wonder about these lives and their interconnections, and understand how they themselves are part of these ecosystems, and potentially disruptive of them. Where possible we encourage you to create access to this sort of experience for children, in the settings in which you find yourselves. This might be through allowing a part of the outdoor area to become wild, planting only local plant life, and allowing these to grow freely once established. Even better would be to establish a connection with a nearby patch of woodland, forest or bushland to which your groups could undertake regular excursions. Doing so repeatedly helps children build a sense of connection, as well as noticing ongoing change due to the seasons or human disturbance. Ensuring that you visit these sites with only basic equipment that might be useful (e.g. magnifying glasses, cameras, guidebooks) ensures that children are not distracted from the rich play and exploration that is possible in natural environments.

We see this immersive form of nature play as a way to extend on many important aspects of learning right across your curriculum. For example, building compassion for insects (through choosing not to destroy them or their homes) helps generate conversations about how we can be respectful of all creatures, including other human beings. We do this by talking about the things we might share even with an insect, like the desire for community, the need for water and food or enjoyment of sunlight. In doing so try to avoid any tendency to anthropomorphise other creatures. This is a common reaction but can prevent us from understanding and noticing how differently they behave. Sustainability work can be an opportunity to deepen children's emotional awareness, as many children will not have much experience of the natural world and may react with fear or disgust in response to natural phenomena. Helping them move through these reactions (such as fears of spiders or snakes) through gradual exposure and increased knowledge frees them to enjoy and learn from natural environments.

Concluding remarks

We believe that young children have a vital stake in a safe and stable climate, and will benefit from growing up understanding the complexities of ecosystems and our human place within these. This is becoming recognised at a more formal level, with many countries, such as Korea, Australia and Sweden, including sustainable practices as part of their early childhood curriculum documents (Davis, 2015, 21). We have given you some frameworks for thinking about these issues, as well as some practical strategies for engaging in this work with young children.

The threat of climate change is an invitation to the human community to learn new ways of relating to the world, rather than the extractive-exploitative paradigm that has been common within the neoliberal worldview. One thing we can do about this often overwhelming issue is to support young children in developing these new ways, through supporting their development of an ecological identity (Pelo, 2013). By being honest about some of the damaging practices humans have created, we can invite them to join us in becoming 'problem-solvers and solution-seekers' (Davis, 2015, 23), who will grow up understanding not just what is wrong, but why we must do things differently. The earth is a wondrous place, full of self-repairing and intricate ecosystems. These continue to support abundant life, despite the damage we have inflicted on them. The planet has nurtured humankind for many millennia – it is time we returned the favour.

Questions for reflection

- Climate change raises fundamental questions for us about how we live our lives, and the ways that others might be affected, even if we are not. What feelings did this bring up for you (anger – sadness – irritation – hopefulness)? How might you use those feelings constructively to reflect on your own experiences and capabilities in regard to teaching for sustainability?
- It helps to have a working definition of what you will be trying to achieve as an educator, in terms of sustainability. Formulating your own statement about what you believe can be a good way to start. What does sustainability mean

to you? What language used in this chapter has helped you understand these concepts? What language might you use with the children you work with? We like the pithy summary made by a young person from Australia – 'enough for all forever' (quoted in Davis, 2015, 10). How would you describe it?

Activities for educators

- Start a project with children to implement a more sustainable form of technology in your educational setting. This might be a water tank, some solar photovoltaic panels or a basic solar hot water heater. It could involve putting in a new window or skylight, to avoid the need for more electric lighting. Make sure that this is a learning activity throughout. Who could you ask to come and help with this? How can you investigate which changes will be most beneficial in your environment? Think about the problem as widely as possible, and make sure your solution does not have unintended sideeffects. Who will manage the technology once it is in place? Make sure the children are included in this management, and share the knowledge widely with them, with families, and with colleagues, to ensure that everyone feels confident in its use (this is a form of educational sustainability). How can you use your experience with this type of sustainable upgrade to help others? Do families want to do a similar thing at home? Can you share your experience with other early childhood settings in your local area? Remember to use the whole process as a learning experience, including any mistakes that you make, or problems that occur while implementing it. Environmental changes often require resourcefulness, and children enjoy thinking up solutions to problems, as we saw in chapter 9.
- Have you ever examined your carbon/ecological footprint? Searching for carbon footprint calculators online will bring up a range of tools for helping you evaluate your impact on the planet. There are even ones for children to use themselves. Some of these calculators show you how many planets would be needed, if every person on the earth had the same lifestyle as you. This can be a useful reminder of how wealthy you are in global terms, even if early childhood educators are not well paid generally. Make time to do a climate audit of your life, even if this feels scary. Get a friend to help you, if some of the questions around energy use look like they will be tricky. This sort of information can support you to live more simply yourself, but also to change practices at work to minimise environmental impacts there. We can all make a difference!
- What areas of environmental knowledge do you feel ignorant about? What is stopping you from understanding this better? There are many areas of knowledge around sustainability that can be challenging, such as the economic issues that drive damaging practices. Sometimes the things we are most tempted to avoid thinking about are the ones we most need to learn about. Make an agreement with an early childhood colleague (or group of colleagues) to investigate this issue further, perhaps through a reading group

or watching a video together. Talk about this together, exploring how you might put these new ideas into practice in your home or working life.

Key readings

Davis, J. (2015). What is early childhood education for sustainability and why does it matter? In J. Davis (Ed.), *Young Children and the Environment* (pp. 7–31). Port Melbourne: Cambridge University Press.

Monbiot, G. (2017). *Out of the Wreckage: A New Politics for an Age of Crisis*. London: Verso.

Pelo, A. (2013). *The Goodness of Rain: Developing an Ecological Identity in Young Children*. Redmond: Exchange Press.

Raworth, K. (2017). *Doughnut Economics: Seven Ways to Think like a 21st-Century Economist*. London: Random House.

Warden, C. (2015). *Learning with Nature: Embedding Outdoor Practice*. London: SAGE

Online resources

Earth charter – This children's version of this document offers seeks to engage children in these important principles of sustainability and peace. www.littleearthcharter.org/

Iearn – This sites connects educators and students worldwide in educational collaborations which help the planet. https://iearn.org/

Doughnut Economics – This video is a talk by Kate Raworth about her progressive and sustainable economic proposals www.youtube.com/watch?v=CqJL-cM8gb4

Further reading

Atmosfair. (2017). Project standards: Atmosfair carbon offsetting project. Retrieved from www.atmosfair.de/en/zulassung_und_standards

Bourdieu, P. (1990). The scholastic point of view. *Cultural Anthropology, 5*(4), 380–391.

Diamond, J. (2005). *Collapse: How Societies Choose to Fail or Survive*. Camberwell: Penguin.

Godley, W., & Lavoie, M. (2007). *Monetary Economics: An Integrated Approach to Credit, Money, Income, Production and Wealth*. Basingstoke: Palgrave.

Hage, G. (2017). *Is Racism an Environmental Threat? Debating Race*. Cambridge: Polity Press.

Knight, S. (2013). *Forest school and Outdoor Learning in the Early Years* (2nd ed.). London: SAGE.

Little, H., Sandseter, E., & Wyver, S. (2012). Early childhood teachers' beliefs about children's risky play in Australia and Norway. *Contemporary Issues in Early Childhood, 13*(4), 300–316.

Nicholson, S. (1971). How NOT to cheat children: The theory of loose parts. *Landscape Architecture, 62*(1), 30–34.

United Nations (1992). *Agenda 21: UN Conference on Environment and Development*. Rio de Janeiro: United Nations Department of Economic and Social Affairs Retrieved from www.un.org/esa/sustdev/agenda21.htm.

United Nations (2015). *Paris Agreement*. Paris: United Nations Framework Convention on Climate Change.

12 Changing the world

Figure 12.1
Source: Pixabay. Licence: Creative Commons CC0

Questions for consideration
- As a voter, do you know your chosen political party's policies on early childhood education, and on the balance between children's rights and those of parents? How might you engage with your party to change or improve their policies? Are your concerns serious enough to consider changing your vote?
- How does your society treat children? Are they valued at home and in the wider society? How are children's needs recognised, by businesses, government or in societal infrastructure?

- How democratic is your own educational site? How are children involved in decision-making? In what ways could you expand their decision-making contributions?

Vignette from practice

Out in the playground it had been a more than usually accident-prone day, with a number of children needing minor first aid. Two friends, Keesha and Anna, in their first year at school, had gone to the school nurse to get a bandaid, having grazed their knees getting tangled up while running holding hands. Safely bandaged up, they were admiring their matching bandaids, when they realised that Keesha's showed up more vividly on her darker skin than on Anna's lighter skin, something Anna was impressed by.

When they told their teacher, Kye, back in class about this, Kye realised this was a good opportunity for some activism. Kye explained about 'flesh-coloured' bandaids, and how these were only made in one basic shade, which tended to match lighter coloured skin.

'That's not fair', Barkhado said. Barkhado's family is from Somalia, and he could see the bandaids didn't match his skin at all.

'You're right' said Kye. 'What should we do about it?'. There were many suggestions, from 'Make our own!' to 'Ask them to make bandaids in lots of skin colours!' While some of the group decided to make their own bandaids using materials from the maker-space, Kye sat down with some others to write a letter to the company that made them. Having asked Keesha and Anna to go back to the nurse and find out which company made them – they came back proudly with the empty box, which was helpful, allowing a demonstration of some of the information on packaging. Having located the website, they found a complaints form to fill in.

There were lots of good suggestions, but after much discussion they kept the message pretty simple, explaining that it's unfair to have bandaids that match some kids and not others, and to ask for skin colours that matched everyone. Kye asked Barkhado to press the submit button on the form, in recognition of his contribution to their action. Everyone was excited about the thought of special bandaids for everyone, but Kye was not so sure.

About a month later (Keesha said it felt like 'forever!'), they finally got a reply from the company. This said, 'We have received your request, but do not believe this is a problem. We will be mailing some see-through bandaids to your school, which you should receive in 3–5 working days.'

Kye knew the children were disappointed, but felt it was a useful lesson to learn about persistence, and a reminder that not everyone listens and understands.

(Inspired by Derman-Sparks, 1989, 80)

Introduction: Making change

In this final chapter of our journey together, we look at what it means to become an activist. This involves putting together all the sociological knowledge you have gained from previous chapters, and working out what this means for you, in your setting and in this moment. What do you need to be doing, to make the world a better place for children? What issues are important to you and to your local community?

What do we mean by activism?

Those who have never thought of themselves as activists might find this term a bit confronting, but it doesn't need to be. Some people may believe their role includes advocacy on behalf of children. Advocacy is important, but often implies speaking out, without necessarily making change. There are many issues we might want to address in our sector, or in the wider world. An activist mindset says that these are not someone else's problem or the government's problem, but the responsibility of all of us, as Ann Pelo and Fran Davidson (2000) have demonstrated so effectively.

To be active might involve anything from protesting locally about a tree being cut down outside your school or preschool, to trying to do something at a global scale, such as helping the lives of refugee children. Whether big or small, activism involves making change in the world, speaking up and thinking hard about where you invest your time and energy. Like most of our educational work it involves particular skills and attitudes, which you can develop with practice. Fortunately we believe children are instinctively inclined to be activists, because most children have strong opinions about what is fair and unfair, as we saw in the vignette. Not everyone agrees on this, of course, with Anna possibly thinking it was unfair that she could not have a contrasting bandaid.

Sociology as activism

The discipline of sociology began as a type of activism, as scholars started to look at the emerging world of the industrial revolution and notice it was creating winners and losers, and tried to work out why. Karl Marx is one of the most well-known sociologists. Marx grew up in a middle-class household in Germany, in the nineteenth century, and studied philosophy and political theory. Marx articulated the emergence of a new organising principle in society, the *capitalist mode of production*, in which the wealthy came to hold power through owning 'the means of production' (factories, mines, businesses), and profiting from the labour of workers (Marx, 1887 [1867]). Even though Marx was wealthy enough to benefit from such a society, his intellectual work was a type of activism in believing that this capitalist system was fundamentally unfair. Marx believed such a system was inherently unstable, and needed to make way for a much fairer system when circumstances were right.

Marx's analysis has been foundational for sociology in the modern world, although contemporary sociologists sometimes lose sight of the heart of Marx's ideas, which is that it is unfair for owners of factories to profit from the labour of workers while paying them much less than their work is worth. This gap between the value of labour and the cost of wages is called 'profit', and tends to be thought of as a good thing because capitalism has become so widely accepted. One of the consequences of capitalism is that, in the search for profit, decisions are made that are bad not just for workers, but for the planet itself. Under capitalism, natural resources are extracted without thought for the biosphere, or the other creatures that share the land being exploited. Things like pollution, climate change, habitat destruction and depletion of groundwater are viewed as 'externalities' within most capitalist business models, and seen as irrelevant in the pursuit of profit.

Whether you agree or disagree that capitalism is a good way to organise the world, you may well be concerned about the forms of damage we are doing as a human species to planetary ecosystems. Given the large number of human beings now on the planet (more than seven billion), any activities our species engages in now have a much larger impact than in the nineteenth century, when the global population was only one billion. The scale of our impact increases with our population, and the sorts of materially wealthy lives we are attempting to lead. Many contemporary sociologists examine ways of organising the world which are less damaging to earth systems (e.g. Hage, 2017).

Other sociologists investigate our gendered systems, including workplace discrimination and the gender pay gap (e.g. Budig & Misra, 2010). Building on the work of early sociologists such as Marx, many examine the systems of social class that exist and the sorts of denial and silencing that happen around persistent economic inequalities (e.g. Connell, 2013). You may be interested in work within the sociology of education, which explores how schools and other educational institutions are structured, and what can be done to make these fairer (Osgood, 2012; Vincent, 2017). In more recent years, childhood itself has been seen as an important focus of study due to a realisation that ageism is a persistent issue, and marginalisation of children's rights is ongoing (James, Jenks, & Prout, 1998).

A brief history of early activism in our field

The early childhood field has a history of activism, because education for the youngest children is still a comparatively recent phenomenon. The existence of early education today is due to the efforts of early activists who believed this was important. Johann Pestalozzi was born in the middle of the eighteenth century in Switzerland. As someone who had grown up poor, Pestalozzi was inspired by the need to provide education for poor children who at that time were either sent to work or given only basic religious instruction. His ideas influenced a number of people, including Elizabeth Mayo in the UK, and Friedrich Fröbel, who in turn inspired others. Pestalozzi was perhaps the first to advocate for individual understanding of students, and the idea that education was not just intellectual, but also about social and emotional learning. He seemed to care deeply about his students, which may have had as much impact as the specifics of his educational methods (Brosterman, 1997).

Mayo used Pestalozzi's ideas to develop systems for training infant teachers in London – a new development at that time. In this context, infant or nursery education referred to children up to the age of seven, reminding us of the very different perceptions of children's skills and abilities at that time, and the still limited understanding of this as an important part of education. The Hadow report (Board of Education, 1933), which investigated the provision of education in the UK in the 1930s, explored the limited services for nursery-age children (birth to five) at that time, as well as recommending separating provision of schooling up until the age of eight. Susan Isaacs was a progressive and critically minded psychologist whose work informed the Hadow report. Her work sought to question taken-for-granted notions about child-rearing, and to advocate for a nursery school system which developed children's independence and critical-thinking skills (Isaacs, 1932). It was around this time that early educators such as Isaacs were advocating for 'scientific ideas around child development' – this is a useful reminder that what can be a progressive idea in one era may turn out to have unexpected downsides later on, as we saw in discussing child development in chapter 2.

Fröbel took Pestalozzi's ideas back to Germany, where he developed the idea of the *kindergarten* and many of the basic elements of early childhood practice, such as block play, art, singing and music, still widely in use today. Although banned early on in Germany – due to a misunderstanding by Prussian authorities at that time – these ideas were taken up widely across the world in the nineteenth century, including much of Europe, and as far away as Japan and the USA. The concept of kindergarten was brought to the USA in the mid-nineteenth century by Margarethe Schurz (after a brief stint in the UK) to serve an immigrant German community in Wisconsin, and from there to the wider North American community, with Elizabeth Peabody opening an English-speaking kindergarten in 1860 in Boston (Brosterman, 1997). Many early feminists, such as these, saw the kindergarten movement as an unimpeachable way to advance women's rights, and children's education. Less helpfully, early concepts of early childhood education, such as the idealism and romanticism of Fröbel, were used to entrench the 'naturalness' of women taking up this role, extending on their responsibilities for child-rearing at home, as discussed in chapter 10.

A more helpful activist tradition arose from the social democratic movements in Scandinavian countries during the twentieth century, which aimed to create a more equal society, in part through supporting education and childcare (Lakey, 2016). Rising prosperity in these countries in the postwar boom and activism for gender equality led governments to introduce broad-based provision for early education. Countries in the Scandinavian region now tend to have guaranteed government-supported provision for all children aged one to six, prior to schooling, which implement a progressive and play-based educational programme led by qualified educators. This in turn has helped support more progressive gender equity in these countries, with fathers expected to participate meaningfully in domestic and child-rearing duties, as a consequence of female workforce participation being higher than in other comparable nations (Abhayaratna & Lattimore, 2006).

The early childhood educator as activist

We hope you are reading this book because you want to make a difference in the lives of children, and believe that education is a great way to do this. You may also have strong ideas about how you think early education should be organised, what sort of curriculum is best for young children or what form of society best supports children's wellbeing. These can all be activist projects. The idea of 'play-based learning' was once a strange idea, and it was only through the work of activists that it became widely accepted as a means for learning. In this section we will look at some early childhood educators whose names you may know, but that you may not think of as activists.

Maria Montessori

Many people around the world have heard of Montessori education, with schools based on her methods existing in more than 110 countries worldwide. Fewer people know that Maria Montessori, whose theories they are based upon, was an early feminist and activist, challenging existing norms of her time, and advocating for women's rights throughout her life (American Montessori Society, 2017). Even as a young person, Montessori, raised by educated parents, refused to accept the limits of her time and was willing to attend an all-boys technical college to further her early dreams of becoming an engineer. When she decided instead to become a doctor – such study was barred to women at that time – it took much persistence and advocacy to enable this to happen, and she was amongst the first group of women to graduate as medical doctors in Italy, in 1897. Training as a psychiatrist, she worked initially with children with intellectual disabilities and realised how inadequate the educational programmes were for such children at the time. Using contemporary ideas, she investigated new ways to support and educate the children at the centre she directed, seeing impressive progress in their learning. Always willing to take on new challenges, she saw that there were similar problems in the education of poor children, and so opened the first *Casa dei Bambini* (children's house). This radical and experimental programme saw Montessori learning as she went, observing what methods and activities worked best for this group of disadvantaged children. The methods she developed are still widely used today, and have impacted hugely on the wellbeing and education of many thousands of children.

The activists of Villa Cella

Again, many have heard of the educational centres of Reggio Emilia in Italy, but few have heard of the ordinary people – an activist community – who planted the seeds of this vibrant democratic educational approach (Edwards, Gandini, & Forman, 1998). In the first days after the end of the Second World War, in the collapse of Mussolini's regime in Italy, many people wanted to do something constructive given the horrors they had experienced. The women of

218 *Changing the world*

Figure 12.2 These student teachers in Canada were activists of their day, carving out new roles for women in education in the 1890s.
Source: Archives of Ontario. Licence: Public domain

a small village, Villa Cella, decided that they would open an *Asilo de Populi* – a kindergarten of the people. They believed this would help the children of the village learn and thrive and look to a future beyond the war, which was all many of these children had known.

The only economic resources the villagers had were military equipment abandoned by the German army in their retreat – a tank, some trucks and some horses, which they sold to provide their initial funds. They decided to build the kindergarten with their own hands, on top of their regular work. They did not know where they would find money to run it, but were determined to try. The land was donated by a local farmer, and they built the kindergarten with materials salvaged from bombed houses, with the resourcefulness shown by early childhood educators everywhere. They were fortunate that word of their efforts spread, and a young school teacher – Loris Malaguzzi, also an activist – heard about what they were doing, jumped on his bike and came to see it for himself. Malaguzzi became a key advocate of the work these villagers were doing. He supported them as they opened more *Asili de Populi* and began to experience recognition but also opposition, as they expanded. All activists need determination, and this group of educators struggled for ten years before getting acknowledgement and support from the regional government. Even with this support, there was long-term opposition from the Catholic Church, for whom the idea of secular education was threatening. When this opposition reached its peak, the educators of Reggio Emilia invited church representatives to visit their kindergartens, opening up an intense seven-month dialogue. This was exhausting but immensely productive, helping move this situation from conflict to cautious acceptance. These days Reggio Emilia educators continue to advocate for better education for children, and still research their own practices with the aim of enriching their work with children.

The Anti-Bias Curriculum Taskforce

At around the same time as the activists from Villa Cella, again inspired by the end of the war, some families in California started an early childhood programme of their own. This was Pacific Oaks Children's School in Pasadena, based on Quaker values of community, equality and peace. The strengths and progressive orientation of this programme led to it being chosen as one of the locations of the new Head Start programmes funded by the Johnston administration in the 1960s, to improve the situation of children in poverty. The collective experimentation of these educators established what is now known as *Anti-Bias Curriculum*, a programme of early childhood education designed explicitly to challenge racism, sexism, ableism and economic inequalities (Derman-Sparks, 1989), and the source of the vignette at the start of the chapter. Louise Derman-Sparks is one of the leading advocates of this approach (as Malaguzzi was for the Reggio Emilia preschools) and has written and collaborated widely since that first publication about this sociologically inspired pedagogy and curriculum (Derman-Sparks & Olsen Edwards, 2010; Derman-Sparks & Ramsey, 2011). The methods and ideas of anti-bias curriculum have become widespread, in the USA and further afield, and have expanded over time to include additional concerns, such as LGBT+ rights.

Anti-bias is fundamentally an activist's curriculum, acknowledging at its core the bias built into the education system, and encouraging educators to actively counteract this bias with children every day. This approach has four central goals, which build upon each other, beginning with the individual child and working outwards. The first goal is for children to have confidence and pride in their families and social identity. The second supports children becoming comfortable with difference, and making connections across boundaries. The third asks them to recognise and name unfairness, as well as acknowledging how this can hurt. The last goal helps children learn the skills to act, collectively and individually, against this unfairness, becoming activists themselves (Derman-Sparks & Olsen Edwards, 2010).

Advocating for and with children

There are many ways educators may want to be activist. Some will feel most comfortable advocating on behalf of children, perhaps raising issues of concern for them with educational authorities. Others will choose to work with their group of children on activist projects that matter to young children. Some may even want to proactively engage with young children about current issues which the whole nation is considering or being challenged by, such as legalising same-sex marriage, and asking them to consider their views on these issues as citizens.

We tend to think of young children as *future* citizens, but such a view disenfranchises them, assuming that they should not have any sort of legitimate voice until they are of legal voting age. Education and health are two of the main roles of government, representing significant expenditure, and these are both areas where children have a legitimate and immediate interest. They are affected by the policies being made by parliaments and other governing structures, and so deserve a say in matters that concern them closely.

In our early education settings

The first place to practise being an activist is in your workplace, and you may notice you do not agree with all of the practices at your site, or believe that some of these systems do not fully support children's rights or choices. Your voice as an educator can act as an amplifier for the voices of children, making change more likely to happen. For example, many preschool services still have inflexible sleep routines, causing stress to children as well as to those adults tasked with encouraging children to sleep when they do not want to, or preventing them from sleeping when they do. Workshopping with the children what they would like to see happen, if they can articulate this, and then coming up with some concrete suggestions, will then allow you to take these to the management or committee who have ultimate responsibility for your service. This will depend very much on your local environment, as these sorts of rules always happen in a wider cultural context. With sleeping, we know that in some nations, such as Italy or Spain, a midday rest is a valued community institution and supported by parents and staff alike. On the other hand, in contexts such as the USA or Australia many parents actively wish their children not to have a sleep during the day. As always with any activism it helps to think through the possible steps needed to make this change, because your aim is always to make it easier for those in authority to say 'yes' to your ideas rather than 'no'. By having a focused plan for change, which you can explain simply and clearly, you reduce the usual human tendency to stick with what they know best.

In our local communities

Moving out geographically, we think that all our services should have strong connections in their local communities, with children living locally, or making regular excursions to local landmarks or playspaces (Monbiot, 2017). Children may notice things in their community that bother them, such as dangerous or noisy roads, or an excess of garbage accumulating at their local playground. To a critical educator these sorts of noticings are great opportunities for activism, with children being encouraged to write letters or emails to their local council, or even make a time to go and talk with them (although this may be intimidating for some). Don't be afraid to experiment with your activism – you never know what will have an effect, and it is important for children to experience unsuccessful activist projects as well as successful ones. Maybe you want to make signs to put up nearby, encouraging cars to slow down. Depending on the families using the service, you may even have enough energy to get working on a traffic-calming urban transformation project, such as a *woonerf* (see breakout box).

> ### *Woonerf* – Living streets
>
> This idea emerged in the Netherlands in the 1970s. *Woonerf* are streets designed to blur the boundaries between zones for vehicle users and pedestrians, encouraging all in that space to proceed slowly and with care for others (Baker, 2004). This may appear dangerous, but the early experiments were so successful they have been applied in many different countries. *Woonerf* design encourages people to share space respectfully, allowing roads to be safer for everyone, especially children and cyclists. In a delightful paradox, the busier the street gets, the slower everyone must go, improving safety for all (see also online resources).

In our town or city

Depending on the size of your city, there may be issues at this level that you want to be active about. If you work with children who have migrated from war zones (see chapter 9), or have experienced other forms of trauma, you might want to engage in projects connected with peace and conflict resolution. You might consider lobbying your local mayor to become part of the Mayors for Peace project, which aims to get city authorities working together to support a world without war or nuclear weapons. Founded by the Mayor of Hiroshima in 1982, this project may be suitable for classes that have read children's books that focus on anti-war issues, such as the story of Sadako (Coerr, 1977). This could be a story which local newspapers become interested in or which a group of parents would be willing to take up and develop beyond your own efforts. Grounding such efforts for peace in our own efforts to relate respectfully (see chapter 6) is a good way to keep this sort of project relevant in the classroom.

Nationally

Young children will tend to know their nationality, particularly if they are migrants, and these sorts of activist projects will vary greatly depending on the issues that may be current in your own country. If there is a national election coming up this could be an opportunity to talk with children about the sorts of issues that affect them. Consider inviting willing parents to come and talk with the children about their own political opinions, and why they vote the way that they do. This can be a touchy subject for some people, so making sure that you have talked this through thoroughly with other colleagues and families will help this remain a respectful conversation. Ensuring that you hear from those aligned with all significant parties as well as independent candidates can help keep the conversation open. It is always useful to be explicit with visitors that they must not undermine the wellbeing of any children in the class, such as through careless comments about immigration.

In Australia, for example, educators may wish to engage children in conversations about the ongoing struggle for justice for Aboriginal and Torres Strait Islander people, given more than two hundred years of colonial occupation and the lack of any treaty process or formal recognition. Such issues may already be part of your regular curriculum, in reading stories or going on excursions which educate about Indigenous cultures and histories. At election times, this offers the possibility of exploring policies which impact negatively on First Nations people, and the often inadequate responses by political parties who remain invested in the status quo. Taking up challenging issues like this will not be likely to have much direct impact in your nation (although activists tend to be optimists). They can be a valuable way to promote greater justice long term, through helping non-Indigenous children to connect Indigenous peoples' experiences to their own knowledge of what is fair and unfair. Wherever you are located you might want to undertake a unit of work about connection to place and land, looking at the history of your area, who has lived there, and the political impacts of migration and colonisation in recent centuries.

Internationally

It may seem overwhelming to expect yourself or the young children you work with to be an activist about issues happening on a global scale. However, as we saw in chapter 11, we can no longer pretend that the impacts of human population and consumption have little influence on the planet's environment. Global human-induced climate change is a reality we are all living with, and whose consequences are already seriously impacting on the lives of the world's most marginalised populations. The children we work with will witness the seriousness of this crisis throughout their lives, and their adult existence may well end up looking very different from ours today.

As educators we can help children to think about these problems for themselves, and find new ways of relating to the natural world, and to each other. Our activism may feel local, in taking steps to live more sustainably, but the consequences add up to a global scale. As part of this work you may decide with your group that you want to speak directly, as citizens, to your elected representatives. You could write letters with children about particular aspects of the environmental crisis and send them to key politicians. This will also involve managing expectations about the likely response, which can be disappointing. We could see this in the vignette, where the children were very hopeful about a positive outcome, but were dismissed. Kye knew this was likely, but had believed the activity would be good for building community and talking honestly together about racial unfairness. We can always be thinking pedagogically, finding positive ways to stay focused on our goals, even when we experience setbacks.

Advocating for and with educators

We have talked about advocating for children, but educators themselves are the lynchpin of the early childhood education and care system, and need to be respected and valued. Are you an activist for the early childhood workforce, demanding respect and appreciation for the work that we do, and the sorts of wages and working conditions that would make excellent work more possible? In this section we will look briefly at some of the important reasons why we should be more aware and active about these issues.

Even if we feel that our wages and conditions are good, there are many in our field who are not so fortunate, driving high levels of burnout, with staff leaving the field for less stressful or better paid work (Jovanovic, 2013). This is especially true for our early childhood colleagues in some national contexts, particularly Majority World countries. In less economically privileged contexts, many workers may be paid very little, due to low rates of government support and the limited capacity of many parents to afford higher costs for care (Yulindrasari & Ujianti, 2017). Even in Minority World contexts it is often the most marginalised women (including those from migrant or non-dominant cultural groups) who are working in the least well paid positions, simply because their home-country qualifications are not recognised or they are experiencing systemic racism. A significant proportion of early childhood staff are working for less than the minimum wage, either through underpayment by employers, or through working longer hours that they should for a fixed salary (Osgood, 2005; Pocock *et al.*, 2008).

The gender pay gap is an issue that affects women worldwide, across all occupations and roles (Lips, 2013). Feminist economists have shown that there are financial penalties not just for less-valued work such as carework or 'dirty work', but simply for any work that is seen as primarily female work (England, Allison, & Wu, 2007). We could call this *systemic sexism*, because it is not about specific discrimination by specific people in most cases, but the result of taken-for-granted notions about who is most valued, and whose work matters most. Even if you identify as male, and are reading this (statistically most readers of early childhood texts will be female), then you should be disturbed, because there is a gender pay gap in favour of males even in the early childhood field, where the vast majority of the workforce are female (Wahlquist, 2017). We are sure you would prefer to achieve higher rewards through hard work and commitment rather than through unearned privileges.

Globally there are pressures on all governments to reduce the costs of education, whether in the early years or at tertiary level. Those in power try to lower expenditure by depressing the wages and conditions of educators, which is the major item in any educational budget. We believe that education is one of the things any society should be investing most in, supporting and valuing educators at all levels.

The most effective response to this challenge is to join your local childcare or education union and encourage others to do the same. Unions exist to support the rights of their members, arguing for fairer pay rates or defending workers who are sacked without good reason, even if historically many resisted advocating for women's employment or equal pay. Given the power imbalance between employers and educators, unions exist to redress this imbalance through collective organisation. The right to join a union and legal support for unions in the workplace were major activist achievements in the first half of the twentieth century in many countries. If you are troubled by the politics of your local union, then start a new one, or lobby that union to have better policies and practices. That is what being an activist is all about!

The last thing you need to know, in terms of being a workplace activist, is that the stresses of working in early childhood are often huge, with significant responsibilities, and often limited support structures. This can result in educators treating each other badly, as a way of dealing with their stresses, a phenomenon Freire called 'horizontal violence' (2014 [1968], 62). Recognising this as a problem not with each other, but with the way the early childhood system is set up to be stressful or unsupportive, enables this anger to be channelled into activism. We can work to support each other to make changes, rather than making our work even harder than it needs to be.

The educator as researcher

As educators we may feel poorly prepared to support children in activism, and without enough knowledge to do this well. This should not be used as an excuse to avoid these important issues. As with anything we do not know, or feel overwhelmed by, our job is to model a learning orientation to children, taking on our own research about the issue concerned. There are many ways to do this, but working collectively with other educators will help make your activist journey more enriching. Miriam Guigni and Kerry Mundine (2010) have collected many engaging stories about activist projects in early childhood. Part of this research is not simply about knowledge, but also about the pedagogical skills that are necessary to be an activist educator, in learning how to share ideas with children, investigate problems and possible solutions, and learn from children's own optimism about the possibilities for change.

Anyone can be a researcher, no matter what your educational background has been or how confident you are. All it takes is to think of a question that has puzzled you, and then to think of some ways to investigate this question, hopefully with the children you are working with involved too (Pelo *et al.*, 2000).

This research can be short term (less than a week), or something that captures your attention for years and years. The question is there to keep you focused, and to act as a provocation, allowing you to revisit it from time to time and ask, 'What do I *now* know about this question?'

If your question were to be 'How do I become an effective activist?' then you might decide to tackle this by inviting people into your classroom whom you know to be committed activists from within your local community. Perhaps they have campaigned to prevent a local open space being sold to developers? Perhaps they got active around the issue of same-sex marriage? Perhaps they have worked for many years to support the rights of children with disabilities? Having these activists come and talk with your group of children allows them the chance to celebrate any successes and reflect on what they still want to achieve. You may also be impressed at the sorts of insightful questions that children will want to ask.

In any research, if your commitment is to a more equal world, you need to think about how you are doing this collaboratively rather than in an exploitative way. We can call this 'researching with', rather than 'researching on'. In this, you might initially consult with those who your research question affects, asking if this is the right question or a useful question to be asking. You might also want to ask for their suggestions about how to investigate this issue. Perhaps they will want to be part of the research work, or perhaps this is something that is your own responsibility (e.g. 'How does my whiteness stop me from seeing racism in my everyday life?'). Whatever happens, it is worth checking in with others about your progress, and reporting about what you are learning or discovering, so that the benefits of the research are shared.

Final thoughts

Throughout this book, we have explored different aspects of early childhood work, and the ways that sociology can make sense of what we see around us. These could be the temper tantrums of a two year old, the resistance of some family members or the misplaced policy-making of governments. Whatever it may be, we believe the tools and insights of sociology can help reveal new ways of being an educator and better ways of achieving meaningful early childhood education for all of those involved – children, educators, and families. Bringing you the best of contemporary research and practice, we have provided some different theoretical perspectives from which to examine our everyday actions.

While we are always aiming for a 'good-enough' early childhood system, there are many ways we can strive to make it better, just as the activists of Reggio Emilia have been doing for 70 years. One persistent problem across the Minority World is that our educational workforce is not representative of those we teach. If you are an Indigenous child or a child with a disability, for example, then you will be less likely to have educators who have firsthand experiences of the challenges you may be facing in life. In most countries with a European heritage the workforce is predominantly white, female, middle-class and able-bodied. We are not

Figure 12.3 Demonstrations can still be an effective way of making change, and activism on behalf of children can attract wide-ranging support.
Source: Phil Roeder. Licence: Creative Commons 3.0

yet representative of those who come through our doors. What can you do, from your position within early childhood education, to support more diversity in your workplace? As a start, you might encourage a wider pool of volunteers or work-experience students than those you usually accept. Once you have recruited some good people, how do you work to support them specifically, using your sociological understanding? Systemic racism or other 'isms' can impact on people in many ways, including educators' voices or expertise being taken less seriously. People with disabilities have much to offer as educators in understanding the challenges and joys of being different, but your environment needs to offer no additional barriers preventing them from contributing. With male educators, they have more to offer than just the stereotype of a 'male role model'. Older workers often have a lifetime of experience to draw upon, even if they are new to the early childhood field, and if your organisation is willing to employ people close to retirement they may prove to be an unexpected asset. We believe the best early childhood team is a microcosm of your community, modelling respectful and collegial relationships to all the children that you are working with.

Lastly, we hope you will join us in advocating for the early childhood field as part of your everyday practice. We believe that the early years offer a vital foundation for all children, capturing their enthusiasm for life, and helping direct this curiosity and inquiry into productive directions. We need programmes that are supported to do this, which will mean advocating continually for effective funding levels not just for services like your own, but for all parts of the early childhood field. This funding needs to be guaranteed in the long term, to allow for good planning and provide sufficient support to allow for fair and equitable pay rates for those working as early educators. Beyond the material conditions of our work, we hope you will always seek to build respect for early childhood practice, through demonstrating in your own pedagogy the intellectual and emotional engagement that children need and deserve. We are our own best advocates when we demonstrate each day what great early childhood education can create, nurture and inspire. It can transform the world!

Questions for reflection

- What will you do now with what you have learnt in this book? As with most activities we get better with practice, and activism is no different. If you want to be an activist then get out there, be bold and willing to make mistakes!
- Were you surprised to learn about the activism of some historical early childhood figures? What might you achieve in your life in transforming the early childhood system, which future educators might learn from?
- What are you curious about in your work today? Write down some ideas and then try turning them into a research question. Now how could you go about investigating that idea?

Activities for educators

- As a beginning educator or early childhood student you will have a group of friends or colleagues whom you want to work with. There are many possible activist challenges to take on in our field, but the best ones are ones we can work on together. When you next have the opportunity (a staff meeting, a get-together) ask each of your (potential) co-workers to write down their five ideas for changing the world, whether big or small. Writing these on sticky notes is an easy way to make this activity work better. Now see what common ground you can find between these ideas. Are there any that everyone shares? Think about which ones might be achievable in the short term, and which ones may take longer. Can you agree on one goal that most people think is worth trying right now? Write down your shared goal as clearly as possible, working together, to make sure everyone is on the same page about it. Now think of some concrete steps you can take to achieve this goal. Who else could you ask to join you? What other supports may be available? What else do you need to know (perhaps others are already working on this issue that you can join up with)?

- Think about your own five goals from the previous activity. These are part of your values as a teacher, and as educators we tend to be at our best when we teach from the heart of what we value. How do these goals align with the goals of your workplace, or with your local or national curriculum frameworks? How can you turn these goals into curriculum, into activities you might work on with children? Think about how you might change the power dynamics in such activities, so that all children get to share in the leadership and work of these activities. Good luck!

Key readings

Derman-Sparks, L., & Olsen Edwards, J. (2010). *Anti-Bias Education: For Young Children and Ourselves*. Washington, DC: NAEYC.

Guigni, M., & Mundine, K. (2010). *Talkin' up and Speakin' out: Aboriginal and Multicultural Voices in Early Childhood*. Sydney: Pademelon.

Monbiot, G. (2017). *Out of the Wreckage: A New Politics for an Age of Crisis*. London: Verso.

Pelo, A., Davidson, F., & Roth, S. (2000). *That's Not Fair! A Teacher's Guide to Activism with Young Children*. St Paul, MN: Redleaf Press.

Yulindrasari, H., & Ujianti, P. R. (2017). 'Trapped in the reform': Kindergarten teachers' experiences of teacher professionalisation in Buleleng, Indonesia. *Policy Futures in Education* (Onlinefirst), 1–14.

Online resources

The Letterbox Library – This social enterprise has been selling multicultural and equity-based children's books for more than 30 years. www.letterboxlibrary.com/

Mayors for Peace – This local government initiative supports local officials to connect worldwide in the quest for peace. Global action on climate change is also happening at a local government level. www.mayorsforpeace.org/english/

Living Streets – This charity advocates in the UK for living streets, like the *woonerf* idea, to support more walking, encouraging better health and sustainable transport. http://livingstreets.org.uk/

Further reading

Abhayaratna, J., & Lattimore, R. (2006). *Workforce Participation Rates: How does Australia Compare?* Canberra: Commonwealth Government of Australia.

American Montessori Society (2017). Maria Montessori biography. Retrieved from https://amshq.org/Montessori-Education/History-of-Montessori-Education/Biography-of-Maria-Montessori

Baker, L. (2004). Why don't we do it in the road? *Salon*, 21 May.

Board of Education. (1933). *The Hadow Report: Report of the Consultative Committee on Infant and Nursery Schools*. London: HM Stationery Office Retrieved from www.educationengland.org.uk/documents/hadow1933/hadow1933.html - 01.

Brosterman, N. (1997). *Inventing Kindergarten*. New York: Harry N. Abrams Inc.

Budig, M., & Misra, J. (2010). How care-work employment shapes earnings in cross-national perspective. *International Labour Review*, 149(4), 441–460.

Coerr, E. (1977). *Sadako and the Thousand Paper Cranes*. New York: G. P. Putnam & Sons.
Connell, R. (2013). Why do market 'reforms' persistently increase inequality? *Discourse: Studies in the Cultural Politics of Education, 34*(2), 279–285.
Derman-Sparks, L. (1989). *Anti-Bias Curriculum: Tools for Empowering Young Children*. Washington, DC: NAEYC.
Derman-Sparks, L., & Ramsey, P. (2011). *What if All the Kids are White? Anti-Bias Multicultural Education with Young Children and Families*. New York: Teachers College Press.
Edwards, C., Gandini, L., & Forman, G. (Eds) (1998). *The Hundred Languages of Children: The Reggio Emilia Approach – Advanced Reflections*. Westport, CT: Ablex Publishing.
England, P., Allison, P., & Wu, Y. (2007). Does bad pay cause occupations to feminize, does feminization reduce pay, and how can we tell with longitudinal data? *Social Science Research, 36*, 1237–1256.
Freire, P. (2014 [1968]). *Pedagogy of the Oppressed [Pedagogia do Oprimido]* (M. Ramos, Trans.). New York: Bloomsbury.
Hage, G. (2017). *Is Racism an Environmental Threat? Debating Race*. Cambridge: Polity Press.
Isaacs, S. (1932). *The Nursery Years: The Mind of the Child from Birth to Six Years*. London: George Routledge & Sons.
James, A., Jenks, C., & Prout, A. (1998). *Theorizing Childhood*. New York: Teachers College Press.
Jovanovic, J. (2013). Retaining early childhood educators. *Gender, Work and Organization, 20*(5), 528–544.
Lakey, G. (2016). *Viking Economics: How the Scandinavians Got it Right – and How we Can, Too*. New York: Melville House.
Lips, H. M. (2013). The gender pay gap: Challenging the rationalizations. Perceived equity, discrimination, and the limits of human capital models. *Sex Roles, 68*(3), 169–185.
Marx, K. (1887 [1867]). *Capital [Das Kapital]* (Vol. 1). Moscow: Progress Publishers.
Osgood, J. (2005). Who cares? The classed nature of childcare. *Gender and Education, 17*(3), 289–303.
Osgood, J. (2012). *Narratives from the Nursery: Negotiating Professional Identities in Early Childhood*. Abingdon: Routledge.
Pocock, B., Elton, J., Preston, A., Charlesworth, S., MacDonald, F., Baird, M., … Ellem, B. (2008). The impact of 'Work Choices' on women in low-paid employment in Australia: A qualitative analysis. *Journal of Industrial Relations, 50*(3), 475–488.
Vincent, C. (2017). 'The children have only got one education and you have to make sure it's a good one': parenting and parent–school relations in a neoliberal age. *Gender and Education*, 1–17.
Wahlquist, C. (2017). Female childcare workers paid 32% less than male workers, new data shows. *Guardian Online*, 4 Sept.

Glossary

This glossary helps explain any unfamiliar words you will find in the text. Some words you may already know, but we will be using them in specific ways in this book to cover the experience of those in many different countries. We know we will be talking to people teaching in different sorts of contexts, and we want our language to feel inclusive.

Childcare (daycare, nursery, early learning, creche): At times we will need to talk about children's spaces in the years before school. We will call these spaces *childcare*, or *family childcare* if they happen in private homes.

Children's spaces As sociologically minded educators, we think a lot about power, and how this is enacted in language. Rather than language like *children's services*, which conjures up ideas of businesses designed to allow parents to work, we sometimes ask you think about our environments as *children's spaces* – places that belong to children, and nourish a sense of their own worth.

Classroom There are not many useful words to describe the immediate teaching spaces in which we work. For many readers, the word 'classroom' will conjure up the idea of formal schooling. In this book we will use classroom to mean any early childhood learning environment, including a room for babies in a childcare setting, a school classroom, or sometimes a natural setting, as with Forest Schools. To us, a classroom is anywhere a child is learning supported by an educator.

Early childhood educator (practitioner, teacher, carer, caregiver, pedagogue, worker): This one is pretty simple. We are all in the business of education, whether we are degree-qualified teachers, or caregivers working outside the formal educational sector. Those working in the early childhood field come with a variety of qualifications and experience, but we will describe everyone as (early childhood) educators, unless we need to be more specific.

Family childcare (family daycare, FDC, home-based care): This is a specific sort of preschool education, which provides education to children in family homes, by educators who usually live fulltime in those spaces. These provide flexible care for families, and tend to operate over longer hours than *preschool*, but increasingly is regulated similarly, and with the same curriculum.

LGBT+ (Lesbian, Gay, Bisexual, Transgender, Queer, Intersex, sex and gender diverse, SOGI): We have used the language of LGBT+ to talk about the significant group of people who identify as diverse in terms of their gender, sex or sexuality. As there are many different names that can be included in this acronym, we use the '+' sign, to acknowledge all those who are included but not directly referenced. We think it is a useful term, because it has been adopted in countries around the world to describe sex and gender diverse people, including places where the language spoken is not English. LGBT+ usually describes all those who would not identity as both cisgendered and heterosexual.

Majority/Minority World (developing/developed, Third/First World): When talking globally we will sometimes draw a contrast between the small number of the world's wealthiest nations, where fewer people live (the Minority World), and contrast them with the rest of the world, where most people live (the Majority World). We use this language because it reminds us that despite the habitual dominance of wealthy countries, the majority of the global population does not live like this, and we prefer a world where everybody's lives matter. Most of the Minority World became wealthy by colonising and exploiting Majority world countries, stealing their resources and sometimes their people (such as Africans abducted for the slave trade).

Neoliberalism (modern capitalism, Minority World hegemonic practices): We use this word to describe the contemporary state of politics and governance in the Minority World, but also within global institutions such as the World Bank or the International Monetary Fund. On the rise since the 1980s, this is a particular way of thinking about the world which privileges some narrow economic ideas (e.g., the importance of 'the market') at the expense of social equity or environmental awareness. It remains in place because it privileges the ruling classes, who use money and influence to steer governments into making decisions which advantage them. The name (meaning 'new liberalism') takes ideas from 19th century liberalism, such as free speech and freedom of choice, but uses them not to expand democratic ideas, but to concentrate power in the hands of the privileged.

Out of School Hours Care (OSHC, before-care, after-care, breakfast club): These programs tend to be for school-aged children, and aim to extend the hours of formal school programs. They allow family members working business hours to be able to drop off and pick up children who may be too young to walk to school themselves. They generally offer a more leisure-focused program, but with educational activities.

Parent (family member, caregiver, guardian, carer, mother, father, mom/mum, dad): When talking about parenting, we mean this as inclusively as possible, to include all people who take up the social role of parenting, including guardians, foster-carers, older siblings and other relatives. We believe that the whole community has a role in raising children, including educators and extended family. We see all this work as *child-rearing*, or *care-giving*, which can happen in a family or in a variety of children's spaces. When we use the word *parenting*, we will be talking about the care and education of children that occurs in families. When we use the term caregivers this can be inclusive of educators and families. Our view of parenting extends beyond 'biological' parents to same-sex families, adoptive families, extended families, and stepfamilies. We don't use terms such as 'birth mother' because some people with a uterus who give birth identify as male.

Pedagogy (critical pedagogy, pedagogical space): We think this is a valuable word. The word 'teaching' can often make people think of one teacher at the front of a classroom talking *at* children, whereas teaching happens in many different ways and different contexts. Pedagogy is a broader word and helps us focus on the *practices* of teaching, and the theories which underpin them.

Preschool (kindergarten, long day care, childcare): Sometimes we will want to talk specifically about education in the years before formal schooling, and there are many words for this across the world. Here we will borrow a word used in a variety of contexts – preschool – but use it in the way it is used in Sweden (*förskola*), to describe a range of early childhood settings from birth up to starting school.

Site (setting, space, context): Early childhood education happens in lots of place, from private homes to large public schools. When we want to talk about education generally, we will use the word *site*, to be as inclusive as we can of the different physical environments where we work.

Social class (ruling class, middle class, working class): As discussed in chapter 1, we use particular language to refer to particular locations in social space, based on people's access to economic privilege. This needs noting because language around social class makes people feel uncomfortable. We use the language of 'working class', to describe those who have the least money and access to economic privilege and so must work hard to survive. We use the language of 'ruling class' to describe those with significant wealth (often talked about as *the 1%*) because these groups often control access to the media or have most influence on local and global political processes. 'Middle class' describes those, ranging from tradespeople to professionals, who earn a reasonable income and do not experience financial stress, but who are not particularly influential in society. In social surveys, most people will identify themselves as middle class, whatever their level of wealth or poverty, because of discomfort with the extremes of economic situations.

Year 1, Year 2, Year 3 (first year, second year, third year): The first year of formal education has many different names across the world, including *kindergarten*, *reception* or *foundation*. For simplicity we describe the first year of school as *Year 1*, and so on. We know that children start schooling at very different ages in different countries, from four through to seven, so even these labels will describe very different ages. It will give a sense of the sorts of teaching that may be possible at each level from 'transitional' teaching in Year 1 to an expectation in Year 3 that children are familiar with the school setting and capable of focused work.

Index

Note: This index covers the main body text and 'Vignettes from practice' only. Figures, tables, and vignettes are denoted by italic, bold, and bold italic text respectively.

ability 9–10, 34–35, 56, 191, 219
able-bodied 6, 15, 47, 53, 128, 182, 226
Abrahamic religions 139–140, 141, 145
'active play zones' 121
activism *212*, **213**, 213–225, *218*, *226*
advocacy 72, 74–75, 160, 214, 217
AEDC/I (Australian Early Development Census/Instrument) 81, **85**
ageism 11, 31–33, *32*, 88, 158, 161, 215
agency: of children 13, 44–53, **44**, *51*, 56, 164, 205; of educators 27; and health 65, 66, 67, 69; and participatory research 81, 82, 89; and wellbeing 81, 82, 89, 93
see also disability, social class, structure-agency continuum
agender 6, 71
ahimsa 140, 149
Ailwood, Joanne 185
'alone time' 120
anger 102–103, 106, 109–110, 171
Anti-Bias Curriculum 219
anxiety 100, 111, 145
ARACY (Australian Research Alliance for Children and Youth) **85**
art, and spirituality 152
Asilo de Populi 218–219, *218*
atelierista 126
Australian Early Development Census/Instrument (AEDC/I) 81, **85**
Australian Institute of Family Studies **85**, 89–90
Australian Research Alliance for Children and Youth (ARACY) **85**
autism spectrum 37, 105, 121
autonomy 27, 65, 81, 89, 93

babies 17, 24–26, 28–29, 30, 31–33, *32*; dis/ability 34–35; indigeneity 36; privilege 34; race 36; relationships with 36–37; social class 35–36; working with 37–39, *39*
'banking model' 13, 14
behaviour guidance **156–157**, 157–174
behaviour management 65, 91, 164
belief systems, and sociology 144–146
Ben-Arieh, Asher 84
biomedical models, of disability 34, 63, 64–65, 67, 72
biophilia 199–200, 205, 206, 208
Blackmore, Jill 123
Bourdieu, Pierre 14–15, 16, 35–36, 46, 48–49, 101, 144, 198
British Columbian Provincial Curriculum 73
Buddhism 139, 140, 143, 146, 148, 152
building design 120–121
built environments 71
bullying ***2–3***, *3*, ***69***, 69
Burman, Erica 16, 30, 163
businesses 26, 28, 40; early childhood service as 126; schools as 123, 125
Butler, Judith 29

Cannella, Gaile 118
capabilities, children's 11, 26, 31, 33, 54, 81, 88, 158–159, 162, 163; class backgrounds 152; disabilities 166; knowledge-making processes 89; poorer backgrounds 167; race backgrounds 152, 167
capital: cultural and economic 35–36; emotional 101, 108, 109; social 35

capitalism 214–215
carbon budget 197
caregiving 24, 30, 37, 181
Casa dei Bambini 217
change 197–198, *213* see also activism
child abuse 90–92, 165
Child and Youth Well-being Index (CWI) 85
child development theory 16, 30–31, 34, 45, 64–65, 80–81, 163
child neglect, reporting of 89–91, **90**, 165
Child poverty in perspective: An overview of child well-being in rich countries 85
child protection 89–92, **90**, 90–92
child wellbecoming 87, 88
child wellbeing 82–89, **85**, **86**, *88*
childcare 28, 47, 91, 183, 216, 224
'child-centred' practice 50
childhood, new sociology of 81–82
child-rearing 29, 127, 145, 152, 179, 216
choice: in educational settings 50–56, *51*, *54*; theories of 46–47
Christianity 139–140, 146, 148
civil society 123–124, 125
class 50, 56 see also middle class, ruling class, social class, working class
classrooms 35, 52–56, *54*, 68, 128–129, 151–152, 157, 182
climate 125, 188, 196–197, 198–199, 200, 209
colonialism 8, 47, 117–118, 125, 130
commons, the 125, 126
community: and activism 187, 217–219, *218*; charitable giving 146; children's engagement in the 124; classroom 182; connectedness **85**, **86**; cultural wealth 38; and equality 142; *habitus* 48, 49; indigenous 129, 141, 186; and inequality 102; Japanese culture 103, 170; learning 38, 56, 57, 157–158; services run by the 125, 126; values 189, 219
'comparison test' 161
compassion 117, 139, 149, *149*, 160, 164, 169, 208; educator 164, 174
competencies 31, 33, 202, 205
compulsory schooling 14
'concerted cultivation' 179–180
connectedness **85**, **86**, 146–151, *147*, *149*, *150*
'conscientização' 13
consent 70, 92, 96
considerateness 160

consistency 161–162, 172
constraint, theories of 48–49
control, child's desire for 45–46
corporal punishment 91
Cottingham, Marci 101
creativity 26, 31, 81, **116**, 117, 152, 204, 205
creche see childcare
Crenshaw, Kimberlé 6
critical consciousness 13
critical pedagogy 13–15, 27, 57, 128
critical psychology 16, 105
critical thinking 33, 216
Cruz, Merlyne 13
cultural heritage, and race 7–9, *8*
cultural practices 8, 24, **77**, 118, 139, 141, 152; and spiritual beliefs 145–146
cultural spaces 116, 125–126, 127
cultures 25, 28, **77**, 100, 139, 144; colonising 125; community 102; dominant 14–15, 18, 49, 167; family 102; gendered 183; hybrid 117–118; indigenous 118, 146, 222; institutional 186–187; material 129; native 118, 146, 222; school 72; technologised 150–151
curriculum 72, 73, 92, 128–129; formal 15, 117, 128, 143; hidden 15, 117; national 27, 92, 228; null 15, 20, 160, 182; Swedish 27
CWI (Child and Youth Well-being Index) 85

dadirri 148
Dahlberg, Gunilla 33, 129, 131
Danish Child Protection Policy 91
DAP ('developmentally-appropriate practice') 30
Davidson, Fran 214
Davies, Bronwyn 13, 15, 53
Davis, Julie 198, 202, 209, 210
daycare see childcare
deep listening 148
Department of Education and Child Protection 92
depression 30, 76, 100
Derman-Sparks, Louise 213, 219
Descartes, Rene 151
developed world see Minority World
developing world 69, 183, 198–199, 223
developmental psychology 26, 30, 163
'developmentally-appropriate practice' (DAP) 30

diet 17, 67, 68–69, 104–105, 141, 145
disability 9–10, 34–35, 53–54, *54*, 128, 166, **177**, 183, 225
disciplinary power 47, 51–52, 124, 137–138, 146
discourse/s 12–13, 14; agency 46–48, 49, 52, 53, 56, 57; emotions 107; health 65, 67, 72, 76; inequality 163, 167; learning environments 118, 123, 126, 128, 129; relationships 27–28, 29, 30, 34; resistance 46–48, 49, 52, 53, 56, 57; safety 207; spirituality 137, 143, 144; wellbeing 81, 87, 92
discursive regime 49, 52
dispositions 31, 33, 202, 205
distance from necessity 198
distress: childhood 30, 57, 109, 148, 161, 164–165; adult 113, 144–145, 164
distribution of resources 159–160
diverse families 93, 176–191, *176, 184, 189*
diversity 93, 153, 166, *176*, **177**, 177–191, *184, 189*; ecological 121, 199; expectations 38; practices 38; theory 179–180; in the workplace 128, 226
dominant discourses *see* discourses
Down syndrome 17, 208
dualisms 151–152

early childhood education: *Anti-Bias Curriculum* 219; and child-rearing 179–180; and 'concerted cultivation' 179–180; cultures 186; dominant discourse in 30; educator diversity in 226; educator engagement in 227; 'folk theories' 11; influence of Friedrich Fröbel on 216; history of 16; perception of 50; and physical environments 116, 123; practices 186; rationale for 123; responsibility for 125–126; and social indicators 87; and sociology 3, 225; and standardisation 125; and theory 24
Early Childhood Environment Rating Scale 130
Early Development Index/Instrument (EDI) *80*, 80–81, **85**
early learning *see* childcare
Early Years Framework 72
Early Years Learning framework (EYLF) 92
ecological identities 202–203, 205, 208, 209

economic inequality 14, 48, 55, 159, 215, 219
economics 123, 125
EDI (Early Development Index/Instrument) *80*, 80–81, **85**
education: early childhood *see* early childhood education; 'gender-complex' 56; performance in 28; sociology of 49, 215; strengths-based 31–32; sustainable 194–209, *194, 196, 201, 207*; unintentional discrimination in 52
embodied learning 108–109
emoji 89, 93, 94–95
emotional capital 101–102
emotional *essentialism* 101
emotional labour 100–101, 104, 184
emotional learning 103, 108, 215
emotional management 101, 104
emotions 28–29, 94–95, *98*, **98–99**, 99–101, 102–113, *106, 112*; sociological understandings of 99–103
environments: agency in classroom 52–56, *54*; built 71; evaluating 129–131; inclusive 126–128; learning 38, 93, *115*, 116–131, *119, 122 see also* natural world
epigenetics 25
equal rights 160
Erikson, Erik 30
Estes, David 82
ethnicity 8, 17, **136**, 137; emotions 103; Judaism 141; and migration 187–189, *189*; stereotyping 167
excitement, pedagogical response to 111–112, *112*
extended families 186
EYLF (Early Years Learning framework) 92

families: disadvantaged 35–36; food insecurity of 73, 74; impact on life chances 17–18; poor 33; privileged 55; relationships within **85, 86**; working with 172, 176–191, *176, 184, 189*; working-class 55; violence within 91, 165
family service orientation **90**, 90
fear, pedagogical response to 111
feminism 13, 15, 29, 52–53, 183, 184, 216, 223
fields 48
First World *see* Minority World
folk religions 140–141

'folk theories' 11
forest schools 124, 186, 208–209
'forever families' 190
formal curriculum 15, 117, 128, 143
Foucault, Michel 11–13, 15; disciplinary power 47, 51–52, 124, 137–138, 146; discourse 46–47, 48; discursive regime 49; *regimes of truth* 47; *surveillance* 120
Fraser, Nancy 55, 159–160, 162
free air life 208
'free play' 52
Freire, Paulo 13–14, 128, 224
friluftsliv 208
Fröbel, Friedrich 215
Frønes, Ivar 84
frustration, pedagogical response to 109–110

gender 6–7, 10, 13, 16–17, **98–99**; babies 28–30; and emotions 102–103; and in/equality 142, 183–184, 216, 223; mixed gender classrooms 52–53; and non-dualistic thinking 152; and performativity 29, 107; and sex and sexuality 71
gender identities 6, 7, 10, 71
'gender-complex' education 56
gendered behaviours and beliefs 167
gendered systems 215
Generative Curriculum projects 129
genetic heritage 25, 189
Germov, John 64
government 27, 33, 39–40, 67, 137, 220; education provision 125, 126, 143, 216, 220, 224
greenhouse gases 196–197
grief, pedagogical response to 110–111

habitus 46, 48–49, 52, 56, 144, 167
Hadow report 216
health **62**, **69**; biomedical model of 63; children's 17, 25, 35, 220; choice and constraint *61*, 62–76, *66*, *68*, *74*; social determinants of 69–71; social model of 63; social view of 64–66, *66*; sustainable education 196, 198; and wellbeing 80, 83, 84–85, **85**, **86**, 87; World Health Organisation definition of 63
health advocacy 74–75
health education 67, 72–73
Health Promoting School model 72
healthism 65, 66, 67
healthy lifestyle 17, 67

Heckman, James 123
Hedges, Helen 26
heritage, cultural and racial 7–9, *8*
heteronormativity 10, 28
hidden curriculum 15, 117
Hinduism 140
Hochschild, Arlie 99–100, 101, 103, 183
hooks, bell 15, 27, 35, 167
Horn, Sarah 165
Hurricane Katrina 198

impairments 10, 35, 121, 128, 159, 182, 190
inclusive environments 126–129
independence, in children 38, 92, 216
indigenous peoples: behaviour guidance 170; definition of 9; educating about 222; healthcare 71; racism 36, 48, 55; spiritual practices and traditions 140–141, 146, 148, 149; stereotyping 167; sustainable living 151; trust 179
individualisation 137
individuation 160
inequality 3, 4, 5–6, *8*, 14–15, 17, 56; class 7, 48–49; climate change 198–199; cultural heritage 7–8, *8*; dimensions of 191; economic 16, 159; environments 116–117; gender 6–7, 16, 27–28, 102–103, 183–184, *184*; health 73; political 159; race 7–8, *8*, 48, 49–50, 199; sexuality 27–28, 49–50; social class 7, 48–49
innocence, children's 3–4, 92
institutional cultures and practices 186–187
institutional racism and sexism 49–50 *see also* racism, structural
institutionalisation 33
intelligence 14, 49, 81, 169, 177
internalisation, of regulations and rules 137
internalised healthism 67
intersectionality 6
intimacy 180
intimate life, sociology of 28–29
intimidation 3
Isaacs, Susan 216
Islam 27, **136**, 139, 141, 146

James, Alison 81
joy, pedagogical response to 111–112, *112*
Judaism 139, 141–142

Kafer, Alison 53
Kagan, Shelly 82–83
Keeping Safe 92
kindergarten *see* preschool
kitchen gardens 206
kōhanga reo 186

language nest 186
Lareau, Annette 55, 167, 179–180
leadership 123, 160, 184, 186
learning environments 38, 93, *115*, **116**, 116–131, *119*, *122*
LGBT+ 127–128, 145–146, 189–190, 219
lifestyle 17, 65, 188
Little, Helen 207
Living Streets 221
Lóczy Institute 32–33
'logics of parenting' 180
long day care *see* preschool
loose parts play 204–205

McMahan, Ethan 82
Majority World 69, 183, 198–199, 223
Malaguzzi, Loris 218–219
mana 118
manaakitanga 170
managing behaviour, principles of 160
Maori culture and language 118, 141, 170, 186
marginalisation **2–3**, 5, 90, 118, 215
marketisation 123
Marx, Karl 214–215
masturbation 10
material cultures 129
'maternal responsiveness' 16
Mayo, Elizabeth 215–216
Mayors for Peace project 221
media 3, 26–27, 28, 29, 148, 204; and dominant discourses 47, 143; and health 72 148
medical interventions 65
mental disability 9–10
mental illness 17, 35, 183
metacognition 151
middle class 7, 28, 35, 132, 179–180, 214, 225–226
migration 8–9, 144, 187–189, *189*, 222
Miller, Darla 110
mindsets 31
Minority World 17; child abuse and protection 89–90, 92; childhood 195; climate 188, 197, 198; colonialism 118; developmental psychology 163; educational workforce 225; gender 183; hegemonic practices 15, 123; LGBT+ 127–128; marginalised women 223; social support 67
modern capitalism 15, 123
Mohanty, Chandra 125
Montessori, Maria 217
Moss, Peter 128, 129, 131
Murray, Susan 180

National Association for the Education of Young Children (NAEYC) 30, 161
national curricula 27, 73, 92
national frameworks, for child protection 90–91
natural environments 9, 71, 198, 208–209
natural growth, of children 179–180
natural world 121–122, *122*, **195**, 195–196, *196*, 199–200, 209, 222; and ecological identities 202–203, 205, 208, 209
neoliberalism 15, 123
neutrois 6
Nicholson, Simon 204–205
non-dualistic thinking 152
'normal' child, the non-existent 163
normalisation (disciplinary power technique) 131, 137–138
normalising (making something regular) 14, 47, 143, 158, 163
null curriculum 15, 20, 160, 182
nursery *see* childcare
Nussbaum, Martha 152–153, 159

obesity 66–67, *66*
Open Science Collaboration 31
over-protectiveness 54

Pacific Oaks Children's School 219
Paris agreement, on climate change 196
parenting 91, 137, 178, 179–180, 185; social 189–191
Parten, Mildred 30
participatory parity 159–160
participatory research **80**, 82, 89
partnerships 127, 182–183
passeggiata 126
Peabody, Elizabeth 216
pedagogy 3, 38, 56, 116, 126, 160; and spirituality 146–151, *147*, *149*, *150*; critical 13–16, 27, 57, 128
Pelo, Ann 202–203, 209, 214, 224
performativity 29
Pestalozzi, Johann 215–216

Petrie, Pat 128
physical activity 75, 77
physical disability 9–10
physical spaces 116, 120–123, *122*, 124, 127
Piaget, Jean 30
Pikler, Emmi 32–33, 40, 120, 160
place-making 119–123, *122*, 124, 127
play-based learning 52, 217
political inequality 159–160
postcolonialism 47, 117–119, 131
poststructuralism 11–13
post-traumatic stress 164–165
poverty 7, 33, 70, **85**, 90, 159, 198, 199, 219
power *2–3*, 3, 5, 11–15, 26–27; children's lack of 158; in classrooms 93; disciplinary 47, 51–52, 124, 137–138, 146; in guiding children's behaviour 168–169; reflection in dominant discourses 46–48; and health inequality 73–74, *74*; in research process 82; resistance to 51–52; subjectification 46–48
practices, institutional 186–187
pre-birth 17
preschool 28, *74*, 75, 92, 120, 151, 170; quiet time and sleep 181, 220
privacy, children's need for 120–121
privilege *4*, 5–6, **69**; ability 9–10, 34–35; and children's care needs 34–36; class 7, 18 35–36, 49, 55–56, 166–167; cultural 7–8, 187; disability 9–10, 34–35; dominant discourses 47, 143, 163; economic *8*, 16, 100, 223; gender 6–7, 53; and health 73–74, *74*; indigeneity 9; migration 9; race 3, 7–8, 19, 118, 166–167; social class 7, 18, 35–36, 49, 55–56, 166–167; stereotyping 167; *symbolic violence* 14–15; and values 132
'problem behaviour' 169
problem-solving skills, children's 168–170
protective force 164
Prout, Alan 81
Provincial Early Learning Frameworks 72
psychology *see* critical psychology, developmental psychology, social psychology
'psychosocial' life stages 30
Puwar, Nirmal 127

Quaker values 219
quality regimes/systems 28, 130–131

racial heritage 3, 7–8, *8*
racism, structural 7, 34, 36, 47–48, 55, 118, 167, 188
Rands, Kathleen 56
Raworth, Kate 125, 197, 199
reciprocal respect 160
recognition 159–160
refugees 5, 55, 71, 164–165, 187, 188
Reggio Emilia, early childhood services of 126–127, 217, 219, 225
regimes of truth 47
regulation (disciplinary power technique) 137
regulations, for service provision 27, 121, 137, 207
religion 17–18, 138–142, 142–146, 153; dominant discourses 47; health 71; philosophical perspective on 151–152; exercise of power by 27–28, 137–138 *see also* connectedness
Report Card: The Wellbeing of Young Australians **85**
research methods 88, 89
resistance 5, 7, 12, 14, 51–52, 56, 57, 93, 117
responsibilisation 67, 76
'right to roam' 208
rights, of the child 62, 88, 92, 158, 161
risk 206–208, *207*
Rostrom, Elinor 125
ruling class 7, 15, 36, 49, 179

sadness, pedagogical response to 110–111
Said, Edward 117, 118
St Leger, Lawrence 72
Savage, Catherine 170
Sayer, Andrew 28, 100, 108, 178
Schurz, Margarethe 216
scientific method 139
Second Opinion: An Introduction to Health Sociology 64
'second shift' 183
secularism 138, 142
Sen, Amartya 152, 159
sexism 48, 49–50, 56, 219; hetero- 145–146, 189; systemic 223
sexual abuse 165
sexuality 6, 10, 18, 27–28, 71, 92, 127, 187
Sidorkin, Alexander 117
Sihkism 142

silence, as meditative practice 148–149, 152, 203
singing 37, 75, 216
Skeggs, Beverley 50
social class 7, 55–56, 70, 100, 102–103, 184, 215; Pierre Bourdieu on 35–36, 48; bell hooks on 35; Annette Lareau on 179
social constructionism 101–102
social justice 36, 121, 123, 142, 150, 152–153
social media 148, 204
social models 34, 63, 64, 66, 72
social parenting 189–191
social psychology 16
social spaces 122–124
social structures 26–28, 143
'socialisation' 13, 25–26
society, civil 123–124, 125
Sociological Imagination Template 76, **77**
sociological thought, and religion 143–144
sociology: as activism 214–216; and belief systems 144–146; definition of 3
Socrates 139
spaces, children's 124
spirituality **85**, **86**, *136*, 138–142, 142–143, 145–146, 152–153; and art 152; and everyday life 152–153; and pedagogy 146–151, *147*, *149*, *150*
Srinivasan, Prasanna 13
stereotyping 127, 166–167
stigma 10, 16, 73, 161
stillness, as meditative practice 148–149, 152, 203
stress: childhood 104, 111, 121, 153, 164–165; adult 35, 104, 153, 181, 184, 223, 224
structural racism 7, 34, 36, 47–48, 55, 118, 167, 188
structuralism 12
structure 49, 66, 67
structure-agency continuum 66, *66*
subjectification 46–47
surveillance 120
sustainability, pedagogies for 202
sustainable education **195**, 195, *196*, 196–209, *201*, *207*
Swedish curriculum 27
symbolic violence 14–15
systemic sexism 223

tantrums 110, 165, 171
Taoism 143, 146
te ao Māori 170
'Te Whāriki' curriculum framework 31, 72, 92
Teeger, Chana 119
The Biggest Loser 67
theory **24**, 179–180; choice and constraint 46–47; discourse 46–47; *discursive regime* 49; economic 125; postcolonial 117–118; sociocultural 14; 'working theories' 26 *see also* developmental psychology; disciplinary power; power
Third World 69, 183, 198–199, 223
transgender 10, 29, 71, 102
trauma 30, 34, 36, 40, 163–166, 221; and anxiety 111; and conflict 181–182, 221; impact on education 95; and the learning environment 121
truth claims 12, 47, 48
Turner, Nancy 150–151
turtle pond *195*, 205–206

unconditionality 160
United Nations 9, 62, 81, **85**, 85, 88, 92, 158, 202
Universal Design 121, 128
unspoken rules 55
upbringing *8*, 19, 26, 46, 48–49, 55, 91
Uttal, Lynet 180

values: community 125, 126, 129, 131, *136*; conflicts in 145; cultural 125, 127, 129, 187, 188, 189; democratic 142; dominant 15, 127; in education 31, 49, 172; environmental 129; Hindu 140, 142; indigenous 170; *normalisation* 137–138; pedagogical 172; Quaker 219; Reggio Emilia 126–127; societal 72, 73 *see also* connectedness
van Laere, Katrien 123
victim blaming 65, 69
Villa Cella 217–219, *218*
violence 3–4, 117; domestic/family 30, 91, 165; horizontal 224; symbolic 14–15; war zone refugees 165
Viruru, Radhika 118
vulnerability 26, 103, 111, 136

Walkerdine, Valerie 16
war zones 164–165, 221
water cycle/play 201, 206
wellbeing 17, 20, *62*, 63, 79, **80**, 80–95, **85**, **86**, *88*, *94*; in the Early Years

Learning Framework 72; and racism 36; research 89
whanau 186
white privilege 8, 19, 47, 225
Woonerf 221
working class 7, 55; and emotional expression 102–103; and *habitus* 48; parental attitudes 179, 180; stereotyping of 167; Valerie Walkerdine on 16
working conditions 37–38, 47, 50, 99–101, 126–127, 183–185, 223–224
working theories 26, 28–29, 31

yoga 113, 146, 147, 148